EUTHANASIA
OF THE
COMPANION
ANIMAL

EUTHANASIA
OF THE
COMPANION
ANIMAL

The Impact on Pet Owners,
Veterinarians, and Society

Edited by
William J. Kay, DVM
Susan P. Cohen, CSW, ACSW
Herbert A. Nieburg, PhD
Carole E. Fudin, PhD, CSW, ACSW
Ross E. Grey, DVM
Austin H. Kutscher, DDS
Mohamed M. Osman, DVM, PhD

The Charles Press, Publishers
Philadelphia

The Charles Press, Publishers
Post Office Box 15715
Philadelphia, Pennsylvania
19103

Library of Congress Catalog Card Number: 88-071526

ISBN 0-914783-24-6 (cloth)
ISBN 0-914783-25-4 (paper)

Managing Editor: Sanford J. Robinson
Production Manager: David L. Myers
Composition: Cage Graphic Arts, Inc.
Printed by: Princeton University Press
Cover design: Sanford J. Robinson

5 4 3 2 1

We gratefully acknowledge the cooperation of the American Veterinary Medical Association, by whose kind permission the Appendix has been reprinted herein. The *AVMA Panel on Euthanasia* originally appeared in the Journal of the American Veterinary Medical Association, Vol 188, No. 3, Pages 252-268. © American Veterinary Medical Association, 1986. All rights reserved.

Chapter 5, "Animal Euthanasia and Moral Stress," was adapted from Bernard E. Rollin, "Euthanasia and Moral Stress," in DeBellis R, Marcus ER, Kutscher AH, Smith-Torres C, Barrett VW, Siegel ME (editors): *Suffering: Psychological and Social Aspects in Loss, Grief, and Care*. © 1986 by The Haworth Press, Inc. We gratefully acknowledge the cooperation of The Haworth Press, Inc. in granting permission to reprint this material herein.

Contents

PART I   THE ETHICS AND MORALITY OF EUTHANASIA

PART II   EUTHANASIA, PET LOSS, AND CLIENT GRIEF

Editors

William J. Kay, DVM
Chief of Staff, The Animal Medical Center, New York, NY

Susan P. Cohen, CSW, ACSW
Director of Counseling, The Animal Medical Center, New York, NY;
 Chairperson, AMC Institute for the Human/Companion Animal
 Bond; Board Member, Delta Society

Carole E. Fudin, PhD, CSW, ACSW
Founder, People/Pet Problems—Education, Therapy Services; Consulting Psychotherapist, The Animal Medical Center; Psychotherapist
 (private practice), New York, NY

Austin H. Kutscher, DDS
President, The Foundation of Thanatology, New York, NY; Professor of
 Dentistry (in Psychiatry), Department of Psychiatry, College of
 Physicians and Surgeons, Columbia University, New York, NY

Herbert A. Nieburg, PhD
Professor of Community Health, Long Island University, Westchester
 Division; Attending Psychotherapist, The Animal Medical Center,
 New York, NY

Ross E. Grey, DVM
Chairman, Institute of Comparative Medicine, Department of Animal
 Care, College of Physicians and Surgeons, Columbia University, New
 York, NY

Mohamed M. Osman, DVM, PhD
Assistant Professor of Pathology, College of Physicians and Surgeons,
 Columbia University; Director, Comparative Medical Sciences,
 Columbia-Presbyterian Medical Center, New York, NY

Contributors

Jack L. Albright, DVM
Professor of Animal Sciences, Lay and Animal Clinics, Purdue University School of Veterinary Medicine, West Lafayette, IN

Edward Baker, VMD
Animal Skin and Allergy Clinic, Demarest, NJ

Alan M. Beck, ScD
Director, Center for the Interaction of Animals and Society, School of Veterinary Medicine, University of Pennsylvania, Philadelphia, PA

Roger A. Caras
Writer, Kew Gardens, NY

Donald H. Clifford, DVM, PhD
Professor and Director, Division of Laboratory Animal. Medicine, Medical College of Ohio, Toledo, OH; Diplomate in the American College of Laboratory Animal Medicine and the American College of Veterinary Surgeons

David C. Cooke, BS
Director, Abbey-Glen Pet Memorial Park, Warren, NJ; Past President, PADAC (Professional Animal Disposal Advisory Council), Elkhart, IN

Sharon L. Crowell-Davis, DVM, PhD
Assistant Professor, Department of Anatomy and Radiology, University of Georgia College of Veterinary Medicine, Athens, GA

Dennis T. Crowe, DVM, ACVS
Assistant Professor of Surgery; Director, Shock/Trauma Team, Department of Small Animal Medicine, The University of Georgia College of Veterinary Medicine, Athens, GA

Patricia Curtis
Writer, New York, NY

Andrew T. B. Edney, BA, DVM
Secretary, World Animal Veterinary Association; Director of PPPets (Pet People Problems Educational Therapy Services), Animal Study Center, Waltham-on-the-Wolds, Leicestershire, United Kingdom

Harry V. Hagstad, DVM
Professor and Head, Department of Epidemiology and Community Health, Louisiana State University School of Veterinary Medicine, Baton Rouge, LA

Alton F. Hopkins, DVM
Highland Park Animal Clinic, Dallas, TX

Susan A. Iliff
School of Veterinary Medicine, Purdue University, West Lafayette, IN

Eileen Koski, BS
Graduate Student, Division of Sociomedical Sciences, Graduate School of Arts and
    Sciences, Columbia University, New York, NY

Catherine A. Kotch-Jantzer, BS
Pennsylvania State University, University Park, PA

Dan Lago, PhD
Assistant Professor of Human Development and Coordinator of Gerontology
    Center, Pennsylvania State University, University Park, PA

Paul H. Langner, VMD, MS
Department of Veterinary Clinical Medicine, College of Veterinary Medicine,
    University of Illinois, Urbana, IL

David L. Levine, MSW
School of Social Work, University of Georgia, Athens, GA

E. Gregory MacEwen, VMD
Head, Department of Oncology, The Animal Medical Center; Speyer Hospital and
    Caspary Research Institute, New York, NY

Sharon McMahon, RN, BScN, BA, MEd
Assistant Professor, School of Nursing, University of Windsor, Windsor, Ontario,
    Canada

James Moneymaker, PhD
Assistant Professor of Medical Sociology, Georgetown University, Washington, DC

F. Ellen Netting, PhD, ACSW
Assistant Professor, School of Social Work, Arizona State University, Tempe, AZ

John C. New, Jr., DVM, MPH
Associate Professor, Department of Environmental Practice, University of
    Tennessee College of Veterinary Medicine, Knoxville, TN

James E. Quackenbush, MSW, ACSW
Research Associate, Section of Epidemiology, Department of Clinical Studies,
    School of Veterinary Medicine, University of Pennsylvania, Philadelphia, PA

Bernard E. Rollin, PhD
Professor of Philosophy, Department of Philosophy, Physiology and Biophysics,
    Colorado State University, Fort Collins, CO

Marvin L. Samuelson, DVM
Department of Surgery and Medicine, College of Veterinary Medicine, Kansas State
    University, Manhattan, KS

Joel S. Savishinsky, PhD
Chairperson and Professor, Department of Anthropology, Ithaca College, Ithaca,
    NY

Donald C. Sawyer, DVM, PhD
Professor of Anesthesia, Department of Small-Animal Clinic Sciences, College of
    Veterinary Medicine, Michigan State University, East Lansing, MI

Mary-Ellen Siegel, MSW, ACSW
Senior Teaching Associate, Department of Community Medicine (Social Work),
    Mount Sinai School of Medicine, New York, NY

Robert G. Stevenson, EdD
Co-Chair, Columbia University Seminar on Death; Instructor of Death Education
  Programs at River Dell High School, Bergen Community College, and Fairleigh
  Dickinson University, NJ

Bob Szita, MA
Out-Reach Program Coordinator, Staten Island Zoological Society, Staten Island,
  NY

Sylvan Lee Weinberg, MD
Clinical Professor of Medicine, Co-Director of Cardiology, Wright State University
  School of Medicine, Dayton, OH

Walter E. Weirich, DVM, PhD
Director, Department of Small Animal Clinics, Purdue University School of
  Veterinary Medicine, West Lafayette, IN

Cindy C. Wilson, PhD
Assistant Professor, Department of Health Sciences, Arizona State University,
  Tempe, AZ

Preface

Although a routine, well-established, accepted procedure in veterinary practice, euthanasia of very old or incurably ill animals, especially pets, still raises many troubling moral and ethical questions. But this is only one part of the euthanasia issue. The emotional response to this elective form of death is often far-reaching and profound. When a companion animal is "put down" or "put to sleep"—euphemistic terms for euthanasia—all those involved in the decision and implementation of terminating the pet's life share the emotional impact. Under what circumstances, then, is euthanasia the best choice, and how should it be performed? How can veterinarians, helping professionals, and owners cope with the stress of this difficult decision and its aftermath?

In the following pages, 37 outstanding authors—veterinarians, social workers, psychologists, and animal owners—explore the issues of animal euthanasia and owner bereavement from a variety of perspectives. Searching discussions of the ethics and morality of euthanasia precede firsthand accounts of the impact of pet loss upon owners, including children, adolescents, and the elderly. Next, the nature of the human/companion animal bond is examined, with particular attention to the grieving process and the role of the helping professional in resolving owner bereavement. The fourth section of the book is devoted to the experience of the veterinarian and other animal-care workers in coping with the emotional and practical aspects of euthanasia. Finally, a special Appendix provides the reader with comprehensive and up-to-date guidelines from the American Veterinary Medicine Association's Panel on Euthanasia, including specific agents, methods, and safety precautions.

It is the sincere hope of the editors, contributors, and publisher that this book will prove to be of genuine value to all concerned not only for the welfare of animals, but also for the emotional well-being of those who share responsibility for their care.

Dedication

This book is dedicated to
Michael J. McCulloch, MD
and
Karen Ann Bustad

Acknowledgment

This text was jointly prepared by The Foundation of Thanatology and The Carola Warburg Rothschild Society for the Human—Animal Bond of The Animal Medical Center. All royalties from the sale of this book are assigned to The Foundation of Thanatology, a tax-exempt, not-for-profit, public scientific and educational foundation.

Thanatology, a new subspecialty of medicine, is involved in scientific and humanistic inquiries and the application of the knowledge derived therefrom to the subjects of the psychological aspects of dying; reactions to loss, death, and grief; and recovery from bereavement.

Part 1
The Ethics and Morality of Euthanasia

1

Common Fate, Difficult Decision: A Comparison of Euthanasia in People and in Animals

Joel S. Savishinsky

It is hard for many people to accept death as a fact of life. The concept of euthanasia, literally, "good death," may be even more elusive. Just as difficult for many of us is the recognition that the deaths of nonhuman animals can have human consequences and that the loss of an animal companion may exert economic, moral, and emotional effects. When a domestic animal dies as the result of euthanasia, the human implications of the event are particularly compelling because people are then simultaneously the caretakers, the decision-makers, and the instruments of death.

The issues raised by euthanasia in veterinary medicine have assumed new significance in recent years because of the intrinsic worth that many groups in our culture now accord all forms of life. Whether people fulfill the roles of owners, stewards, clients, researchers, care-givers, or life-takers in regard to animals, they must face questions of right and wrong, pain and suffering, power and process, expense and emotion, and technique and responsibility. Furthermore, the issue of animal euthanasia evokes some significant parallels to life-and-death decisions concerning human beings. The implication is that lessons learned from research on euthanasia in the veterinary context could be applied to comparable issues in human medicine. Seven such parallels are implicit; it is worth making them explicit to sharpen the focus of future studies.

(1) *Moral ambiguity*. The decision to take the life of an animal and the

decision to contribute to the death of a human being both activate moral
uncertainty. Only in recent years have the human and veterinary
medical professions begun to develop guidelines to help practitioners
deal with such decisions. A lack of ethical consensus about proper
behavior still obtains, however, and professional codes are not
necessarily helpful to lay individuals whose pets or human relatives are
the subjects of the anguished decisions that must be made. The issues
are also currently addressed from a legal perspective through legislation
on animal abuse, court decisions on "mercy killings," the establishment
of "death committees" in hospital settings, and the creation of "living
wills" that declare how individuals want themselves (and sometimes
their pets) to be treated under terminal conditions or in situations of
medical extremity. The moral ambiguity and controversy that surround
these approaches to death are reflected in the very names and diverse
positions taken by groups active in what they variously term the right-to-
life, death-with-dignity, right-to-die, and animal-rights movements. The
legal, medical, and organizational responses to euthanasia for humans
and animals indicate both the intensity and the similarity in the cultural
impact of these ethical issues.

(2) *Role ambiguity.* When confronted with euthanasia, professionals in
human and veterinary medicine face a role dilemma as well as a moral
one. Their primary mission as researchers, technicians, or clinicians is
to support and enhance human life, not to end it. Yet their humane or
scientific motives for taking a life may be equally legitimate as a means
of alleviating immediate pain or future suffering. The predicament here
is neither a narrowly legal nor a strictly ethical one: it derives from a
contradiction inherent in the medical role itself, and may therefore
require a reassessment of how practitioners see themselves, as well as
how they wish to be regarded by clients and other members of society.

(3) *Clients and patients.* In clinical situations, a euthanasia decision
may cloud the issue of who is the primary client: for the veterinarian,
is it the animal or the owner? For the physician, is it the patient or the
patient's family? In either context, practitioners may find themselves in
a relationship with both the ailing individual and significant others.
When this happens, a physician or veterinarian must decide whose
needs are paramount, what financial and emotional costs people can
afford, and what process and criteria should be followed in answering
these questions. If a human or animal patient seems to express needs
or desires different from those articulated by other members of the
family, are there ways to mediate these differences, and what role does
the practitioner play when issues seem irreconcilable? The problem of

whether the patient must invariably be regarded as the primary client highlights another aspect of role ambiguity for doctors: namely, whether their role as care-givers entitles or requires them to be advocates for their patients. The issue is one that mental health professionals and social workers also face in their practices; they are often called on to help patients, families, and other professionals to deal with these life-and-death questions. No simple or uniform answers exist in any of these fields, but when a decision on euthanasia is at issue, practitioners are especially compelled to be clear about where their primary commitment lies.

(4) *Caring and callousness.* When life and death hinge on the kind of intervention that a professional chooses to make, the emotional consequences do not end with the decision and its implementation. The decision-making process and its aftermath can be intensely disturbing. Ample evidence shows that the processes of grieving over the loss of a pet and grieving over the loss of a person exhibit many similarities. Participants and witnesses to euthanasia with animals indicate that owners and medical personnel are capable of both great caring and disconcerting callousness. Pet owners sometimes praise, sometimes condemn the professionals with whom they have dealt. In turn, veterinary doctors and technicians can testify to extremes of grief, relief, and indifference among their human clients. The same emotional range characterizes people involved in euthanasia decisions concerning human beings. In both contexts, individual reactions reveal marked differences in how well people deal with such situations, and how much thought, energy, and consideration they give to the psychological impact of death on victims and survivors. Considerable variability also obtains in how openly issues of method and responsibility are discussed, and in how professionals and family members feel about the latter being present at the time of death. Rather than characterizing euthanasia as a uniform process involving standard reactions, then, research indicates a need to recognize the diversity of responses by practitioners, patients, and clients.

(5) *Language and meaning.* The personal meanings of death are often encoded in the metaphors that people use to describe it. One of the striking parallels between human and animal death, whether from natural causes or human intervention, is the use of euphemism to deny or soften the reality. When euthanatized, animals are not *killed*: they are put down, put to sleep, or put away. Humans, too, do not *die*: they pass away or pass on. Adults use such a vocabulary in speaking to one another and often become even more indirect or deceptive when

discussing death with children. Students of human and pet death have argued that our cultural tendency to deny death is reinforced by our use of these figures of speech. Since euthanasia creates an occasion in which people are compelled to talk about death more openly, it offers an opportunity to revise our vocabulary, rethink our metaphors, and thereby change the meanings that we attach to death as a human experience.

(6) *Ritual and myth.* As with other forms of death, euthanasia puts an end to a relationship but not to its significance. We deal with human loss by marking it with ritual and by weaving memories into stories and myths. A funeral, a memorial service, a burial, the unveiling of a gravestone, and the sharing of reminiscences are some of the ways we aid the mourning process and move it toward closure. Euthanasia may leave a special residue of guilt and doubt that needs to be dealt with in these other creative ways.

Despite the close ties that people develop with animals, they often are reluctant or unable to accord the death of a pet the due degree of meaning and social recognition. Pet owners may be embarrassed or apologetic about their grief or may repress their feelings for fear of how others will react. Unlike religious patterns for dealing with human death and its aftermath, rituals for pet loss are not culturally established. Some people have designed their own ceremonies and observances for deceased animals, but these are not as widely known or as broadly accepted as religious responses to human death. Medical and mental-health workers, humane educators, and animal-rights advocates may all be able to make a significant contribution here by helping people to create meaningful ways to mark and mourn the deaths of their pet companions.

(7) *Burial and disposal.* Death leaves bodies as well as memories with which to deal. The options available for the disposal of animal remains — cremation, incineration, burial, commercial removal, dumping, abandonment, and donation to a research facility — are somewhat more varied and certainly more informal than the choices that exist for human disposition. But in both cases a decision must be made, and economic, spiritual, and moral factors must be weighed by survivors. The issue of human disposal is more carefully controlled by the law, but the problem of what to do with animal remains is potentially of even greater ecological magnitude. On a crowded planet with finite space and a fragile environment, we may need to reassess our current solutions for dealing with death in the light of changing social priorities.

● ●

Euthanasia is one of the most difficult issues in the brave new world of modern medicine and morality. Whether it is a person or an animal who dies as the result of human intervention, the "good death" that is supposed to result confronts us with several dilemmas and demands:

- to balance the prolongation of life with the alleviation of suffering;
- to redefine our ethical and professional responsibilities;
- to clarify the relationship between clients and care-givers;
- to educate people about human rights and animal rights;
- to recognize people's emotional needs and to sensitize them to the impact of their behavior on others; and
- to devise ways of thinking about, communicating about, and responding to death so that our actions are honest, respectful, and meaningful.

Different cultures express distinctive ideas about what constitutes a "good death," so that cross-cultural as well as cross-species approaches suggest ways in which these issues can be examined. Compared to the American wish to die peacefully in one's sleep, for example, traditional Japanese and Irish cultures see desirable death coming about in very different contexts. In Japan, suicide is a much more acceptable option for elderly people who feel they have become a family burden (Plath 1983). Aged people in rural Ireland hope to be awake, alert, surrounded by kin, and in command of their households, when their final moment comes (Arensberg 1968; Scheper-Hughes 1983). Human and animal death are interlinked in some societies: equestrian peoples from Asian and Plains Indian cultures sometimes killed a deceased warrior's favorite horse so that the two might be honored and buried together and then continue their relationship in the next world (Ewers 1980; Roe 1955; Zeuner 1963). Such patterns express the belief that lifelong ties between humans and animals are not terminated by death, but may be continued through invoking death.

Although the experiences of euthanasia with humans and animals are not identical in any culture, they bear sufficient similarity in our own and some other societies that the lessons learned from one process may be applied to understanding the other better. Recognizing that people are an evolving, integral part of the natural world, we can apply that knowledge to our treatment of life and death in our own and other species. Humans and other living beings share a common planet and a common fate, and our awareness of this truth may lead to more compassionate ways of deciding how our lives will end.

REFERENCES

Arensberg C: The Irish Countryman. Garden City, NY: The Natural History Press, 1968

Ewers JC: The Horse in Blackfoot Indian Culture. Washington DC: Smithsonian Institute Press, 1980

Plath D: Ecstasy years: Old age in Japan. In Sokolovsky J (ed): Growing Old in Different Societies, pp 147-153, Belmont CA, Wadsworth, 1983

Roe F G: The Indian and the Horse. Norman, OK: Univ of Oklahoma Press, 1955

Scheper-Hughes N: Deposed kings: the demise of the rural irish gerontocracy. In Sokolosky J (ed): Growing Old In Different Societies, pp 130-146, Belmont CA, Wadsworth, 1983

Zeuner F: A History of Domesticated Animals. New York, Harper & Row, 1963

ADDITIONAL READING

Cohen S: Words of comfort. People-Animals-Environment 1 (1): 16-17, 1983

Fogle B: Attached-euthanasia-grieving. In Fogle, B (ed): Interrelations Between People and Pets, pp 331-334, Springfield, IL, Charles C Thomas, 1981

Katcher A, Rosenberg M: Euthanasia and the management of the client's grief. Calif Veterinarian 36 (8): 31-36, 1982

Keddie KMG: Pathological mourning after the death of a domestic pet. Brit J Psychiatry 131:21-25, 1977

Levinson B: Pets and Human Development. Springfield IL, Charles C Thomas, 1972

Nieburg H, Fischer A: Pet Loss. New York: Harper & Row, 1982

Quackenbush J: Pet bereavement in older owners. In Anderson RK, Hart BL, Hart LA (eds): The Pet Connection, pp 292-299, Minneapolis MN, Centre to Study Human-Animal Relationships and Environments, Univ of Minnesota, 1984

Quackenbush J, Blickman L: Social work services for bereaved pet owners: a retrospective case study in a veterinary teaching hospital. Katcher A, Beck A (eds): New Perspective on Our Lives with Companion Animals, pp 377-389, Philadelphia PA, Univ of Pennsylvania Press, 1983

Rynearson AK: Humans and pets and attachment, Brit J of Psychiatry 133:550-555, 1978

Savishinsky JS: Pets and family relationships among nursing home residents. Marriage and Family Review 8 (3-4), 109-134, 1985

Stewart M: Loss of a pet, loss of a person: a comparative study of bereavement. In Katcher A, Beck A (eds): New Perspectives on Our Lives with Companion Animals, Philadelphia PA: Univ of Pennsylvania Press, 1983

2

Euthanasia as an Ethical Dilemma

James E. Quackenbush

Euthanasia, a major agent of death in nonhuman animals, occurs with regularity in the three chief areas of concern of veterinary medicine; clinical service, research, and education. While it may be impractical or impossible to determine whether euthanasia, under any circumstances or in any given situation, is absolutely good or bad, right or wrong, it is still possible to examine the decision-making processes involved in choosing euthanasia in order to understand the inherent ethical dilemmas such decisions pose. How do we examine, understand, and determine the ethics of interactions and the implications thereof for the owner, the animal, and the veterinarian? Because the issue is complex and emotional, a searching discussion may yield inconclusive results. Indeed, the reader of this chapter can expect to encounter more questions than answers—which is perhaps as it should be.

Rachels (1978) and others have discussed the ethical dimensions of human euthanasia occurring as an active or a passive process. The practice of causing a person to die, as opposed to allowing the natural course of a disease or injury to progress to a lethal end, is also applicable to nonhuman species. Two additional factors may be considered within that active-passive framework: (1) whether the decision making is voluntary or involuntary; and (2) whether the dying subject actively chooses how his life will end, or whether his fate is determined by others.

We may now construct an analytical paradigm to define various circumstances of euthanasia choices, placing them in particular categories (Beauchamp 1979). Any decision about euthanasia may be defined as follows:

VOLUNTARY-ACTIVE   VOLUNTARY-PASSIVE
INVOLUNTARY-ACTIVE   INVOLUNTARY-PASSIVE

Admittedly this is not a perfect instrument. It will therefore generate controversy, as do most models containing diametrically opposed concepts. But it is a start, a way to begin understanding the considerable complications that arise in choosing to treat, kill, or let die.

In discussing ethics and ethical dilemmas, we implicitly concern ourselves with morals and value systems. Building on the model of active-passive concerns, we can introduce a hierarchy of moral values into the decision-making paradigm. While numerous values must be considered, the following five areas seem particularly suited to the subject of euthanasia (Critical Issues, More Than Just Opinion, I 1983). They also bring the euthanasia dilemma clearly into an ethical context.

1. *Life* In considering euthanasia one must understand that certain extreme positions characterize how life is valued: (a) Life is the ultimate value, and under no circumstances is the taking of life justifiable or acceptable. (b) The quality of a life is the moral priority; if the quality of living cannot be maintained in certain ways at a particular level, it is acceptable, even mandatory, that the life be humanely terminated.

2. *Freedom of choice* The focus is on resolving who makes decisions about euthanasia. To what extent, and how, is the veterinarian a decision-maker? To what levels of participation and authority is the owner entitled? Who is best suited to determine the fate of an animal? How are any conflicts over who decides resolved?

3. *Excellence* Inevitably, one must examine the knowledge, skill, and experience of the clinician and the state of the veterinary profession. To what extent does the clinician understand the life-threatening problem, possess the expertise to treat it, and have sufficient experience to know how to handle it? Also, to what level is the profession itself knowledgeable and skilled to provide a clinical intervention for any given medical problem? Another facet of excellence is degree of effort: given the capabilities of professional knowledge and individual expertise, a spectrum of choice arises between insufficient effort to save a life and overly heroic measures applied despite sometimes minimal expectations of cure or palliation. More simply, how does one choose to stop or continue trying to save an animal's life? Either choice may generate moral and ethical concerns.

4. *Justice* Under many, if not most, circumstances involving the possibility of euthanasia, the availability and distribution of resources, human and material, may play a vital role. When is it appropriate to

redirect clinical skills, experience, and medical resources from one ailing animal to another? Are all animals always entitled to equal shares of available care, or should we establish priorities for access to care? Who makes such a choice and how is it justified? When should economic factors precipitate a choice for euthanasia? What allows us to determine the value of one life over another, or to redirect care and resources?

5. *Trust* Euthanasia decision-making depends a great deal on open and honest communication. The trust that develops between the veterinarian and the owner is based on two premises: truth-telling and promise-keeping. The interactions between veterinarian and animal owner require honesty and follow-through on both implicit and explicit commitments; the veterinarian and owner owe this consideration to one another and both owe it to the animal. To distort the truth or to fail in fulfilling a responsibility constitutes a breach of ethics.

When all of these moral values are integrated with the paradigm of active-voluntary options regarding euthanasia, a complex model results. It is a provocative and difficult framework within which to make euthanasia choices. Yet, one may cite good reasons why such a model, though perhaps cumbersome and time-consuming in practice, nevertheless makes a point. As overtly empirical and fact-based professions the biomedical sciences encounter real decision-making limits within the boundaries of "objective" knowledge. The issue of euthanasia as a treatment option in veterinary medicine, and using the model described here, strikingly illustrates the role of subjectivity in the making of specific life or death choices. In the end, moral values should be accepted as an inseparable component in resolving questions about euthanasia. Such decisions are not made within a moral and ethical vacuum.

A last thought is that every moral consideration deserves attention from at least three perspectives. In veterinary euthanasia the primary characters in the experience should claim careful consideration. Moral values and potential ethical conflicts, those circumstances in which moral values clash, demand attention whether one considers euthanasia from the point of view of the animal, the owner, or the veterinarian. When there is no common ground on which euthanasia choices can be considered, when moral commitments differ among those parties involved, yet another dimension of conflict and ethical concern surfaces. And while no statement is possible upon universal "rightness" or "wrongness," an understanding may be reached that whatever choice is made, for whatever reasons, it should be based on due deliberation and genuine caring—for the animal, the owner, and the veterinarian alike.

REFERENCES

Beauchamp TL: A reply to Rachels on active and passive euthanasia. In Beauchamp TL, Perlin S (eds): Ethical Issues in Death and Dying, pp 246-258, Englewood Cliffs NJ, Prentice-Hall, 1978

Critical ethics, more than just opinion (I). In Ethical Issues in Medical Care: Syllabus for Freshman Bioethics. The Medical Humanities Program (a division of the Department of Community and Preventive Medicine), Philadelphia PA, Medical College of Pennsylvania, 1983

Fromer MJ: Ethical Issues in Health Care, pp 390-396, St. Louis MO, CV Mosby, 1981

Rachels J: Active and passive euthanasia, in Beauchamp TL, Perlin S (eds): Ethical Issues in Death and Dying, pp 240-246, Englewood Cliffs NJ, Prentice-Hall, 1978

3

Medical Research, Euthanasia, and The Animal Welfare Movement

Alan M. Beck

Antivivisectionism does not simply protest the abuse of animals, but is part of a tradition of resistance against establishment power in urban, industrial society. Not inherently misanthropic or malevolent, the animal welfare movement is impelled by a set of ethical considerations based in part on distrust of oversized institutions, fear of change, and religious fundamentalism. Like the "Luddites" of the 1800s who tried to prevent the use of labor-saving machinery in factories, the animal welfare movement also saw a threat implied by progress. In many ways, "antivivisectionists foresaw the cold, barren alienation of a future dominated by the imperatives of technique and expertise. It was not experiments on animals they were protesting, it was the shape of the century to come" (French 1975).

It is human to remember only the best from the past and to fear the worst from the future. One often forgets that for humankind, the best there ever was is the present. The public should be educated to include among its "humane" goals a realization that people are a species worthy of protection. The human race deserves the benefits of advancing medical care and reasonably priced, high quality food. The alternative is a planet regressed more than a million years—a prospect that few would argue is desirable.

Although the literature of the movement speaks of "animals" in the generic sense, the animals that are usually foremost in the minds of most antivivisectionists are pets—dogs, cats, and horses—which are significantly singled out for protection. The defense of farm animals—

cattle, poultry, and swine—may stem from the need of urbanites to keep a sense of kinship with their rural past and to develop a bulwark against modernization and the tyranny of modern life (French 1975; Turner 1980). The animal welfare movement defends farm animals, but overlooks the farmers who depend on animal products for a livelihood.

Historically, the animal welfare movement, and antivivisectionism in particular, has been associated with agitation against organized medicine and an anti-scientific attitude. Most of the rank and file of the movement came (and comes) from the urban middle class or clergy; often professionals, semi-professionals, or people living on inherited income; and people identifying with the aristocracy (French 1975). About 60% of adherents are female. Antivivisectionism attains highest visibility during periods of affluence and freedom from hunger and disease.

Materials from related movements, notably those devoted to slaughterhouse reform, humane trapping methods, and even prevention of cruelty to children, occasionally appear in antivivisectionist periodicals, but response to such materials apparently has not been sufficiently strong to broaden the appeal. Today, the movement embraces such causes as protest against seal killing, intensive farming, trapping, and euthanasia.

Peter Singer, in his book *Animal Liberation*, which is often referred to as the bible of the movement, makes the case that speciesism is analogous to racism and sexism by declaring that ". . .we would be on shaky ground if we were to demand equality for blacks, women and other groups of oppressed humans while denying equal consideration to nonhumans" (1975). One wonders whether blacks, women, and other people appreciate the analogy.

THE RELIGIOUS ISSUE

There is a strong religious component to the animal welfare movement; by restricting progress by means of experimentation, people reaffirm their fundamental belief in God as the sole director of life. The movement is self-characterized as the guardian of human morality, insisting that to inflict pain is immoral. The cultural myth that scientists are often atheists, and therefore immoral, is well established. Vivisection is presented as further evidence of the scientist's denial of a supreme being uniquely privileged to bestow or withdraw life. In addition, the scientist's objectivity is viewed as cold and lacking compassion, a natural target for moral militants.

Fundamentalists regard disease as the divinely ordained consequence of sin: man is destined to his alloted share of pain, but animals are not so ordained. Medicine is viewed as a misdirected field, "grovelling in the entrails" of animals, serving a "culture of cowardice," and ignobly shrinking from the necessity of pain and death (French 1975). Science is judged to encourage a selfish human obsession with health and self-preservation. The animal welfare movement proclaims that the true path to salvation is prevention of disease through sanitation ("cleanliness is next to godliness") and leading "the Good Life" (Turner 1980). In *Slaughter of the Innocent,* a book often quoted by members of the movement, Ruesch (1975) stated "every real expert is aware that nothing is known for sure except what Hippocrates already knew: that the best protection also against this infection [referring to rabies] is cleanliness."

At times, as in Nazi Germany, the movement has been closely allied to anti-Semitism (French 1975; Goering 1939), although many Jews were and are involved. The anti-Semitism may stem from the anti-power, pro-fundamentalist nature of the movement. Jews, like scientists, are often considered atheistic, or, at least, "non-Christian."

Paralleling the belief in one God, the humane movement identifies with the individual animal, not with the animal population, whereas science, public health, farming, and conservation all focus on the population. The animals that are differentially singled out for salvation by the humane movement are those that (1) retain juvenile characteristics even as adults (neotonic), (2) are social, or (3) are perceived to be intelligent. Clearly, these animals demonstrate the attributes of humans, and often of the most worthy humans. Concern is thus lavished on calves, deer, and seals (which appear juvenile); dogs, wolves, horses, and poultry (which are social); and primates, dolphins, and swine (which are perceived to be intelligent). Only small, extreme groups protest to save rodents, goats, or invertebrates.

Such concern for the individual has led also to a distinction between pets and other animals of the same species. Many perceive their dogs as additional family members (Beck and Katcher 1983). It is not conceivable to treat some pets as people while using former pets as "guinea pigs." Pound seizure law, a major victory for the movement, maintains the right to use breeder-raised dogs and cats for research, but not former pets. In reality, the pound seizure law creates a new class of "puppy mill," which raises animals for research, and leads to the death of many more animals. Such inconsistency is at odds with the logic of the scientist, but seems acceptable to the humane movement.

WHY THE MOVEMENT IS NOT PARTICULARLY SUCCESSFUL

The movement has not been particularly successful in shaping public attitudes because only two reasons are adduced for protesting the use of animals in research: it is immoral to cause suffering, regardless of the results, and the results of the research are not useful anyway. Often both arguments are combined.

First, there is no uniformity of opinion regarding the morality issue. Attitudes range from the belief that animals, like people, are born with rights, to the opinion that animals only possess rights as given by people. Second, many thinkers have been convinced by results in bacteriology, immunology, pharmacology, and anesthesiology that experimentation on animals provides useful material. Scarcely any medical achievements have been obtained without the use of animals in some way, yet movement literature makes such claims as "There never has been and there never could be a single experiment that saves thousands of lives" (Singer 1975). The statement completely misses the additive nature of scientific progress. Often the value of research is denied outright: "And as far as the U.S. is concerned, for all the formidable therapeutic arsenal at the disposal of its citizens and the feverish activity of their doctors, Americans don't live longer today than their parents—but they suffer much more" (Ruesch 1975). This statement is simply untrue.

In addition, the movement perpetuates two fundamental flaws: lack of agreement within its ranks and misjudgment of public attitudes toward medical science (Turner 1980).

First, the movement is unwilling to compromise in arguing for a total ban on animal experimentation. Isolated cases of abuse are argued as evidence against the entire system. One faction will deny all support to another at the first sign of compromise or differing levels of commitment on a given issue. Such division leads to a proliferation of groups, the draining of resources, and aggravation of public distrust of extremism.

Second, the movement employs the full repertoire of nineteenth century methods for focusing public opinion on an issue. *Love and Anger: An Organizing Handbook* (Morgan 1980), published by the Animal Rights Network, contains guidelines for rallies, sit-ins, symbolic actions, legal defenses, and even diagrams on how to picket. Regardless of the issues, this style of antivivisectionist agitation, including gory posters, distortions of truth and vitriolic publications, discourages potential supporters and encourges public withdrawal.

Moreover, the movement underestimates popular admiration for, and dependence on, medical science. Despite transient disappointments with science and technology, the scientific community has been remarkably successful in maintaining its funding, freedom, and lack of accountability. In fact, scientific prestige has grown enormously in both England and America, despite the antivivisectionist movement.

When presenting its side of the story, it is important for the scientific community to identify the population to be addressed. Animal activists themselves are virtually unconvincible regarding animal suffering. The target for the medical community must be the general public, students, technicians, and political leaders. New susceptibles in the general public must be presented with the case for animal research in an honest and clear way that does not unnecessarily polarize the issues (Verdeber 1984). Portraying the animal welfare movement as uncaring or irresponsible is neither productive nor fair.

The vast majority of the public is sympathetic to research but needs to be assured that the matter of animal suffering is not ignored. The public should be aware of existing guidelines: using as few animals as possible (reduction); using lower life forms when possible (substitution); and finding as many non-animal procedures as possible (replacement). They should be assured that the search for alternatives to animal experimentation is an area of active interest and research (Rowan 1977).

More research is needed to develop methods that will lessen scientific dependence on animals, to determine the nature of accommodation to environments, and to pinpoint the triggers of animal stress. It is unproductive to argue that animals do not suffer or that they would not prefer to be free. Researching how animals accommodate to any environment may reveal that animals do accommodate to whatever conditions they encounter, so that incarceration per se is probably not inhumane. It may be inhuman—but then animals are not, after all, human.

It would be useful to investigate how the perception of scientists influences the issues. If scientists were honestly portrayed as caring and animal-loving people, would the issue change? The defensive posture often assumed by scientists and their institutions may aggravate the situation and alienate public support. There must be honest commitment to protecting animals against pain whenever possible, including sensitizing those involved in research.

THE RATIONALE FOR MEDICAL RESEARCH

Life has changed for the better because of the use of animals for research and experimentation. The advances of medicine in the last century indeed halted the first wave of antivivisectionism. Perhaps people have grown impatient with the pace of medical progress, now that science is tackling chronic diseases and such self-imposed afflictions as overeating, environmental pollution, auto accidents, and radiation. Research in these areas, too, however, requires the use of animals, and progress, however slow, is being recorded. The truth is that few significant medical advances do not include the use of animals for research.

Medical research has good reasons for using animals, and they should be shared with society. They include the following:

1) Animals are part of an intellectual "food" chain, not unlike the protein food chain; our very survival, as we know it, has depended on the use of animals for both food and knowledge.

2) Science has no choice, for there is no better alternative. Computer modeling, unicellular systems, tissue culture, and human studies will replace animals in some areas of research and reduce the number of animals used in many others, but these devices cannot substitute for the whole organism. There may never be a substitute for using a whole, living organism in some areas of research, training, and testing.

3) Animals are different from people in the ways in which they respond to the death of others. Singer, in *Animal Liberation* (1985), stated "If the experimenter would not be prepared to use a human infant, then his readiness to use nonhuman animals reveals an unjustifiable form of discrimination on the basis of species. . . ." The argument that it is wrong for science to perform procedures on animals that can suffer, when it is unwilling to use infant, retarded, or comatose humans, misses a vital point. The death of a human, any human, decreases the quality of life and health of many people. In our society people mourn for the death of all people in ways not observed at all among laboratory and farm animals (Hoff 1980). As the movement itself makes a distinction between lower and higher forms of animals, society distinguishes between even higher animals and people.

4) The decrease of disease and consequent suffering that has been achieved by medical research is desirable to the vast majority of the public. Would people trust medical professionals who did not use animals in their training, or pharmaceuticals and vaccines not first tested on animals?

THE MAJOR ISSUE: PAIN AND SUFFERING OF THE INDIVIDUAL

For the animal welfare movement the major issue is not death, but suffering. Millions of dogs and cats are killed annually in animal shelters with the support of the humane movement, because of the perception that they are better off dead than suffering the indignities of homelessness. It is interesting that the notion "better off dead than underfed" has never been challenged by an animal equivalent to the "Right to Life" movement protecting the human's absolute right to live regardless of the circumstances. In fact, there is virtually no commitment at all about living conditions in humane shelters, because most of their animals will die relatively soon after arrival. There is virtually no quarrel with the number of animals that die in research or in farming. Objections are raised against only the *way* animals are maintained and the *way* they die.

In this light one can easily see why the euthanasia issue is so very important, perhaps disproportionately so, when compared to the many other issues associated with the relatively new field of human–animal interactions.

CONCLUSION

Although in terms of achieving its goals the animal welfare movement has not been particularly successful, it is nonetheless a political force requiring attention. At the very least, the imposition of new regulations, whatever their merit, can create issues of added cost for biomedical research and animal control.

Pound seizure laws require that research animals be raised and purchased, rather than allowing scientists to use the thousands of animals killed daily in shelters. Obviously, specially bred animals cost more, and SPCAs no longer gain income from selling animals to research facilities. Often they must even pay for the removal of dead animals.

The banning of high-altitude chambers in favor of intravenous methods of euthanasia adds greatly to the cost of animal control. As a result, SPCAs may be required to provide fewer services for living animals simply to make the last seconds of dying animals' lives appear more peaceful.

The euthanasia movement is, in part, an extension of the animal welfare movement. Like members of the larger humane movement, euthanasia proponents focus on the pain and suffering of individual creatures, while tending to ignore broader social issues such as why we are killing so many animals, what is the impact on animal control, and why there is such a turnover of animals in our society. In order not to lose perspective, we should recognize the many issues to be addressed. We must understand that our concern for how animals die is part of the broader issue of how we all live and die.

REFERENCES

Beck AM, Katcher AH: Between Pets and People: The Importance of Animal Companionship. New York, G. P. Putnam's Sons, 1983

French RD: Antivivisection and Medical Science in Victorian Society. Princeton NJ, Princeton Univ Press, 1975

Goering H: 1939. A broadcast over the German Radio Network describing the fight against vivisection and measures taken to prohibit it (28 August 1933). In The Political Testament of Herman Goering, 1939

Hoff C: Immoral and moral uses of animals. New Eng J Med 302(2):115-118, 1980

Morgan R: Love and Anger: An Organizing Handbook. Westport CT, Animal Rights Network, 1980

Rowan AN: Alternatives to laboratory animals in biomedical programmes. Animal Regulation Studies 1:103-128, 1977

Ruesch H: Slaughter of the Innocent. New York, Bantam Books, 1975

Singer P: Animal Liberation. A New York Review Book, dist by Random House, 1975

Turner J: Reckoning with the Beast: Animals, Pain, and Humanity. Baltimore, The Johns Hopkins Press, 1980

Verderber RF: Depolarization of Humane Animal Care Groups. Lab Animal 13(6):47-51, 1984

4

The Use of Animals in Research: Attitudes Among Research Workers

Eileen Koski

The use of animals in laboratory experiments, particularly experiments that entail either inflicting pain or euthanatizing research animals, has been the subject of controversy since the nineteenth century (Key and Rodin 1984). In recent years the animal rights movement has made increasing attempts to regulate, limit, or even abolish outright many, if not all, forms of animal experimentation (Chambers and Hines 1983; Griffin and Sechzuer 1983; Paton 1983). The efforts of groups such as People for the Ethical Treatment of Animals (PETA) have even resulted in criminal convictions on charges of cruelty (subsequently dismissed on appeal) against an animal researcher in the case of Taub vs. the State of Maryland in 1981 (Curran 1983).

The "animal liberation movement" actually consists of a loose coalition of groups ranging from relatively conservative humane organizations to more radical groups. The literature that is critical of animal experimentation ranges widely from such moderate positions as that of Hoff (1980), who stated that experimentation involving injury to animal subjects should be limited to those from which "substantial benefits" are expected and escalates to calls for the abolition of all animal exploitation, including the use of animals as a food source (Singer 1985). The arguments used in the debate also range from instances of blatant failure of animal models to predict human responses accurately —as in the case of Thalidomide (Whittaker 1979)—to complex philosophical discussions of the moral status and rights of living creatures and of parallels with other human experience, such as Singer's (1975) equating of "speciesism" with

21

racism and sexism.

The pro-experimentation literature attempts to stress the concern of most scientists for their animal subjects (Adams 1981) while using two basic arguments to support the claim that animal experimentation is justified. The first premise is that human life is more important than animal life and that it is, therefore, wholly justifiable to use animals to alleviate human suffering, even if animal suffering is the means to that end (Fox 1986). The second argument is that animal-rights activists actually exercise double standards, since they condone the use of animals for food but not for research; and that they condemn the use of animals in research while also demanding protection from the possible dangers of new chemicals, new drugs, and various consumer products (McMillan 1979). It is usually stressed by researchers that animals should be treated humanely in the course of experiments and subjected to the least distress possible, if only out of consideration for how the animals' comfort may affect the results of the test (Soma 1983). Even pain researchers, who must, by the nature of their study, inflict pain on their animal subjects without using anethesia, claim that such research can be conducted within reasonable ethical guidelines (Covino et al 1980; Dubner 1983).

I have found minimal evidence in the literature to suggest that animal researchers continue to grapple with the ethical or moral dilemma posed by animal experimentation once their guidelines for justification and humane conditions have been met. Sechzuer (1983) does allude to the fact that researchers must contend with such ethical dilemmas, but even he feels that modern research techniques have minimized the issue. Based on firsthand observations and conversations with animal researchers over the past six years, I have discovered that many animal researchers may actually be far more ambivalent toward their use of animals than the literature indicates. The following study was conducted to examine this impression.

METHODS

Background and sample selection

I have worked in close proximity to animal experimentation for several years: initially in a cancer research facility where rats, mice, and rabbits were used and, more recently, in a cardiology research laboratory where dogs, as well as some guinea pigs and rabbits, are used. During this period I have observed working interactions between researchers and their animal subjects, and I have discussed the use and misuse of animals in research with technicians, postdoctoral fellows, and faculty members, including physicians and research scientists. In an attempt to distill my impressions I conducted several more formal interviews with additional researchers and technicians. Two of these interview subjects were involved with primate research.

The final sample consisted of fifteen respondents. This small sampling was not intended to be representative of animal researchers in general, but rather to provide a basis for subsequent observations.

With the exception of the formal interviews, the subjects were all people with whom I had regular contact in the workplace, although the nature of our professional interaction was completely independent of any animal experimentation.

DATA COLLECTION

The data were gathered principally by means of observation and discussion. I neither observed nor actively participated in any of the experiments, although I did observe several of my subjects interacting with their animal subjects prior to or following experiments.

The discussions all took place in a completely informal context. I stated simply that I was not completely opposed to animal experimentation, but that I did have some reservations, and that I was interested in their feelings and thoughts on the subject. The more formal interviews were conducted with the intent to elicit differences, if any, that might be attributable to different job categories or different backgrounds, such as clinical medicine vs. basic research.

As this inquiry was strictly exploratory, I tried to minimize any direction in the questioning in order to elicit the broader range of issues that might arise. However, four general questions were always asked:

1. Do you feel the animal research you are doing is justified, and if so, why?
2. Do you have any resistance to using particular species; if so, which species and why?
3. How do you feel about using pound animals as opposed to animals bred specifically for research?
4. Do you place any restrictions on the kind of experiments with which you will be involved?

RESULTS

In general, the most interesting observations emerged from lengthy, informal, and wide-ranging discussions. The formal interviews did not provide the same sort of qualitative data that I had been able to obtain from the direct observations and more casual discussions. Specifically, the responses to formal interviews closely approximated the traditional arguments found in the literature, without the reservations expressed by the other interviewees.

In addition, the only time I encountered defensive behavior by my subjects was during formal interviews with people I did not know well. Not all of the formal interviews were characterized by defensive behavior, but none of the informal discussions were. This defensive behavior usually took the form of questions posed to me, such as "Do you eat veal? Do you know how veal calves are raised?" "Do you wear leather, fur, ivory?" "Do you wear eye make-up? Do you know about the Draize test?" or statements such as "People do worse things to each other than we do to animals."

One of the subjects stated emphatically that she would have been more defensive and would have also relied on the traditional scientific arguments to support animal research had she been specifically interviewed for this study, but that she, as well as some others, were willing and able to be more frank with me because I was known to them.

Is animal research justified?

All of my subjects felt that the knowledge gained by animal experimentation justifies some experiments, despite the animal suffering that might occur. This reaction was expected, since animal researchers are, by definition, self-selected for the ability to justify animal experimentation. However, considerable variation appeared, both in the limits placed on that experimentation and in the ease with which this justification was accepted.

Not surprisingly, the strongest convictions and the least ambivalence were expressed by senior faculty members who were firmly committed to animal research as part of their careers. Two physicians expressed the opinion that exposure to human suffering during medical school and residency training had the dual effect of impressing researchers with the compelling need for increased biomedical knowledge and of desensitizing them to excess involvement with their subjects. (While this reasoning sounds plausible, I did not find any appreciable difference between the behavior or reactions of physicians and of research scientists). Junior faculty, postdoctoral fellows, and technicians, who did not necessarily expect to conduct animal experimentation indefinitely, expressed greater reservations.

The actual reasons offered for involvement in animal research did vary somewhat. The senior faculty members simply stated that there was no other way to obtain the information that they needed in their research. One, a researcher in chemical carcinogenesis, said that she never used animals unless absolutely necessary, but that toxicity testing mandates the use of live animals. This researcher also stressed that the cost of maintaining live animals for study was a major deterrent to using live animals if the information could be obtained in any other way.

One junior faculty member and several postdoctoral fellows indicated that the animal experimentation was part of their training. It was, however, made clear that animal experimentation was not an unavoidable part of all training programs in their field, but rather something that had to be accepted if a particular training program were selected.

Two technicians stated that they were interested in research and in animals and wanted to work with laboratory animals to ensure that humane conditions were maintained. Another technician bluntly stated that it was difficult to find work in the research area that he preferred.

Species-specific limitations and pound animal use

None of my respondents reported any moral reservations about the use of rodents, although one postdoctoral fellow was distressed by the fact that some of his colleagues were unable to euthanatize the animals neatly and quickly, thus inflicting more pain than necessary. The majority of interviewees reported their greatest difficulty was in working with dogs and primates. Several people categorically rejected the idea of conducting primate research, stating that primates were "too close" to humans and too intelligent. When I specifically asked four cardiologists about the transplant of a baboon's heart to a human infant, three cited the hierarchical supremacy of the human infant as a self-evidently sufficient reason for the sacrifice of the baboon. (Interestingly, only one expressed concern about the experimental use of the human infant.) The fourth cardiologist, while not totally rejecting this use of a baboon, did find that it raised troubling ethical questions about the possible future breeding of primates specifically as organ donors.

Many of my subjects were currently involved with research in which dogs were used. One particular difficulty experienced by more than half of these subjects was that they were or had been dog owners. Several subjects expressed considerable conflict between the close attachments they had formed to their pet dogs and their treatment of canine experimental subjects. One technician stated that he could not keep a dog as a pet as long as he was involved in this type of research because of "the way a dog looks at you. I couldn't look it in the eyes, knowing what I was doing during the day." One research fellow, talking about his relationship with his dog, remarked, "I don't talk to him about work; he doesn't know what I do for a living." This was said with a laugh, but the researcher admitted that he found it difficult to reconcile his affection for his dog with the way he handled similar animals at work. One technician kept two pet dogs who had both been rescued from their intended fate as experimental subjects.

In the case of dog owners, it appeared necessary for the researchers to differentiate between their pets and the dogs used in research. Several people pointed out that many of the dogs used in research are abandoned strays, destined to be destroyed anyway. Despite the fact that pound dogs may have been pets and the fact that a purebred strain of dogs might produce more consistent laboratory results, virtually all of my subjects preferred the use of pound dogs precisely because of their almost certain fate at the pound. In fact, several people objected strenuously to breeding dogs purely for experimentation when so many dogs are euthanatized annually by humane societies without benefit to anyone, including the dogs.

Several people also cited the poor physical and emotional status of the laboratory dogs to differentiate them from their own pets. I often heard that "most of these dogs are in such bad shape it is a kindness to put them down." That this was a powerful defense became clear whenever a particularly lively, friendly, or attractive dog was delivered to the lab. In some cases, active attempts were made to find homes for such animals rather than using them in experiments. Such rescues were sometimes rationalized by stating that a particular animal was "too small" or "too hairy" for the experiment in question. Some dogs had apparently been pets; some even obeyed simple commands, like "sit." These dogs were reportedly more troubling to work with since the researchers could not help wondering how the animal had devolved from pet to research subject.

Dog owners were not the only researchers, however, who found working with dogs problematic. The main objection was that the researchers felt it is perfectly clear that dogs are intelligent and, in many cases, suffer badly from the research procedures. This issue grew even more difficult when a dog was studied for a long period rather than subjected to a single procedure and sacrificed. Several researchers observed that one reason the long-term studies are more difficult is that a relationship with the dog develops, even when a particular dog may initially have been disliked.

This attachment phenomenon was not restricted to dogs. One researcher used a single rabbit for antibody studies for over two years. The rabbit had been named and well cared for. Although this same researcher had sacrificed large numbers of mice, rats, and other rabbits during this period, he became very distressed at the thought of euthanatizing "Jack" and made extensive efforts to find a home for the rabbit.

The second major explanation for the difficulty of long-term studies was that the researchers watch the animals suffer as a result of the experiments. One faculty member reported her considerable distress at encountering dogs in long-term studies who were obviously suffering, and yet greeted her with excited barking, jumping, licking, and tail-wagging, even though she was the source of their pain and usually only visited the dogs to draw blood or inject drugs.

Long-term studies did not appear to pose any difficulty if the animals did not show any distress. A second researcher who conducted long-term antibody studies with rabbits demonstrated that it was possible to inject a rabbit without the animal exhibiting distress. The rabbits were housed in a clean environment with what appeard to be an adequate amount of space per animal. Her rabbits had good appetites and did not display any of the usual indicators of animal distress, such as avoidance, whining, lethargy, or aggressive behavior. This researcher said that the animals did whine or cry when blood samples were drawn, but that since blood samples were only taken every few weeks, she did not feel that the animals were subjected to an objectionable degree of suffering, considering their overall condition and treatment. This same researcher, however, did point out other rabbit research subjects that apparently were not in good condition: one in particular had damage to its forelimbs that appeared to have been caused by poor techniques in withdrawing blood samples. This researcher objected strenuously to allowing animals to be injured by careless researchers, particularly when a procedure could be carried out without causing residual distress to the animal.

In general, none of my subjects expressed as much distress about conducting experiments on anesthetized animals that would be sacri-ficed without ever regaining consciousness or experiencing pain as they did about experiments that did involve pain and suffering for the animal. All of my subjects insisted that research animals should be treated humanely and should be prevented from suffering as much as

possible. Some, however, were more emphatic than others. Two technicians stated that their primary reason for involvement with animal
research was to ensure that the animals were treated with respect and
care. Some of my informants only stated concern about whether or not
the animal experienced pain, but several were also concerned with the
animal's psychological state. One postdoctoral research fellow spent
several minutes gently stroking and talking to his research animals
(mice, rats, and rabbits) to soothe them before giving them injections or
drawing their blood. He was much distressed by researchers who found
it necessary to strap an animal into a restraining device for this
purpose, objecting that the procedure terrified the animal
unnecessarily.

Limitations on research types

The final limitation placed on experimentation by my interview
subjects had to do with the purpose of the research being conducted.
Most were concerned that some studies are repeated more often than
necessary. For example, several cited the fact that in the United States
drug trials on animals are required for drugs that have already been
thoroughly tested in Europe. These researchers objected to both the
death of animals in those repetitive studies and the delay in making new
drugs available to patients. Many researchers did not object to animal
studies that are designed to produce new information, but were
disturbed by studies that were performed for "the sake of a publication."

Several people were deeply concerned that animal models are not
necessarily applicable to the human problems being studied, citing,
particularly, toxicity testing on mice and rats. The alternative of using
a more closely related animal model, such as primates, introduced
serious issues, ranging from the higher mental status of the animals, to
the dramatic increase in cost. The concept of animal experimentation
to benefit animals was equally troubling to some, since that rationale
entailed selecting one animal to die so that another might live. Some
found this notion even more distressing than the conduct of animal
research for human benefit, since they could not even rely on the
rationale that animals were being sacrificed for the benefit of a higher
life form. One technician asked, "How can we possibly say that the life
of one particular dog is more valuable than that of another?"

Any use of experimental protocols on human subjects in this country
is subject to stringent restrictions and regulations. Some researchers
perceive the effort to impose similar restrictions on animal research as
a threat (Visscher 1981). None of my informants objected to the

imposition of stricter controls on animal experimentation; most welcomed the possibility. One surgeon even suggested that surgical experiments on animals should be performed only by surgeons, since he was concerned that some animals die unnecessarily because of researchers' poor technique. All of my subjects who were involved with dogs expressed strong support for better regulation of animal vendors and complained that many animals are sick when they arrive at the research facility. With respect to dogs not specifically bred for research, some subjects also expressed a desire to be provided with information about the source of each animal to eliminate the nagging fear that the animal might be a stolen or lost pet.

One technician felt that improvements in the treatment of research animals was probably the best means of meeting the assaults of antivivisectionists and assuring the continuance of animal research. One faculty member claimed that she welcomed the intervention of the animal liberation movement and the possibility of increased government regulation of animal care facilities. "Without such regulations," she observed, "we could not justify spending scarce grant money on upgrading animal-care facilities." This sentiment has been expressed in the pro-experimentation literature as one of the few positive results of the animal rights movements (Visscher 1979). This same researcher also suggested that the desire to improve conditions for the animals also alleviated some of the researchers' guilt, since they could at least say, "but we treat them well and they don't suffer."

CONCLUSIONS

The image of animal researchers often propagated by animal rights activists is one of cold scientists who inhumanely, even cruelly, inflict pain on innocent animals. I have heard several of my subjects called "murderers," and seen them harassed for the work they do. The information I have gathered clearly indicates that, far from being cruel, some animal researchers are concerned about the treatment of their animal subjects and are troubled by the ethical and moral implications of their actions.

A sample this small cannot be conclusive about the attitudes of animal researchers in general; however, it should be clear that the ability to justify animal research does not necessarily imply a total lack of ambivalence on the part of a researcher. It is also evident that some animal researchers are supportive of many aspects of the animal rights movement and feel that, as researchers, they also stand to gain by improving the treatment of laboratory animals.

REFERENCES

Adams PM: The scientist's concern for animal welfare. Psychopharmacology Bulletin 17(2):91-93, 1981

Chambers KT, Hines C: Recent developments concerning the use of animals in medical research. J Leg Med 4(1): 109-129, 1983

Covino BG et al: Ethical standards for investigations of experimental pain in animals. Pain 9:141-143, 1980

Curran WJ: Biochemical laboratories and criminal liability for cruelty to animals. New Engl J Med 309(25):1564-5, 1983

Dubner R: Pain research in animals. In The Role of Animals in Biomedical Research. Annals of the New York Academy of Sciences 406:129-132, 1983

Fox MA: The Case for Animal Experimentation: An Evolutionary and Ethical Perspective. London, Univ of California Press, Ltd, 1986

Griffin A, Sechzuer JA: Mandatory versus voluntary regulation of biomedical research. In The Role of Animals in Biomedical Research. Annals of the New York Academy of Sciences 406:187-200, 1983

Hoff C: Immoral and moral uses of animals. New Engl J Med 302(2):115-118, 1980

Key JD, Rodin AE: William Osler and Arthur Conan Doyle versus the antivivisectionists: Some lessons from history for today. Mayo Clin Proc 59:189-196, 1984

McMillian B: Vivisection: do we have double standards? Nursing Times 75(10):397-398, 1979

Paton WDM: Animal experiment: British and European legislation and practice. In The Role of Animals in Biomedical Research. Annals of the New York Academy of Sciences 406:201-214, 1983

Sechzuer JA: The ethical dilemma of some classical animal experiments. In The Role of Animals in Biochemical Research. Annals of the New York Academy of Sciences 406:5-12, 1983

Singer P: Animal Liberation—New Ethics for Our Treatment of Animals. A New York Review Book, dist. by Random House, 1975

Singer P: Ten years of animal liberation. New York Review of Books 31(21,22):46-52, 1985

Soma LR: Anesthetic and analgesic consideration in the experimental animal. In The Role of Animals in Biomedical Research. Annals of the New York Academy of Sciences 406:32-47, 1983

Visscher MB: Animal rights and alternative methods—Two new twists in the antivivisection movement. The Pharos 42(4):11-19, 1979

Visscher MB: Current attempts to prevent the use of animals in medical research. JAMA 245(2)1223-1224, 1981

Whittaker A: Vivisection: the case against. Nursing Times 75(10):395-396, 1979

5

Animal Euthanasia and Moral Stress

Bernard E. Rollin

For as long as human beings have thought about their bodies, it has been recognized that exposure to noxious physical, mental, and emotional experiences has negative effects on health. There exist, for example, classic literary descriptions of the way in which personal tragedy can "age" individuals and destroy their physical well-being. Only in the last half-century, however, has an attempt been made to deal with this phenomenon scientifically. The result has been a bewildering and rapidly increasing literature dealing with "stress" in humans and animals.

Although the literature is vast and exhaustive, it is extremely difficult to pin down precisely what is meant by stress. The term is sometimes applied to environmental situations (cold or heat stress), sometimes to psychological situations (explicitly in humans and implicitly in animals)—e.g., emotional stress, separation stress, sometimes to the effect of those situations on the physiology of the person or animals, and sometimes to a combination of all the above. Very often, stress is discussed from a physiological point of view solely in terms of what Hans Selye (1978), in his pioneering work, called the General Adaptation Syndrome (GAS). This syndrome involves activation of the pituitary-adrenal axis (i.e., the interrelations between ACTH and glucocorticoids) to deal with long-term stress and activation of the sympathicoadrenal axis (i.e., mechanisms mediated by the catecholamines, epinephrine and norepinephrine, to deal with "fight or flight" in short-term stress situations). Because of the influence of Selye's work and the tendency of researchers to look primarily at the mechanisms he delineated, there has sometimes been a tendency to *define* stress in terms of those mechanisms. Doing so is problematic, for two reasons. First, some situations that activate the axes, such as eating, are not what we would normally call stressful; second, various other bodily systems, such as the reproductive and digestive systems, are directly affected by the existence of stressful conditions. The definition of stress in the scientific literature is highly vague and obscure, and the entire concept is desperately in need of conceptual clarification. Much of the use of the concept relies covertly on common-sense notions of what is "stressful" or what makes a person feel physically, mentally, or emotionally uncomfortable. Despite the fact that much of recent scientific literature has, through a misguided obsession with "objectivity," attempted to speak of stress only in terms of objective, observable physiological effects in man and animals, I believe that there is an irreducible psychological component of the concept, which gives it its intrinsic plausibility and which is implicitly appealed to by scientists when it is applied to animals.

For our purposes, it is not necessary to resolve this conceptual muddle. It suffices to point out that in humans and animals, it has now been documented that what common sense calls stressful conditions can have profound physiological effects. All workers in the laboratory animal field know (or should know) that failure to control stress can lead to profound skewing of metabolic and physiological variables, and can put all forms of animal research into jeopardy. It has been pointed out that virtually any stimulators can be a source of stress to the laboratory rat, and it is well known that heat, cold, noise, crowding, light, darkness, temperature, air quality, infection, restraint, trauma, fear, surprise, disease, and a host of other variables can be sources of stress to an animal (Isaac 1979). Recent work has indicated just to what a profound extent animals' physiology and behavior can be affected by variables that are usually not even acknowledged—walking into an animal room, petting the animal, the personality of the animal technician, and so forth. The results of Gartner et al (1980) are especially dramatic because, if taken seriously, they put into question the value of much biomedical research. They show that merely moving a rat in its cage is enough to create a blood plasma profile indicative of microcirculatory shock reaction. Increasing attention is also being paid to the effect stress can have on behavior, especially among farm animals. Behavioral pathologies under stress have been described for a wide variety of farm, zoo, and laboratory animals.

In any event, it has become increasingly clear that stress can have incalculably pernicious effects on human health. As mentioned earlier, there is virtually no aspect of the human body that cannot be deleteriously affected, directly or indirectly, by prolonged stress. Cardiovascular health, blood pressure, susceptibility to infection, susceptibility to cancer, reproductive ability, gastrointestinal activity, ulcers, post-surgical or other wound recovery, migraine, headaches, colitis, irritable bowel syndrome, skin diseases, intellectual abilities, emotional states, nervous and mental diseases, kidney diseases, arthritis, allergies, asthma, alcohol, and drug abuse are all directly tied to stress factors. In addition, a person's exposure to stress obviously can wreak havoc in one's family life, sex life, career, social relations, self-image, life satisfaction, productivity, and so on. In short, no area of one's life is untouched by the effects of stress.

As the extraordinary effects of stress have become better known, society has paid more and more attention to the sources of stress and to controlling its destructive consequences. High stress occupations, such as test pilot and corporate executive, have been recognized, and people whose personalities are likely to lead them to court stress have been defined, and suggestions and alterations have been made to deal with these problems. For example, an attempt is made to reduce stress for those in high-stress jobs by providing them with more free time. Similarly, corporations have become increasingly conscious of high-stress positions in their organizations, and have made workshops and exercise rooms available to their personnel in an attempt to mitigate these stresses.

Furthermore, techniques of stress management have been developed. These include meditation, breathing techniques, yoga, exercise, imaging, and biofeedback. Unquestionably, these techniques are of value for many people in a variety of stressful occupations, whether the stresses are physical or psychological. Whether one's stress comes from facing physical danger, as test pilots do, or from psychological pressure like that of trial lawyers, surgeons, or journalists who must meet deadlines, there is little doubt that these simple techniques can be invaluable for teaching people to relax. This is especially true when the source of stress is of a short-term nature, like that which occurs when one is about to take a test. In this regard, it is interesting that the highest catecholamine levels ever measured in humans occurred in graduate students taking doctoral exams (Best, personal communication). Very likely some of these techniques may also be helpful to those whose jobs present a never-ending series of stressful crises.

There is, however, another source of stress, or kind of stress that has been very nearly ignored in the literature. This sort of stress, which differs from the stresses discussed so far, is encountered by those whose jobs require that they kill animals for reasons other than the alleviation of intractable pain and suffering; i.e., for reasons that are not to the direct benefit of the animal. I refer to this as moral stress. The groups most obviously susceptible to this sort of stress are veterinarians, humane society workers, laboratory animal veterinarians, and laboratory technicians. In my own experience, I have heard this form of stress described at length by members of each of these groups.

For veterinarians in pet practice, the demand that they kill healthy animals for the convenience of their owners is a constant source of stress. No veterinarian in small-animal practice can escape this situation. As I have discussed elsewhere (Rollin 1981), people want animals killed for the most appalling reasons: they have no use for a litter of puppies and only wanted their children to witness the "miracle of birth"; they have undergone psychoanalysis and are no longer "poodle persons" but "Doberman persons"; they are moving and don't want the difficulty of finding a place that takes pets; they are going on vacation and don't wish to spend the kennel fee, since it is cheaper to get a new dog at the pound; the animal no longer matches their color scheme; the dog barks, urinates, chews, chases children, digs up the yard, is too old to jog with them, and so on. In fact, euthanasia is the largest cause of pet animal death in the United States. Veterinarians cannot turn their backs on these cases, for they know that doing so simply pushes them on to a colleague or to a pound down the street. Even worse, veterinarians' failure to engage the issue can lead to abandonment of the animals or do-it-yourself "euthanasia," such as the time-honored gunny-sack-off-the-bridge technique or even the release of animals onto the freeway. Exactly the same problem holds true for workers in humane societies. Among laboratory-animal veterinarians and technicians the complaint is again the same, but compounded by the fact that they are often engaged in inflicting pain, disease, and injury on animals, for reasons that do not benefit the animals, before the final act of killing them. I have had extensive experience with all three groups: I teach at a veterinary college and I lecture to veterinarians all over the world; I have interacted with humane society workers at two conferences on euthanasia (one of which I helped organize) and at humane societies all across North America; and almost daily I communicate with laboratory animal people across North America and Europe. As a result, I have come to certain conclusions regarding this much-neglected problem.

In the first place, there is probably no analogy to this sort of stress in people whose jobs require primary concern with humans—even in the notoriously high-stress profession of dentistry. Although the fact that dentists are universally feared as inflictors of pain is a major source of stress, at least both patient and dentist know that there is good reason for pain, that it is of ultimate benefit to the patient, and that it is, after all, an unfortunate consequence of a therapeutic modality. No such recourse exists for those who work with pet or laboratory animals. The

death and pain they are required to inflict are not excused by the fact
that they are benefiting the objects of their ministrations. In every case,
there is another choice—the particular animal could conceivably live or
not be used invasively or, as one vet bitterly told me, could be out chas-
ing butterflies.

The stress on these workers is further augmented by a bitter irony: the
fact that the people most affected by the stress are those who care most
deeply about the creatures they must hurt or kill. If one is totally
insensitive, if one does not care deeply about animals, if one is hard or
even sadistic, there need be no stress whatever in these occupations. But
consider those who become veterinarians because they wanted to make
things better for animals (75 to 85% of veterinarians in my experience);
those who became shelter workers because they wanted to help animals
(over 90%); or those who became laboratory animal technicians because
they liked to take care of animals (70% of the people in the field). For
such people, the stress is unrelenting, unceasing, and unbearable
because the source of stress is constant, overwhelming, and inescap-
able. It arises from a sense of discord and tension between what one is
in fact doing and one's reason for choosing that field, between what one
feels one ought to be and what one feels oneself to be, between ideal and
reality. It is for this reason that I call this moral stress.

It is obvious to anyone who has experienced this sort of stress that it
is qualitatively different from either physical or mental stresses of other
sorts. Whereas other stresses impinge on the periphery of what one
does, this sort of stress strikes at one's very core. It is equally obvious
that no amount of stress management techniques can really help deal
with this sort of stress. In actual fact, to apply these techniques to this
sort of stress is roughly analogous to using amphetamine for exhaustion—both may help individuals carry on for brief periods but fail to get
at the root of the problem. In either case, failure to get at the root of the
problem allows the problem to become progressively worse, so that one
may finally drop from exhaustion or, analogously, find the stress too
great to bear. At that point, one's useful life in the vocation in question
is over.

My intuitive grasp of this problem was dramatically confirmed in
dealing with animal welfare workers whose primary job is performing
euthanasia on dogs and cats. It is known that such people experience
enormous stress and suffer many consequences of it. At a euthanasia
conference held at Colorado State University, the well-meaning but
misguided planners had scheduled a session with a psychologist to
teach the participants techniques of stress management that they could
employ when faced with the stresses of their jobs. For example, the

psychologist advised them to relax during the actual killing by imagin-
ing some pleasant scene, such as a desert island. Needless to say, this
suggestion evoked considerable hostility. Workers remarked that the
psychologist clearly didn't have the slightest notion of what they were
experiencing, if he thought that that sort of technique was at all relevant. ("It's like putting a band-aid on a bullet wound," one lady told me.)

In my presentation, I raised serious questions about the relevance of
such "band-aids" to the performance of euthanasia on healthy animals.
As I described it, the source of stress for these people is based, in the
final analysis, on their belief that it is wrong to kill healthy animals.
Even though the workers could say they were saving the animals from
something worse, that didn't really help, first because they couldn't
know this for certain, and second because they were still killing healthy
dogs and cats that they did not think ought to be killed, but instead
should be out doing doglike or catlike things. I also argued that their
stress is based on the tragic self-awareness that those who cared most
about animals had essentially been "conned" by society, as one person
put it, into doing one of the worst things to animals, taking their lives
to clean up society's mess. Everything I said was fervently confirmed
by the participants.

Furthermore, I continued, there is really only one way to deal with
this stress, and that is to feel that one is expending every effort to make
one's own job obsolete. In other words, these people had to feel that they
were not only society's hatchet men, but that they were doing something
positive, whether by educating the public, attempting to pass legislation,
or taking other action to eradicate the need for killing healthy animals
in the future. Thus, I argued (and again, this was confirmed by the
participants' responses) that the only way to control the stress of such
a job was to be absolutely clear about why one was doing it, by having
a plan to change the society that makes the job necessary, and by doing
whatever one could to implement that strategy. Thus, in this case, the
response to moral stress is articulation of one's moral principles, and
articulation of the manner in which one hopes to realize them.

I submit that a similar situation causes moral stress for pet animal
veterinarians, laboratory animal veterinarians, and laboratory technicians who were drawn to these fields because they like, care about,
and wish to help animals (or even partly for these reasons). The
situation is, in fact, much worse for laboratory animal people, not only
because they must cause pain as well as death, but because of increasing
attacks on the use of animals in research. The moral stress is not only
internal, but external; with more and more people raising questions
about the legitimacy of the research enterprise, it is difficult not to feel

morally insecure about what one does. This is somewhat true of shelter workers as well. Members of both groups have told me repeatedly that they hide the nature of their work from friends and even family, and are often criticized for it by people close to them who know what they do. Such a situation is clearly untenable. It generates not only stress and makes job satisfaction increasingly difficult, but isolates people in this field from one of the most basic mechanisms for alleviating stress— talking about it to anyone who will listen.

In summary, six facts are the major sources of moral stress on people who must kill healthy animals:

1. These people have been drawn into their work partly by genuine moral concern for animals. (If one has no concern for animals except as tools for human benefit or scientific research, this sort of stress will not arise.)
2. Laboratory animal veterinarians and technicians are required to inflict pain, disease, and suffering on healthy animals, as well as to kill healthy animals.
3. Except for those that are starving or suffering, animals themselves do not benefit from the killing.
4. Society often disapproves of or does not support these activities, even though their justification is often in their alleged benefit to society. Pet owners and society in general prefer to believe that humane societies are able to find good homes for the vast majority of animals.
5. People in this field often feel compelled not to discuss their work with "outsiders."
6. These workers often feel they must suppress their rage and moral indignation at owners and clients.

Taken together, these facts seem formidable. It is not surprising that some people in these fields protect themselves by enclosing themselves in a carapace, by abandoning the moral concern that is the chief source of the moral conflict that generates their stress; by thinking of themselves only as "scientists" or public servants; by shutting off their feelings for animals; or by convincing themselves that animals don't suffer or that their suffering doesn't matter. As protective devices, such moves are quite comprehensible. But do they represent the best answer to dealing with the stress?

In my view, there is a way of dealing with moral stress that is better for people in the field, for society, and for animals, even though it is far more difficult. This method requires that one not forget the reasons one was drawn to care for animals but, on the contrary, remember them in Plato's sense of remembrance—not only recall them, but systematize them into a rational and defensible moral position (Rollin 1983).

In my view, all those drawn to pet practice, humane work, or laboratory animal work either wholly or partly by feelings that the suffering, pain, and lives of animals matter must, first and foremost, articulate for themselves in rational terms their ideal ethical position regarding the moral status of animals in society. This ideal is important in much the same way that we need ideals for science, ethics, and politics, not as blueprints for instant social change, but as yardsticks to tell us where we are deficient.

In my work with each of these groups, I have tried to develop that ethic in terms of the fundamental rights of animals. That need not be anyone else's ethic; for example, some people may simply believe that animals ought not to suffer or die unnecessarily or for trivial reasons. I know from past experience that most people in each of these groups hold some notion like mine, that animals have value in themselves, not just as tools for us, and that aspects of their nature ought to be protected. However, the point is that these individuals need to have some rational and defensible articulation of their basic feelings of concern for animals.

Having articulated to oneself a moral position, workers in this field must then ask themselves whether or not they are doing everything in their power, individually and collectively, to actualize that ethic. Few people in any of these fields have taken these steps. Until recently, few people in humane work had developed an ethic. Even though most of them had realized that something is wrong in a society that kills 15 to 20 million healthy dogs and cats a year, few had gone beyond the tired old saw of "spay and neuter." However, as progressive humane societies like the one in San Francisco have shown, individuals armed with an ethic can dramatically raise the animal adoption rate and awaken the public to the realities of animal-related problems. One must not resign oneself to doing society's dirty work: as long as someone will do it, the dirty work will keep coming. It is essential to feel and to know that one is somehow striking at the sources of the problem, not merely at its symptoms, and working toward a world in which no one must do such a job. Meaningful public education directed at adults, not merely children, and efforts to legalize the rights of pet animals, perhaps by licensing pet owners, are major steps in the right directions.

There is also much positive work to be done by pet veterinarians. Organized veterinary medicine has tended to sidestep animal welfare issues. A growing number of veterinary schools (but still a minority) are incorporating ethics courses into their curriculums, and the key question in veterinary ethics is, of course, the moral status of animals. Ideally, no veterinarian should emerge from veterinary school without having formulated a clear picture of the value of animal life and suffering, and of the hard realities of such ethical questions as the euthanasia of healthy animals. Furthermore, veterinarians who value animals in themselves, as the vast majority of veterinarians do, must emerge as animal advocates and educators. American veterinary medicine is culpable for its failure to use its Aesculapian authority on behalf of the welfare of animals in society; all too often, it has gone with the flow of social and economic pressure. But as society begins to engage the hard questions of the moral status of animals in society—whether these are pets, food animals, or laboratory animals—veterinarians must inevitably provide leadership in this area. This means that veterinarians must be far more than medical practitioners. They must, for example, be counselors on behavioral problems because, as noted earlier, euthanasia for behavioral problems is the single largest cause of death among pet animals. This, in turn, means that behavior must loom large in veterinary curriculums. At the moment, few veterinary schools have required courses on this subject. Veterinary education must adapt to the changing view of animals in society. Accordingly, curricula must highlight, not ignore, ethics, behavior, and the complex social dimensions of veterinary medicine.

Individual practice too can be dramatically changed to harmonize with veterinarians' view of themselves as animal advocates. Far too few veterinarians take seriously their role in educating clients on behalf of animals. With the Aesculapian authority they bear as medical professionals, such a role is natural. Assuming such a role need not mean financial loss. I know veterinarians in California who have clients who do not yet own animals; these clients pay the veterinarians to advise them on the selection, training, and assimilation of an animal into the family even before they acquire an animal. Veterinarians must be trained, if possible, to do what good veterinarians have always done intuitively: to plead the cases of animals whose owners wish them to receive euthanasia for bad reasons, and to seek alternatives for such animals. Veterinary schools would profit greatly from having successful local practitioners as adjunct faculty. Too often, veterinary education is more concerned with teaching about laser surgery or monoclonal antibodies than with developing techniques for persuading clients.

Finally, organized veterinary medicine, beginning at the local level, must work to create social policy in the form of legislation or ordinances to elevate the status of animals, and to make the acquisition and destruction of an animal at least as difficult as getting a driver's license.

Initiating rational legislation in this area is in the veterinarian's self-interest, not merely the animals'. Not only would such action mitigate moral stress, it would forestall the extreme legislation that can emerge from crisis situation—for example, the legislative banning or severe restriction of animals after a dramatic dog-bite case, after a crusade against dog feces, or after a zöonotic epidemic.

Precisely the same sort of strategy should be relevant to individuals in the laboratory animal field. The situation for these people is more difficult, however, for there is virtually no hope of creating a society in which there will be no need to hurt or kill animals for scientific research. Therefore, the moral stress and the correlative tendency to callousness is very great, although one must never minimize what pet veterinarians must feel when they are casually asked to kill animals they may have delivered or, on some prior occasion, fought to save from disease or injury. Laboratory animal workers sometimes get to know their animals individually as well, and give them names instead of numbers. However, when such concern is divorced from a reasoned stance of animal advocacy, it can increase moral stress when the animals one has cared for so deeply must be hurt or killed. It is doubtless for this sort of reason that many people choose to leave the field, ironically eliminating from it those who care the most. A better way, a more productive way, it seems to me, is to stay in the field and try to ensure that the interests of the animals are served as fully as possible even while the animals are being used. In essence, this too means becoming an animal advocate and seeking out ways in which things can be made better for animals within the context of scientific research. We are very far from protecting the interests of animals in research—witness our use of animals for multiple surgery and the fact that the overwhelming majority of research protocols in the U.S. do not employ analgesia for painful procedures on laboratory animals, even when their use would not affect the scientific data. (The use of anesthetics is, of course, mandated.)

This in turn means not apologizing for research or for the status quo, not accepting the official line that all is fine in animal use in this country, but recognizing that there are problems, and trying to fix them. As a prominent laboratory animal veterinarian recently told the American Association for Laboratory Science, our job is to care for animals, not to defend research. Many times, of course, veterinarians and technicians are powerless to effect changes they clearly see as necessary, especially when they are dealing with high-powered, well-funded medical researchers who don't care about animals. It is for this reason, among others, that I have argued for the laboratory animal veterinary community's support for legislation: to give laboratory animal workers some power, which they sorely need.

There is no conflict between caring about animals and working in research once one is committed to the inevitability of the invasive use of animals and has accepted a role as an animal advocate. Those in such a position are all that stand in the way of animals being treated solely as tools. If research goes on, let it at least go on in a way that does not ride roughshod over the interests of creatures who cannot defend themselves. Only in this way can moral stress be overcome, transformed from a drain on vitality and well-being to a creative challenge, and from there to a positive moral force. In attempting to minimize the suffering and unnecessary death of research animals, laboratory animal workers minimize their own suffering. If research is to continue, as it surely will, let it be done by those who care and to whom the suffering and death of animals is of profound moment. I submit that we are living at a critical historical moment. Never has society been more conscious of the ethical dimensions of its treatment of animals. As a Harvard University study (1982) put it, animal welfare shows every indication of being the Vietnam of the decade. It is in our hands to ensure that this international moral stirring is not vainly dissipated, and that its inchoate and largely uninformed emotional energy is channelled in a constructive direction for the genuine betterment of animals, as well as for the health and welfare of our own bodies, minds, and souls.

REFERENCES

Animal Rights Movement in the United States. Harvard Univ Office of Government and Community Affairs, 1982

Best J: personal communication

Gartner D, Buttner D, Dohler K, Friedel R, Lindena J, Trautschold I: Stress response of rats to handling and experimental procedure. Laboratory Animals 14:267-274, 1980

Isaac W: Causes and consequences of stress in the rat and mouse. American Association for Laboratory Animal Science Seminar on Stress. Atlanta GA, 1979

Rollin B: Animal Rights and Human Morality, Part IV. Buffalo NY, Prometheus Books, 1981

Rollin B: The Teaching of Responsibility. CW Hume Memorial Lecture, Potters Bar, Hertfordshire, Universities Federation for Animal Welfare, 1983

Selye H: The Stress of Life (revised ed). New York, McGraw-Hill, 1978

Wolfe T: American Association for Laboratory Animal Science Seminar on Perception of Pain and Distress in Laboratory Animals, Cincinnati OH, 1984

6

Euthanasia and the Human/Animal Compassion Bond

James Moneymaker

Before examining the issue of euthanasia in veterinary medicine, let us consider some arguments for and against euthanasia in humans, in order to provide a moral and ethical context. In any discussion of euthanasia, a distinction must first be made between active and passive methods. Active euthanasia refers to cases in which an individual is killed, for example, by a lethal injection, in response to his or her own request to be put out of misery. Passive euthanasia occurs when the individual is simply allowed to die, either through starvation or refusal by medical personnel to administer further life-saving techniques. An important point is that although active euthanasia involves the actual killing of an individual, and is therefore deemed morally reprehensible (as well as illegal in the United States), the act is nevertheless perceived by many to be necessary. On the other hand, passive euthanasia is commonly considered morally acceptable, especially in those cases when the victim wants to die.

Further distinctions in types of euthanasia are also recognized. The most simply stated cases involve voluntary euthanasia, in which the individual is in complete control of his faculties and asks to be killed. Nonvoluntary euthanasia occurs when the individual is either semiconscious or in a permanent coma, and thus is unable to make any judgment concerning his condition. The problem here is to show that the individual is so deeply in coma that there can be no question of any cure—i.e., that the condition is irreversible. Although this person may still be alive in the biological sense, life was technically over when all signs of consciousness were lost. Finally, involuntary euthanasia occurs when the individual informs his physician and family that he does not wish to die, but is nevertheless killed or allowed to die (Rachels 1975).

It is reasonable to observe that killing people violates their "right to life"; however, if they ask to be killed, then their death is no longer a violation and those who committed it cannot be held morally responsible. In addition, other obvious exceptions to the sanctity-of-life argument demonstrate that killing need not be absolutely immoral. For example, someone about to be murdered must act in self-defense, and many people favor capital punishment for vicious murderers. The sixth commandment is not interpreted to forbid killing in a "just" war. Today, many religious leaders favor active euthanasia: the American Humanist Association found that more religious leaders signed the petition in favor of euthanasia than persons in any other category (*The Humanist* 1974). Even Roman Catholic thinkers are reassessing their traditional ban on mercy killing; the celebrated Catholic philosopher Daniel Maguire (1975:36) stated, "...it may be moral and should be legal to accelerate the death process by taking direct action, such as overdosing with morphine or injecting potassium, and so on."

How can one reply to the view that if active euthanasia were legalized, a real potential of serious abuse would arise? Sometimes referred to as the "slippery slope" or "wedge" principle, this view holds that once we accept killing in some cases, we have stepped onto a slippery slope or wedge that will inevitably slide us further down until all respect for life is lost (Sullivan 1976). However, it is unrealistic to argue that if we start killing people to put them out of their misery, we may ultimately kill many more for reasons of convenience. We would not be courting disaster if we were to set up a social policy legalizing active euthanasia. Naturally, some abuses may occur, as is always the case with a new social policy, but would not the advantages outweigh the abuses? The question should not be ignored.

In the case of the terminal patient who wishes to be killed rather than endure a slow, agonizing death, active euthanasia seems morally acceptable and should be legal for the same reason that it is used today in veterinary medicine: because the veterinarian must employ mercy killing to end the suffering of a creature when that suffering cannot be alleviated. To elect euthanasia extends mercy to the victim and is therefore more ethical than allowing the patient's suffering to continue.

As for individuals who are in a semiconscious or comatose state, their reactions to the situation are nonexistent. More important, the continuation of life through artificial means is both pointless and wasteful when those same medical resources could be better applied to serve those who can still be helped. Certainly, the same attitude should pertain to animals.

One thing is clear: public opinion concerning euthanasia probably parallels attitudes among medical professionals, whether dealing with the lives of humans or animals. Although no medical society in the United States has endorsed the legalization of euthanasia, ordinary compassion seems to favor following such a procedure for the incurably ill. Moreover, many people feel that an "easy way out" should be available for the aged and incurably ill. The numerous problems invoked by the unnatural prolongation of the lives of the aged and the hopelessly afflicted suggest the need for a less rigid application of the moral and legal prohibitions against euthanasia.

ANIMAL EUTHANASIA

The entire range of attitudes toward euthanasia may be extended to veterinary medicine — as well as to pet owners who choose euthanasia for their animals who are in great pain or incurably ill.

One problem is that countless pet owners may begin to regret the decision to euthanatize their animals. Often, bitter regrets produce feelings of guilt, which may ultimately result in permanent anxiety, neuroses, or even psychoses. It is not ordinarily the actual death that produces guilt and anxiety in the owner, but rather the uncertainty of the evidence provided by the veterinarian upon whose professional advice the owner acted.

A further problem is the ever–present possibility that while the owner is deciding to have a pet euthanatized, a new drug may be discovered to eliminate virtually all pain associated with certain incurable diseases.

It is important to recall that animals and humans differ in significant ways. A dog can be relieved of its suffering, but lacks the human capacity to transform suffering into meaningful achievement. Indeed, were "Helen Keller a horse, born blind and deaf, it might have been best to shoot her" (Maguire 1977:298). It is the human capacity to transcend a situation that gives human suffering a qualitative distinctiveness over that of nonhumans.

Nevertheless, the common origin of our own and other species prompts the recognition that other species have capacity for pleasure and pain (consciousness) that is similar to that of humans. As Albert Schweitzer observed, ". . . let us not forget that some of the more evolved animals show that they have feelings and are capable of impressive, sometimes amazing acts of fidelity and devotion" (Free 1982:41). Theirs, however, is an instinctual consciousness, neither rational nor critical. Animals cannot possess knowledge in the human sense, nor can they exercise real choice. Their values are provided by their physical form and by their surroundings. They can choose only between the means or purposes that are already fixed or determined for them by instinct. Unlike humans, animals cannot choose among ends as well as means. Perhaps this is a divine gift to them that humans do not enjoy. Because humans are moral beings, we know the difference between good and evil, and are condemned to bear the moral responsibility of making ethically correct judgments. We cannot be guided by our unconscious nature. We must learn how to discern the values necessary to assist our nonhuman companions in both life and death.

> The important thing is that we are part of life. We are born of other lives; we possess the capacities to bring still other lives into existence. . . So nature compels us to recognize the fact of mutual dependence, each life necessarily helping the other lives which are linked to it (Free 1982:27).

Consciousness of self and the ability to understand and choose between alternatives is crucial in the dialectic concerning the justification of euthanasia for any animal whose future existence is likely to be pathetic. If an animal is not conscious of self and its future appears miserably wretched, then the only humane, compassionate course is to alleviate the creature's suffering by euthanasia. The issue is not one of diminishing happiness, but of eradicating further suffering through death. Even when consciousness of self is present, the animal is not capable of understanding its future prospects or of choosing whether to live or die; it should be deemed morally right and necessary for others to make this choice for the animal. This choice, however, is justifiable only if it is truly made out of compassionate interest for the being who is absolutely incapable of making the choice for itself. Whatever we choose, we are responsible for the forseeable consequences that result, just as we are equally responsible for the fate of an animal we allow to continue to exist in a miserable state.

Ultimately, the law of humanitarian compassion speaks for all living things, as did Albert Schweitzer when he wrote: ". . .we need a boundless ethics which will include the animals also" (Free 1982:27). Suffering is evil, and the abolition of pain justifies even means traditionally regarded as "immoral."

REFERENCES

Free AC (ed): Animals, Nature, and Albert Schweitzer. New York, The Albert Schweitzer Fellowship, 1982

The Humanist. 34(4):5, 1974

Maguire DC: A Catholic view of mercy killing. In Kohl M (ed): Beneficent Euthanasia, pp 34-43. New York, Prometheus Books, 1975

Maguire DC: Deciding for yourself: the objections. In Weir R (ed): Ethical Issues in Death and Dying, pp 284-310. New York, Columbia Univ Press, 1977

Rachels J: Active and passive euthanasia. New Engl J Medicine 292:78-80, 1975

Sullivan JV: The immorality of euthanasia. In Kohl M (ed): Beneficent Euthanasia, pp 12-33. New York, Prometheus Books, 1975

7

Symbolic, Historical, and Cultural Aspects of Animal Euthanasia

Paul H. Langner

A symbol is defined as "a token of identity" by virtue of resemblance, accepted cultural convention, or "an object or act that represents a repressed complex through unconscious association rather than through objective resemblance or conscious substitution" (Webster 1965). Symbols are inherent in the serial, multiple euthanasia of animals because of the resulting conscious and unconscious representations that the process conveys to humans.

Euthanasia is defined as "an easy death" (Webster 1965) or "a quiet, painless death without fear or anxiety" (*Guide to the Care and Use of Experimental Animals* 1980). More specifically, "regardless of whether individual or mass euthanasia is undertaken, the procedure followed must [produce] death without signs of panic, pain, or distress" and must entail "minimum time of loss of consciousness...have minimal emotional effects on the observer and operator...and be safe, reliable, clean, and simple" (*Guide to the Care and Use of Experimental Animals* 1980). This type of humane killing *en masse* is mandated by federal law for experimental and food animals in our society. Even when the process is properly practiced in the mechanical sense, however, the symbolic meaning may be detrimental to both the practitioner and ultimately to the animal involved. This chapter examines some of the historical roots of serial euthanasia of animals and explores the aberrant effects that may currently obtain in food animal production, in research, teaching, and testing, and in stray pet or "surplus animal" control.

To the public at large, the concept of multiple killing is "slaughter," conceived as "wanton destruction" or "massacre," rather than humane euthanasia of animals for justifiable causes (Webster 1965). The idea of planned killing evokes conflict between Eros (the life instinct, the drive toward growth and complex organization) and Thanatos (the death instinct). As Freud (1938) had done, Levinson (1972) interpreted this interaction as the clash between a drive for conscious experience and the entropic direction of natural systems toward a lower energy level of "ultimate. . .inert uniformity." Further, Levinson (1972) pointed out, if these drives are not resolved in the individual, destructive behaviors may result. Two more fundamental mechanisms leading to negative attitudes toward animals on the part of those who perform euthanasia are displaced frustrations and lack of power, which can cause people to see themselves as being controlled by a total institution (Lifton 1982; Owens, Davis, and Smith 1981).

Since we evolved from scavengers to hunters, we have killed animals in a variety of rapid and relatively painless ways for several reasons. Leakey (1977) viewed the hunting of animals by humans as a natural act. Freud (1938) recognized animism, the attribution of similar metaphysical spirits to all creatures, as the belief system of ancient hunter-gatherers. As such, animism preceded religion and science as humanity's original world-view, which directed, or at least influenced, hunters to be respectful and merciful to their prey.

Today, hunter-gatherers such as the Bushmen of South Africa still hunt, kill, prepare, and consume their animal prey with a reverence for the spirit of a fellow creature. According to Vander Post (1961), this reverence has been maintained through the hundreds of thousands of years of the history of this people. In this ancient context, when an animal is killed its death is seen as a moment of truth that is the transition from one realm of existence to the next (Vander Post 1961).

Traditionally, the Bushmen killed one animal at a time, and only after the animal had been rendered unconscious by shooting it with a drug-tipped dart or arrow. Although the American Plains Indians sometimes killed many bison at once, attacking a herd on horseback and forcing the animals to stampede over a cliff (Coon 1977), the Sioux and other Indians of the buffalo hunting culture showed reverence for the kindred spirits of the animals. The buffalo was their sustenance, and they were grateful for its abundance. Their gratitude extended to other animals and to the spirits that they believed created the animals. They expressed reverence in rituals attached to all phases of obtaining and using the animals' bodies, thus honoring the perceived source of life (Vander Post 1961).

Providing a quick, painless death for the quarry without causing it prior apprehension assured meat for the tribe and safety for the hunter. This atavistic principle persists in our culture, as shown in Corder's 1978 novel, *The Deer Hunter*, in which the point is made that a deer should be killed with one shot.

> ". . .as if by magic, a large, black-muzzled broad shouldered buck appeared,. . .a princely animal, mythic against the backdrop of snow and pine and mountainside. It lifted its head to test the air. The shot exploded. The deer sprang straight up in the air, spun around, and then dropped in its tracks, a foreleg twitched once, and then it was still" (p 29).

This example includes manifestations of beauty, dignity, strength, loss, and relief. Here is respect for the nature of the animal, recognition of its individuality and intrinsic worth, concern over achieving a rapid, unstressful, and dignified death, and a sense of relief when this goal is successfully reached. The *process* is of paramount importance here. It is imbued with qualities of tradition and ritual.

Throughout history, humans have considered the ethical concomitants of the killing of animals. The English peasants of Thomas Hardy's day regarded slow exsanguination, without concern for the suffering of the pig or cow, as a means to improve the quality of the meat (Hardy 1967). Other traditions state that "the righteous man knows the soul of his animal" (Levinger 1979). For pious Jews and Muslims, rapid severing of the carotid arteries or jugular veins of sheep and cattle ensured the animals a quick, merciful loss of consciousness. This practice has, of course, been perverted in modern slaughterhouses where the shackle-and-hoist restraint method is used. Today, in laboratories and in humane-society or municipal animal-control settings, rapid, painless death without causing the animals prior awareness and apprehension constitutes what we term euthanasia, or "good" death.

Benning (1976) pointed out the difficult logistics of dealing with huge populations of uncared-for and unwanted pet animals. According to Benning, the right to a rapid, painless death is explicit, the only question being the appropriate means and place. Although Rice (1968) pointed out that animals may become a human's closest tie to the world, Corson (1977) noted that depersonalization contributes to the abuse of animals.

Szaz (1968) decried excessive concern for animals as ignoble and symptomatic of our reaction against a hypocritical viewpoint. Levinson (1972) offered the view that "Man is going through a period of detachment, even estrangement from nature following his conquest over natural forces. The machine dominates man's thinking and life spaces." There is variation and conflict in human regard for animals and, consequently, in our attitudes toward euthanasia of these animals.

Owens, Davis, and Smith (1981) described the plight of euthanasia technicians, who are responsible for providing rapid, painless death to surplus pets but who may themselves experience psychological pain as a consequence of the act. These authors also pointed out (1981:5) the dilemma arising from the fact that "the same public which is responsible for the problem of unwanted animals also has a markedly negative perception of euthanasia" and euthanasia technicians. This situation often extends to animal research personnel (Young 1981). Euthanasia may therefore stimulate many and sometimes conflicting responses.

Animals represent a variety of meanings to humans. Some are seen as predators, prey, gods, or the embodiment of such virtues as strength, beauty, and courage, while others represent small size, weakness, filth, disease, and cowardice (Szaz 1968). Science has described animals as brutes, machines, or victims, depending on the view of the describer (Harvey 1941; Regan 1983; Singer 1956).

Veterinarians generally accept the Darwinian view, which supposes that humans are different in degree, but not in kind, from other animals (Langner 1984). From this viewpoint, the term "allo-animal" seems appropriate for this discussion. This attitude recognizes that humans have a larger neocortex and greater neocortical function, apparently more complex mental activity, and certainly more developed tool-making practices than do nonhuman species, but that our genetic code and everything stemming from it originates from the same source (Langner 1984). Only a small percentage of the chromosomes of chimpanzees (Pan troglodytes) differ from human chromosomes (Desmond 1979). These observations are materially demonstrable and are the basis for considerate attitudes and actions by humans toward nonhuman animals.

Historically, it is obvious that the foregoing views are highly evolved as compared to those of the ancients. Galen, a Greek physician of the second century A.D., in his treatise *Vivisection*, described a procedure in which, without the use of anesthesia, an incision was made to expose an animal's heart; the incision was then closed and allowed to heal. Galen commented that "it is surely more likely that a nonrational brute, being less sensitive than a human being, will suffer nothing" (Singer 1956). In the same treatise, Galen described surgery on a slave, again without benefit of anesthesia, to remove infected bone from the sternum. "We then had little hope for the slave. Yet before long he recovered completely, which would not have been the case if no one had dared excise the affected bone, and no one would have had the courage to do so without previous anatomical experience" (Singer 1956).

In Galen's writing, the salient points for current discussion are the concept of sensitivity, in which he equated animals with human slaves, and comparative anatomical value. These points invite comparison to modern battlefield surgical research to develop solutions for emergent problems. Van Devanter (1983) described the use of anesthetized dogs, followed by trials with human cadavers, in the development of a new procedure to arrest internal abdominal hemorrhage from battle wounds during the Vietnam war.

The experimental use of animals was amplified in the nineteenth century by the work of Claude Bernard (1949), whose view of the operant ethic was that "it is essentially moral to make experiments on animals, even though painful and dangerous to them, if they may be useful to man." He qualified that view, stating that one who conducts experiments on animals—or, in his words, "living machines"—does not hear the animals' cries or see their blood flow; instead, the experimenter "sees only his idea and perceives only organisms concealing problems which he intends to solve."

The concept of the biological *machine* can be traced to the seventeenth century, when Descartes wrote his *Discourse on Method*. He conceived of a biological "machine being so made as to pour forth words," but which could be distinguished from a human being because it "could never arrange its words differently so as to answer the sense of all that is said in its presence" (Harvey 1941). According to this argument, the cries of unanesthetized animals whose chests were cut open by investigators such as Bernard and, in earlier times, Descartes and his contemporaries William Harvey and Francis Bacon, were only involuntary reflexes (Harvey 1941). The ethical position of Francis Bacon sums up the basis of Judaeo-Christian or, at least, the Christian position on the use of laboratory animals: to discover "new ways by which men might establish a legitimate command over nature to the glory of God and the relief of man's estate" ("Bacon, Francis" 1979). Thus, researchers are posited as doing God's work with their human hands.

The image of "vivisection," in which bloody-handed sadists eviscerate unanesthetized animals that are strapped to a surgical table, dates back at least to the eighteenth century. Hogarth's series of engravings "Stages of Cruelty" includes depictions of biomedical research and instruction (Hallie 1960).

Currently, scientific research on animals is most vocally and violently opposed by groups such as the Animal Liberation Front. This organization bases its activities on the logic of Australian philosopher Peter Singer who, in his book *Animal Liberation* exhaustively treated the abuse of animals by humans through "speciesism," which he defined as a prejudice and persecution equal to racism and sexism (Singer 1975;

Thomas 1984). Singer advocated a vegetarian diet for all and urged leaving animals and their environments intact. He developed his argument from the symbol of the victim as interpreted by Bentham, an earlier utilitarian philosopher. "No matter what the nature of the being, the principle of equality requires that its suffering be counted equally with the like suffering—insofar as rough comparisons can be made—of any other being" (Singer 1975). Further, Singer stated that "the capacity to suffer and/or experience enjoyment. . [not] intelligence, rationality. . .[or] skin color. . . is the only defensible boundary of concern for the interests of others." The boundary is implicit, but not objectively explicit in this statement. The suffering of a helpless, persecuted victim is explicit throughout Singer's work.

Later developments of this theme focus on the cortical area of the brain as the seat of conscious "sentience," so that a mollusk, according to philosophers such as Regan (1983), is not, for example, considered to have the same capacity to suffer as a phylogenetically higher creature such as a cockroach. The cortex is the seat of suffering, which, as described, is also the source of entitlement to consideration. This entitlement, in Singer's view, is not owing to intelligence or some other talent or capability. This view is countered by spokesmen for the biomedical research community who, like Bernard (1949), assert that there is no immorality in inflicting pain on lower animals when doing so is necessary to achieve some great good for humanity.

The extreme representation of this pole of the discussion is a wealthy but ignorant "little old lady in tennis shoes" who stops experiments intended to develop life-saving cures for human ills (Langner 1984). Moderates on both sides of center agree that progress in medicine for *both* humans and animals has been, and continues to be achieved through the use of live animals in experimental procedures (Langner 1984). Today, criticism is leveled against the technological imperative that what can be done must be done. The "what" here is, of course, the outcome. The value of the outcome as compared to the moral, emotional, and cultural cost of the process is currently questioned by all reasonable parties to the scientific method—by both detractors and supporters (Langner 1984).

Singer's comparison between "speciesism" in animal experimentation and Nazi physicians' "blatant racism," and use of "dispassionate scientific jargon," when referring to agonizingly painful experiments on concentration-camp prisoners in World War II is increasingly cited today (Singer 1975). It should be noted, however, that there is a vast difference between the Nazi policy of euthanasia of undesirable humans, which was seen as the "cutting out of cancer" and a victory over an enemy, and the policy of the federal law in this country that deals with the euthanasia of animals for necessary purposes of food, population, control, and scientific study (Lifton 1982). Further, Nazi animal welfare laws were extremely strict: animals were not held as "enemies," as were undesirable humans in the Nazi rationalization of genocide.

A recent significant event in the development of animal use in human medicine is the animal-to-human transplant of organs, specifically the heart ("Baby Fae Dies" 1984). The concept of the heart as a pump, which, when transplanted from animal to human, is no more damaging to the deceased animal than if the human had eaten it (assuming nontraumatic death in both instances) is frequently lost. An atavistic aura surrounds the notion of an "alien organ" of an animal entering the body of the human, as indicated in the media (e.g., "Baboon Hearts Could Turn Babies Savage" 1984).

Another historical aspect of the problem is the issue of the profit, either commercial or in terms of academic career advancement, which is provided by laboratory animals and livestock. Multimillion dollar multinational corporations annually breed, raise, and surgically alter millions of rodents that are identical twins, or "congenic," for the study of various human maladies, especially cancer (Fox 1983). Biomedical scientists make their reputations through countless hours spent studying the immune response and other physiologic and pathologic developments in these genetically identical animals (Langner 1984).

These rodents stem from the same line of species that the Pied Piper of Hamelin beguiled out of town with his music and from the same "vermin" that sent the housewife up onto a chair on her way to call the exterminator (Fox 1983). Since virtually everyone is exposed to this mythology at an early age, it may affect individuals' attitudes to and conduct of the euthanasia of these animals.

Representations of laboratory animals in recent years reflect increasing use of probability theory, automated data processing, and the greater size and complexity of the research bureaucracy (Langner 1984). Standardization of genetically equivalent congenic animals in statistically significant sample sizes produces the use of numerical and instrumental symbols as data points, including replicates, subjects, instruments, and "tools" to represent animals (Langner 1984). The symbolic reduction of animal life to chemical compounds reacting with one other according to the physical laws of the universe is perhaps the ultimate representation of scientific "objectivity." This is the subordination of which Corson (1977) warned.

In a more positive vein, laboratory animals may be presented as a responsibility, with the animals seen as dependent beings under the protective stewardship of the scientist or administrator (Langner 1984).

This view is manifested in official documents by statements like that in the *Guide to the Care and Use of Experimental Animals* (1980), which states that "moral as well as legal responsibilities" are congruent with "the welfare of the animals themselves. . . [as well as] the quality of the research results obtained." Ideally, professional success is equated with human stewardship.

Interpretations that relate animals to humans insofar as they are physiologically similar are also positive. By contrast to the absolute reductionist theory, this view allows humans to conceive of other animals as pets, companions, even friends, to be protected because of their sensitivity and vulnerability in captivity. As such, animals may be seen as individuals: unique, irreducibly endowed with the "quality" of animate life (Regan 1983). They are then "objects of moral concern" if not "response-able" moral agents (Singer 1975:265); here is the basis of the current animal-rights movement. Moreover, animals' health, good looks, and vigor may be a source of professional pride and gratification to personnel at all levels of the institutional scientific hierarchy (Langner 1984). In such institutions, euthanasia is usually regarded as a responsibility demanding humane expertise.

At the opposite extreme, in the worst-case scenario, the helplessness of the captive animal may consciously or unconsciously evoke the image of a victim (Bernard 1949). If an individual who works with animals holds this view in combination with the feeling of being enslaved by an odious job, the animals may represent oppression, a "millstone" around the human's neck. Such negative cultural symbols as "vermin," "dirty rat," "yellow dog," "treacherous snake," "man-or-mouse" may become unconsciously operant in this context. In such a negative situation the most positive component may be the paycheck, compelling the human to treat that animals properly, and according to regulations, regardless of what symbols arise in his or her mind, simply in order to receive compensation.

A classic and formerly common example of this attitude is the concept of the animal "diener." From the German for servant, in English dictionaries the word is defined as a laboratory person who "assists in cleaning" (*Stedman's Medical Dictionary* 1976). The implication is that the diener is not even an expert in cleaning, but is only capable of menial tasks under close supervision. "Diener" was also applied to early European hospital janitorial personnel. Because it was their job to remove soiled bandages and amputated limbs from surgical suites, the word came to imply a contaminated or tainted person. Scientists who use the word today tend to operate on the premise of a strict adversarial hierarchy. The disparaging use of the word "diener" to refer to a low-level employee in a setting that involves the care and use of animals implies a lack of cognizance of the overall needs and interests of the animals and of what is required by the facility's organization to satisfy those needs. Scientists who subscribe to this outlook may relate to their animals intensively, but usually in a manner that has to do with their specialized experimental technology (surgical, pharmacologic, or other) rather than in a holistic, caregiving context.

Communication among levels of the hierarchy is influenced by the symbolic meanings of animals. The important factor is recognition of the unique, viable, plastic organism that is in a constantly changing dynamic state, especially during reproduction. An informed, coordinated organization strives to maintain constant environmental conditions and to measure the effect of the experimental variable. This concept conflicts, of course, with the view of the animal as a machine, cast immutably in the form in which it was "produced."

In the upper strata of administration and science, there is the danger of disconnection and alienation from the animals and the people who handle them daily. The professional systems (academic, governmental, and industrial) reward the design and writing of successful grant proposals and reports without requiring actual performance of the experiments descried (Adams 1977). Recently, partly as a result of public pressure and partly through the efforts of scientists themselves, attention has been focused on the "living organism," the individual laboratory animal. This focus is not altogether new: the Animal Care Panel in Chicago was formed in the mid-1950s to improve animal care and use and, even one hundred years ago, Louis Pasteur is reported to have been concerned and empathetic toward the animals he used in infectious-disease research (Brewer 1980).

In almost any large research facility, some scientists personally handle and attend to the needs of their experimental animals daily or several times a week. This practice is the rule, rather than the exception, in small facilities where only one person is needed to provide the primary care for a small number of laboratory animals (Langner 1984). The problem of alienation is intensified in the worst-case scenario in which facilities are managed by large, mechanical, depersonalized, and dehumanizing bureaucracies organized in a rigidly stratified hierarchy (Langner 1984). Alienation occurs both within and among the various personnel levels. In urban facilities, the bottom stratum may be composed of individuals with custodial or janitorial job descriptions who function as primary caregivers (animal caretakers or "technicians"). Entry-level employees in this stratum may be from uneducated, even illiterate, disenfranchised minority segments of urban society, for whom laboratory animal care symbolizes employment-of-last-resort (Langner 1984). An additional negative factor obtains at facilities in which these entry-level employees report to individuals who demean both the entry level jobs, referring to them as "better than digging ditches," and those who hold those jobs, speaking of them in such terms as "low class." The use of such disparaging comments betrays bigoted attitudes or, at times outright racism. Primary caregivers in this situation may perceive themselves as sequestered in their work area with the animals, cut off from sources of information, power, and control, undignified, and unseen as individuals by their employers; they feel forced by circumstances to work with nonverbal, captive creatures whose noxious odors and excrement they must endure (Langner 1984).

Even individuals who work with animals in relatively autonomous situations (e. g., herders with dogs), who enjoy a high level of information and hierarchical control, may find it all too easy to be harsh with the animals or to vent their frustration on them when thwarted by the weather or occurrences beyond their control. A sexist stratification may emerge, especially in mid- and far-western America. Males in these areas typically conceive of their role with animals as that of a competitive, "cowboy" sort rather than as that of a nurturer (Langner 1984). They seek dominance over large, powerful male animals such as stallions and bulls, which to them represent all of nature's forces. Economic exigencies may force this group, as it does the urban minorities, to remain in jobs that involve contact with small animals (rodents), which they dislike. Consequently, they feel powerless in that hierarchy, prey to the vagaries of administrative vacillations and funding withdrawals. Unpredictable, uncontrollable stress heightens their alienation.

The time that personnel within various strata actually spend in contact with research animals, which varies with the type of organization and the structure of each organization's hierarchy, can strongly influence the symbolic value of animals and the procedures involving them, including euthanasia. In the average facility comprising several to many principal investigators and projects, the higher the person's position in the hierarchy, the less contact he or she has with the animals. Strata are often functionally divided into the following positions: (1) primary caregiver, at the bottom of the hierarchy, (2) supervisor (technical); (3) technical manager or scientific professional; and (4) scientific director (principal investigator or administrator). The fourth level, the highest, resembles that of a general in an army, directing the troops on the line from a distant command post. People at this level do not touch, see, hear, smell, or processes raw data from their animals. They plan experiments and funding proposals and interpret results that have already been statistically analyzed. The insulation between these individuals and the other hierarchical strata and between these individuals and their animals varies directly with the size, design, and personalities of the organization (Langner 1984).

Ambiguity within the federal, legal, and academic processes, as seen by persons at the lower levels of stratified hierarchies, may reflect a general hypocrisy and low esteem for laboratory animals. Ambiguity tends to be less pervasive in military-research institutions because of the highly organized systems of the military itself; values, rewards, and punishments are clear at each level. However, the interplay between bureaucratic politics and fluctuating financial support from tax revenues make both government and academic research an uncertain, inconsistent, and often ambiguous process. This fiscal "unknown" is complicated by the desire to maintain, above all, academic freedom of inquiry. Cloudy symbols of correct procedure are thus conjured up by laws and recommendations split between arms of the federal bureaucracy. According to the Animal Welfare Act of 1966, the Department of Agriculture is legally, but not financially, empowered to enforce laboratory animal law. It is the Public Health Service that is financially empowered to withdraw funding for experiments that are in violation of its recommendations, which are not laws (*Guide to the Care and Use of Laboratory Animals* 1980). In addition, both laws and recommendations are frequently so vague (often purposely) that neither a funding agency nor a regulatory agency can consistently apply them. Often, only the mechanism, not the conduct of the euthanasia process, is clear. Finally, professional personnel employed in inspection and regulation are commonly drawn from specialties other than those that deal with biomedical research or with particular laboratory species.

To some degree, acceptance of the Darwinian theory of gradual adaptation of species' phenotypes and genotypes has freed ethical consideration to include all species as objects of moral concern. Dubos (1974) pointed out that the ability of anthropoid apes to communicate with humans by sign language is evidence of the ethical as well as the biological rationale for the Darwinian theory of evolution. This observation mandates scientists to recognize manifestations of animal suffering as similar to their own experience of pain. Now, in fact, pain researchers are advised by their professional organizations to test on themselves experimental procedures known to cause discomfort before using experimental animals ("Ethical Standards for Investigators of Experimental Pain in Animals" 1980:141). The routine use and ethical need for anesthesia in animal research is also well recognized, contrary to the practices of Galen, Bacon, Harvey, Descartes, and Bernard.

The actual process of animal euthanasia, however, is often divorced from biophysical and ethical practice. Both highly-educated investigators and barely-educated janitorial-type animal caretakers experience alienation from ideal goals. Among other causes, such reactions result from the dehumanizing effect of modern depersonalized, mechanized, bureaucratic methods of operating large social organizations (Langner 1984).

The mechanism of rewards for research has become increasingly systematized. Researchers must produce data and secure the approval of their peers for its worth. In academia, the approval must come from journals, and in government and industry from regulatory agencies such as the Food and Drug Administrtion (*Good Laboratory Practices of the Food and Drug Administration* 1980). Multinational and military-industrial-biomedical-academic hydras seem to entangle every facet of research. Pure science for its own sake, justified by brilliance of theory and process, is difficult to find. Results that are salable or publishable, regardless of the means employed, are the rule.

Science as the measurement of estimated uncertainty is threatened by insistence on certainty: predicted ends justify degrading means (*Animal Rights Movement in the United States* 1982). The mandate for certainty and finality is sometimes manifested in the arbitrary euthanasia of groups of animals at the end of an experiment simply because it may be inconvenient to find them a new home. Euthanasia rather than adoption of healthy animals was in fact sanctioned for a number of institutions following the passage, in 1966, of the Animal Welfare Act and the accompanying public scrutiny. Fortunately, this policy decision is now reversing. In their animal request forms, more institutions are offering adoption following the use of animals as experimental subjects.

Most scientists are capable of simplifying and explaining to less-educated colleagues their need to maintain uncertainty and ambiguity in the process of discovering natural laws. Many research organizations, however, for various reasons—mainly expedience—do not encourage or even permit such discourse. Adversary stances may develop between the scientific and entry-level technical strata of the research hierarchy because of this lack of communication. This can occur in municipal pounds and commercial packing companies as well. Better-educated technical supervisors may cut themselves off as much as possible from the hierarchical process in order to endure until retirement, or until they find an opportunity for work at a different institution. To the animal caretaker, the animals may come to be symbols of all that is negative in the workplace. The dehumanization of people that thus occurs, the loss of their human sensibilities, results in varying levels of routine neglect or, in extreme instances, in outright cruelty—"hockey games" in the corridors with brooms for sticks and escaped mice that should be euthanatized as pucks (D. Phifer, personal communication 1984). Well-documented cases in which investigators' ignorance and mismanagement have led to technicians' apathy and neglect of proper procedures have resulted in litigation and withdrawal of financial support (Holden 1981). Slaughterhouses and animal-control supervision also still require vigilance.

It is obvious from examples cited in both popular and scientific literature that actual harm is caused to animals, the social conscience, and the federal budget through actions motivated by attitudes influenced by symbolic representations that have been permitted to develop and remain in people's viewpoints about animals and animal euthanasia. One solution, or response, to this harmful process is radical violence by animal advocates who conduct guerilla warfare (Thomas 1984). The Animal Liberation Front may be illegal and irrational in conduct, but many of its goals are humane and rational. One Harvard University study cited animal rights as "the Vietnam of the '80s" (*Animal Rights Movement in the United States* 1982).

The dichotomy between the mechanistic and what might be called the individualistic view of animal euthanasia in biomedical research, food production, and animal control is apparent. Laboratories, packing plants, and animal shelters accomplish euthanasia with well-planned and well-executed procedures, careful attention to the extinction of each individual life, and respect for the remains. In contrast, other institutions employ poorly-trained people who are assigned, as an entry-level rite of passage, to perform what their superiors may regard as the odious job of killing animals. Mishandling also occurs when animals are housed in the same room as that in which they are killed, when they are killed by mechanisms such as gas chambers rather than by considerate human hands, and when their bodies are dumped in piles several feet high to await disposal by the renderer. These procedures erode the dignity of the humans involved and that of the society that allows them. As Levinger (1979) stated, "the taking of an animal's life. . . involves a great responsibility [requiring] maximal care" and can be done only by one who is educated and has "high moral qualifications."

The application of humane principles to the killing of great numbers of mice and rats may appear difficult, especially in fields such as oncologic immunogenetics, in which the rodents may be congenic, the equivalent of hundreds of identical twins. However, it is of practical as well as ethical import to recognize the real or potential individuality and uniqueness of each animal. This precept is demonstrated when one considers that, given a mutation rate of approximately one in ten thousand births, several mutations may be expected to occur in each *room* of the usual sized colony in a year's time. One such mutation resulted in discovery of the severe combined immune deficiency (SCID) syndrome in mice at the Institute for Cancer Research in Philadelphia a few years ago. Last, it should be observed that what is called euthanasia by law in laboratories and animal shelters is regarded as mere convenience killing by Animal Rights philosophers such as Regan (1983) and activist organizations such as the Animal Liberation Front (Thomas 1984).

A moderate approach to this issue is to continue to improve federal regulation of animal research, an effort that is already underway (*Guide to the Care and Use of Laboratory Animals* 1980). Two additional improvements should be next in line for addition to the "mandatory" requirement for in-service education of animal technicians and caretakers. One is to *specify* the standard of this training: is it to be the Purina Corporation course or the American Association for Laboratory Animal Science course? What standard is "mandatory"? This standard should also define the in-service time that employers must dedicate to training. Time being money, many employers cannot yet see time spent in training employees as a cost-effective investment, but only as an expense.

The second improvement needed is to set specific requirements for organizational communication and documentation of "information flow." Every staff member must have not only the education, but the day-to-day logistical and administrative information requisite to provide adequately for the needs of the animals.

Upgrading these two aspects of the technical program enables the staff to become more conversant with the goals of the organization. Alienation is reduced and cooperation between scientific and technical personnel is increased, to the benefit of both humans and animals. This approach also applies to service veterinarians. Not so long ago, nonspecialized veterinarians consulting for laboratory-animal facilities alienated investigators with evasive statements to the effect that they could "help out with a sick pig, but don't know anything about mice" (personal communication from anonymous investigator, Wistar Institute 1978). Again, education is the solution, in the form of postdoctoral experience in laboratory-animal medicine.

Providing these two aspects of organization would produce obvious economies and is, therefore, a fiscal responsibility. The action might not satisfy the Animal Liberation Front or the antivivisectionists, but it would correct many of the deficiencies that are the source of their more legitimate complaints. If their violent tactics are not answered with rational action like that recommended here, the violence will undoubtedly increase and tragedy will result.

Ironically, the computer, the very machine that has depersonalized much of society, can be used to facilitate the information flow and educational process relating to animal procedures, including euthanasia, particularly in geographically decentralized or dispersed facilities. Computer terminals as simple to operate as children's toys can be strategically placed to make information available even to entry-level primary caregivers. A vast amount of information can be accessed from a central data-store area: education programs; biohazard prevention measures; standard operating procedures; individual research protocols; laws on laboratory animals; emergency and first-aid information; projected workloads, including specifications for replacement of ill or injured personnel; duty assignments; job descriptions; and procedures for ordering equipment and materials (Willis and Miller 1981). Planning for the number of personnel required and their assignments can be placed in computer memory, relieving the ambiguity and uncertainty of the workload. Deficiencies resulting from lack of time, space, equipment, or supplies can be corrected by information storage and retrieval and by rapid communication via computer systems.

Why have these steps not been taken? Critics in Great Britain ask the same thing. They ask why, even with announced revisions and improvements, government inspections "reveal continued problems in . . . basic necessities of human care" of laboratory animals ("Double Talk on Animals" 1984). In the United States, the same kind of bureaucratic inertia that impeded modification of the Draize test laws, even after private industry agreed to finance the demands for reform by animal advocacy groups, now impedes specificity in laboratory animal regulations (regulations that are currently *not* in Title 9, but exist only in the form of Public Health Service requirements for grant recipients, which are delineated in the Animal Welfare Act of 1966 and the *Guide to the Care and Use of Experimental Animals* 1980).

Is this all that impedes this process? Perhaps not. Perhaps we still believe in "certainty." Perhaps we still believe we can remain "decent,'" in the words of Nazi Reichsführer Heinrich Himmler, no matter what we do to "inferior" creatures (Sereny 1976). Let us hope that this is not the case. Science, the amoral measuring tool, which has no more conscience than does a cruise missile, has been used to unleash on this planet the mightiest natural force of the universe, the power of the sun, in a destructive and fearful manner. As the mouse is a potential victim of human force, so are we all fellow victims of the forces of nature that man perverts. To the extent that we forget this, we become like the guards at the Nazi death camps, alienated from our fellow creatures and freed from our rational conscience (Sereny 1976). The mistreatment of animals, and of other human beings, is facilitated by the mental manipulation of symbols that permit—if not create—alienation from the victim.

It may be that *all* humans, not just those with deep attachments to companion animals, need greater harmony with the stream of life in the universe. In the careless dispatch of animals, we diminish all life, including our own. We sanction the poisoning and sterilization of the planet. We deny our inherent respect and love for life and living organisms. To raise all research, slaughter, and animal control processes to the level described earlier in this chapter will take space, time, and expense. It will take attention to the components of the process; the training of personnel; and the careful design and construction of facilities. But this effort is vitally needed—not as a palliative, as most animal-welfare laws in the past have been, but as a positive, holistic approach to continued development of our own humanity.

REFERENCES

Adams RG: The Plague Dogs. New York, Alfred A. Knopf, 1977

The Animal Rights Movement in the United States: Its Composition, Funding, Sources, Goal, Strategies, and Potential Impact on Research. Harvard Univ Office of Government and Community Affairs and Phillip WD Martin, 1982

Bacon, Francis. In Encyclopaedia Brittanica. Chicago, Encyclopaedia Brittanica, 1979

Baboon hearts could turn babies savage. San Francisco Examiner (Dec. 11), p 27, 1984

Baby Fae dies. Science News 126:325, 1984

Benning LE: The Pet Profiteers: The Exploitation of the Pet Owners and Pets in America. New York, Quadrangle/The New York Times Book Co, 1976

Bernard C: An Introduction to the Study of Experimental Medicine. Green HC (trans). Henry Scuman, pp 99-105, 1949

Brewer NR (ed): The founding and early history of the American Association of Laboratory Animal Science. Lab Animal Science 30(4):765-79, 1980

Coon CS: The Hunting Peoples. New York, Penguin Books, 1977

Corder EM: The Deer Hunter. New York, Harcourt, Brace, Jovanovich, 1978

Corson SA et al: Pet facilitated psychotherapy. Comprehensive Psychiatry 18:62, 1977

Desmond A: The Ape's Reflexion. New York, Dial Press, 1979

Double talk on animals. Nature 309:2, 1984

Dubos R: Beast or Angel: Choices That Make Us Human. New York, Charles Scribner's Sons, 1974

Ethical standards for investigators of experimental pain in animals (editorial). Pain 9:141, 1980

Fox JL: Scientist sues over genetically impure mice. Science 221:625-628, 1983

Freud S: The Basic Writings of Sigmund Freud, Brill AA (ed): New York, Modern Library, 1938

Good Laboratory Practices of the Food and Drug Administration. Washington DC: US Government Printing Office, 1980

Guide to the Care and Use of Experimental Animals. Ottawa, Canadian Council on Animal Care, 1980

Hallie P: The Paradox of Cruelty. Middletown CT, Wesleyan Univ Press, 1969

Hardy T: Jude the Obscure. New York, Modern Library, 1967

Harvey W: Exercitatio Anatomica de Motu Cordis et Sanguinis in Animalibus, Leake CD (trans). Springfield IL, Charles C. Thomas, 1941

Holden C: Police seize primates at NIH-funded lab. Science 241:32-33, 1981

Langner PH: Symbolic meaning of laboratory animals for scientists and other research workers. Presented at the American Anthropology Association, Denver CO (Nov), 1984

Leakey R: Origins: The Emergence and Evolution of Our Species and Its Possible Future. New York, E P Dutton, 1977

Levinger IM: Jewish attitude toward slaughter. Animal Regulation Studies 2:103-109, 1979

Levinson BM: Pets and Human Development. Springfield IL, Charles C Thomas, pp 4-33, 1972

Lifton RJ: Medicalized killing in Auschwitz. Psychiatry 45:283-297, 1982

Owens CE, Davis R, Smith VH: The psychology of euthanizing animals. Internat J for Study of Animal Problems 2:19-26, 1981

Regan T: The Case for Animal Rights. Berkeley CA, Univ of Calif Press, 1983

Rice B: The Other End of the Leash: The American Way with Pets. Boston, Little, Brown and Co, 1968

Sereny G. In Despres T: The Survivor: Anatomy of Life in the Death Camps. New York, Oxford Univ Press, pp 51-71, 1976

Singer C: Galen on Anatomical Procedures. New York, Oxford Univ Press, p 192, 1956

Singer P: Animal Liberation, A New York Review Book, dist. by Random House, pp 51-71, 1975

Stedman's Medical Dictionary (23rd ed). Baltimore MD, Williams and Wilkins, 1976

Szaz K: Petishism: Pets and Their People in the Western World. New York, Holt, Rinehart and Winston, 1968

Thomas J: British animal rights: the fight gets violent. New York Times, p A2, Nov 15, 1984

Vander Post L: The Heart of the Hunter. New York, William Morrow and Co., 1961

Van Devanter L: Home Before Morning. New York, Beaufort Books, 1983

Webster's Third New International Dictionary of the English Language, Unabridged. Gover PB (ed). Springfield MA, G & D Merriam Co., 1965

Willis and Miller: Computers for Everybody. Beaverton OR, Dilithium Press, 1981

Part 2
Euthanasia, Pet Loss, and Client Grief

8

An Epitaph for Merlin

Sylvan Lee Weinberg

A dog died today. Not an ordinary dog. It was our dog. It was Merlin. Merlin would have been 14 this week. He was a big, beautiful, reddish-brown, golden retriever. He had the broad chest and dark coloring of the northern goldens. Merlin was gentle and powerful. He ran with speed and nonchalant grace and loved to leap high to pick tennis balls out of the air. When he lay still, he was as regal as a lion and as whimsical as a stuffed animal. He was ours and we loved him.

We got Merlin during the halcyon days when Leslie was seven and Andy was ten. Joan and I were still young enough to believe that time would stand forever still on those shining hours of life's early afternoon.

It was on a summer evening that all four of us had an early dinner at the old Servis and Buhl Restaurant. Excitement was in the air. We were about to go to Yellow Springs to choose our dog from a litter of golden retrievers. We had selected the breed carefully. Big, smart, obedient, lovable—how right we were. But we needed a name. All through dinner we named a hundred dogs. Then one of us said "Merlin." It was a rare moment of family consensus. Merlin The Magician—Merlin the magic dog. On to Yellow Springs.

In the summer twilight we came to a comfortable country house. In the basement behind an improvised barricade, an unbelievable sight. Eleven tawny balls of fur—crawling and frolicking over each other. Two were different from the rest. They were bigger and stronger, more alert, with thicker front paws—suggesting future majestic size. The bigger of the two (just barely) had been promised to a northern Ohio college fraternity who had provided the sire. The other one was Merlin.

The dog books say that some golden retrievers are hunting dogs while others are destined to be family and household pets and to live with humans. Merlin was among the latter. I am sure this would not have been his choice, and at times I felt guilty as if I had denied him his heritage. I hope not. We built a run for Merlin in our backyard. Soon we moved and Merlin had his own quarter acre, fenced and with his own door in our house. We never let Merlin run free. Although Andy and Leslie objected to this, we were afraid of cars or that he might be stolen. Another reason was because of Merlin's only fault. Gentle as he was with humans, Merlin was prone to attack other dogs. In the early years, though, he never missed a chance to get loose. A door ajar — a little daylight — a russet blur of fur — and Merlin was free. In terror that he might not come back, we would scour the neighborhood, but Merlin usually came home several hours later, tired and happy.

Andy took Merlin to obedience school at Wampler's Barn. He won best of breed and barely missed best of show. At the crucial moment, he was distracted by a female dog.

Merlin was at his best at parties. He was in his glory with a house full of people. After making his rounds it would be time to perform. A biscuit on his nose — a disciplined wait and a quick command — a toss of his regal head and the biscuit was in his mouth faster than the eye could follow. There was applause, and a smile as only Merlin could.

Merlin was our companion at a thousand breakfasts. We shared toast. I always thought Merlin liked toast more than bread. Maybe it was really I who liked to hear that crunch. I hope he liked it better too. Merlin ate only dry toast. I had butter and jam on mine. Joan thought butter would be bad for Merlin's arteries and jam for his teeth. Presumably, I was immune to both.

In his later years, Merlin seemed less eager to bolt when a door was left half open. When he did, he came home sooner and more tired.

In the spring this year, Merlin suddenly seemed older. I suspected diabetes, but Dr. Dillman found otherwise. A diet for 'mature' dogs seemed to make him better. Merlin became gray about the face, but his coat was still shiny and rich with thick fur.

When we were out of town, Merlin stayed at his favorite kennel. If we forgot to call and Torok was filled, they offered to keep Merlin in their home. He was everyone's favorite.

When we returned from a three week trip this summer, Merlin wasn't the same anymore. He barely took notice when I came home. Sometimes he tired of toast even before I did. Then heartbreak and ignominy when Merlin couldn't get up without help. Two days ago he fell in his yard and barely struggled to his feet. X-rays showed a tumor in Merlin's abdomen. He had become anemic and painfully weak. The hope that surgery might find a benign or treatable disease was remote indeed. I delayed judgement for a couple of days.

On the last day, Merlin's cry awakened me early. He managed to get up and to go outside and make a last survey of his domain. For the past few days he had barely looked around. This time for a moment, as of old, he walked about majestically, head high and tail erect. A last backward glance, and Merlin came in.

A little later that morning, surgery confirmed what we had feared most. Merlin was no more.

As the world goes, the story I have told is really very unimportant. It is hard to tell whether we mourn Merlin or a part of ourselves, a part of our lives that he had touched and is gone as inevitably as he is gone. Surely the innocence of that summer night, when we chose a name and a dog, will never return.

9

Euthanasia of a Pet: A Personal Experience

Patricia Curtis

My cat Fred's nineteenth birthday found him quite deaf and blind, but still enjoying life. He was always first in the kitchen for meals, purred a great deal, liked to be held, and was treated politely by my other cats. Though he stepped carefully around the house, he could jump unerringly onto the sofa and my bed. He retained his dignity; we called him the "Elder Statesman."

But one morning he failed to appear for breakfast. He was still on the sofa but not asleep, apparently confused, not at all himself. When I set him down, he dragged his left front and back paws, carried his head at an angle, could not find his food bowl, and had to be helped to eat. I guessed what had happened and rushed him to our veterinarian.

"Sometimes cats recover from strokes," said Dr. William Sullivan, attentive physician to my cats and friend to me. "Of course, Fred's age is against him. We just can't tell what will happen." He gave Fred an injection and admitted him to the hospital.

I kept tabs on Fred's condition all that day and the next. I telephoned from home, street corners, the library, editors' offices. Interestingly, nobody in whom I confided seemed to think I was overreacting. No one said "Be thankful it's only a cat," or "But you have other pets. . ." as if the death of my favorite cat, were it to occur, would be a trivial matter. People who knew Fred were especially sympathetic and concerned.

Fred hung on. His condition did not particularly improve, but it stabilized. Two days later, the vet called me. "I think Fred will do as well at home as here," he said. "Another stroke would probably finish him, but on the other hand, he could live comfortably for weeks or months." He hinted, however, that he would cooperate in whatever course of action might lie at the back of my mind. I was struggling with the question of whether it would be a kindness to my pet to end his life.

When I saw Fred, he looked terrible, as the doctor had warned me: thin and wasted, his tabby-and-white coat all matted—but he recognized me and rose to his feet expectantly, as if to say "Let's go home." He gave no sign of being in pain. Quickly, I made up my mind. I wrapped him in his towel (he was too frail to rattle around in a cat carrier), put his various medications and medical instruction sheets in my bag, and, hugging him close, started for home.

I had owned this cat since he was eight weeks old. He had been born in a colleague's greenhouse, the only kitten his aging mother had produced that time, and she had kept him hidden among the plants. He had never been touched by human hands until the day he was brought to me in the office.

Imagine what that experience must have been like for the tiny creature! He had known only the care and warmth of his mother, the serene quiet of the greenhouse. Suddenly, a giant with heavy footsteps had cornered and seized him, popped him into a box, and closed it. He had felt himself carried, heard voices, the noise of a car. Then he faced the terrifying roar of a commuter train, more jostling, and, finally, dark silence as the box was left on my desk. As soon as I arrived home, I opened the box. The kitten looked up at me, dazed and sick with fear.

At home, he disappeared under a chest and stayed there for a full day, not touching the food we pushed to him. Finally, afraid for the young animal's life, I pulled him out, encouraged him to eat, and mothered him. My young son and daughter carried him around, snuggled and petted him. We had one other cat at the time, but she wanted no part of him and ignored him. He had only us human beings with whom to bond, and bond he did. Fred settled in.

He was never an especially playful kitten, but quiet, gentle, and reflective, as if he took life rather seriously. He never gave himself over to play with the reckless abandon of most kittens. He would start to run after a toy, then stop in mid-chase and glance around self-consciously. He would leap for a dangling string if we encouraged him, but rarely originated rowdy games of his own.

By the time he was full grown, Fred and the older cat had reached an understanding, which amounted to mutual tolerance. But as we acquired several other cats, Fred gave each one to understand from the start that he was Top Cat. Fred was young, strong, dignified, and self-respecting, with enormous vitality. By sheer force of personality, he convinced the others to accept his leadership.

If he wanted a snack from another's food bowl, the other cat would step aside. Out of fairness, I always removed and reproached Fred, but I never broke him of this assertive habit. And if he wished to lie in a certain basket when it happened to be occupied by another cat, he would simply stand by the basket, and within minutes, the other cat would get up and vacate it—all without a sound exchanged between them.

Once I took in a friend's cat while she went on a short trip. My cats were accustomed to other pets visiting, and accepted them with grudging grace. But in this case, Cleopatra, the guest, behaved badly; she hissed, snarled, and generally made herself obnoxious. Sometimes such a situation will resolve itself peacefully enough within a few days, but matters just became worse. Poor Cleo obviously did not want to be with us, and my own animals became increasingly upset by her surly presence. I began to regret my hospitality.

The situation came to full boil one day. Cleo attacked Olivia, one of my cats, not merely to express hostility or to try to dominate; she meant business. She pinned Olivia under the desk and was inflicting bodily harm while Olivia screeched with pain and terror. Before I could get at the two cats to pull Cleo off, Fred flew into the fray. He was not especially fond of Olivia, but she was Family, and only over his dead body would any outsider do her harm. Cleo backed off, muttering. I grabbed her, and she spent most of the rest of her visit shut in the bathroom. I was proud of Fred.

When Fred was two or three years old, we witnessed an example of his exceptionally strong will and healthy survival instinct. I have always known enough to protect our cats from falling out of open windows, and none had ever suffered from the high-rise syndrome. One day, however, my son and a friend were in his bedroom and the other boy unthinkingly opened the window from the bottom, something we never did in winter because the screens had been put away for the season. The boys went out, and I did not notice the open window because the blind was down.

Fortunately, someone found Fred on the sidewalk six stories down and rang my doorbell. Fred could not stand, but the moment he saw me, he looked into my face and cried loudly, communicating clearly that he was in real trouble. I rushed him to the Animal Medical Center where he was treated for a serious fracture of one hind leg. We made many trips together to and from the hospital. Throughout his ordeal, Fred's will to recover never wavered. He came through with only a permanent stiffness in the leg.

As he grew older, Fred became more and more loving. He developed a habit of putting his paws around my neck and rubbing his face against my chin, purring loudly. All my cats have been affectionate, but Fred made it known that he was always there for me. He, above all the others, knew when I was tired or depressed, and he would follow me around the house waiting for me to sit down so he could jump in my lap.

He was sixteen years old when his vision began to fail; a year or two later, he lost his hearing. One benefit accrued to his loss of hearing. The only object that ever struck terror in Fred's heart was the vacuum cleaner; I think it reminded him of that commuter train, long ago. But in his last years, he was spared this fright: he could not hear the machine.

Now, as I set him down after bringing him home from Dr. Sullivan's, I knew I had to face the fact that Fred was in the final days of his life. But somehow, I felt he wasn't ready to die just yet. And I believed that after all the years of love and companionship he'd given us, he deserved every remaining chance. I vowed that whatever time he had left would be, for him, worth living.

At first, he was restless, pacing continuously in wide circles. Sometimes he would stand in one spot and yowl; then I'd pick him up, and he would put his good paw around my neck and press his cheek to my chin as he had always done. I never left him for more than a few hours. I became closer to this animal than ever before. In fact, except when my children were infants, I had never been so active in filling another creature's needs. I fell in with the rhythm of his days.

I mixed his pills in his food, and since he could not eat much at one time, I offered it to him at frequent intervals. He ate. He could not always find the litter box, so I placed him in it several times a day. Though he had never before liked to be brushed, now he'd lie in my lap without a murmur while I groomed him. I washed his face with a warm, wet tissue after he ate. He was almost totally dependent — not kittenish, but babylike.

Touch was the only sense remaining to him, and he hungered for it. Once while I was watching television, he slept on my shoulder, head against my neck. He curled up in my lap as I typed. When I'd stand at the kitchen sink, he'd lie across my shoes.

Fred grew better. He stopped pacing, stopped dragging his left paws. He made the jump to the sofa again. Guests one evening marveled at this survivor who went from lap to lap with perfect poise. "This cat wants to live!" someone remarked.

But ten days later, I had been out to dinner and returned to find Fred in bad shape. His paws were swollen, and he plainly did not feel well. I stayed up with him until late, but toward morning I fell asleep. When I woke up, he was lying on my slippers beside my bed. Some blood on his chest seemed to have oozed from his mouth. He was unable to eat breakfast.

Back to Dr. Sullivan's we went, as soon as the office was open. I left Fred there and went home to await the veterinarian's call. I anticipated what he would tell me. "I think Fred has gone about as far as he can go," said Dr. Sullivan, gently. He explained everything that had gone wrong. "His body has simply worn out," he summed up.

Late in the day, I returned to the hospital. The waiting room was full of clients with their cats, but Sharon, one of the staff, led me to a back room and put Fred in my lap. He knew me, but lay in my arms without moving. He seemed to be telling me that he had given up now. It was up to me to make the decision not to keep him any longer, and I made it.

Eventually, all the other clients had left, and it was time. I wanted to sit and hold Fred on my lap, instead of placing him on the table, so Dr. Sullivan, who is very tall, knelt down to get a good angle, and his assistant Sheryl knelt on the other side of me, her hands on Fred. I petted him. The vet took one paw, slipped the needle in—and it was over. There was no cry, no struggle—my cat just stopped breathing. He slipped effortlessly from life to death.

My tears dripped down on his fur, and Sharon and Sheryl patted my shoulder. Dr. Sullivan blew his nose and walked away for a few minutes; he seemed to be having trouble with his voice. Sheryl wrapped Fred's wispy body in a towel, let me have one last look, and carried him away. Then Dr. Sullivn hugged me, and I hugged him and Sharon and Sheryl, and put on my coat.

"Are you glad you took Fred home ten days ago?" asked Sharon.

"Yes," I answered firmly. Fred had seemed to ask to live a little while longer, and I will always remember that reprieve we had.

Much later, when I thought about Fred's death, it sharpened for me a painful knowledge, an awareness that all of us who care a great deal about animals think about with anguish. I became haunted by all the other cats who had died that same day, less humanely, unloved and unmourned.

It is now over one hundred years since the first animal shelter was founded, in Philadelphia. While the ASPCA in New York, under Henry Berg, was the first humane organization chartered in the United States, it was the Women's SPCA of Pennsylvania that opened the first animal shelter, in 1872. In those days the usual method of euthanasia for homeless and unwanted pets was to club them to death. The Women's SPCA ordered that gas be used instead, and thereby established the first humane method of euthanasia for animals in this country.

But what struck me in remembering Fred's death is that our society, after a century, has not yet supplied a humane and decent solution to the problem of unwanted pets who are not adopted into new homes. Our answer is still to kill them. Granted, euthanasia in a shelter is far more humane than leaving dogs and cats to fend for themselves on the street, where they virtually always live short, fearful, suffering lives before they succumb to starvation, disease, or exposure, or are killed by cars or torture. But with what poverty of ideas are we still handling this problem!

Spaying and neutering clinics and humane education have helped. Yet in 1987 some 13 million dogs and cats—many, if not most of them, young and healthy—were put to death. We have forced animal shelters into being mercy killers for our communities. We dump pets when it is no longer convenient to keep them, and when they become too numerous, we simply kill them.

I think we can do better.

10

Euthanasia of Pets: The Impact on Children

Robert G. Stevenson

The death of a pet has long been a topic of interest to teachers, who have traditionally used the lives and deaths of pets as teaching tools. It has been generally assumed that children learn responsibility by caring for their pets and that the death of a pet is a relatively unthreatening way for children to learn about death, grief, and related feelings. By learning to deal with the loss of a pet, children might learn coping skills that would later be helpful in facing the death of a person.

But is this early loss of a pet really less threatening than loss of a human loved one? Children can give love without reservation, and the younger they are, the more likely it is that they will. They can even love and grieve for inanimate objects, such as a lost favorite doll. How much stronger, then, would be the bond of love to a living being who can return that affection? It is clear, then, that the death of a pet will have a strong effect on the child. To what extent will this effect be altered by the fact that the death was the result of euthanasia?

Young children have difficulty understanding the important distinction between the quality of life and the quantity of life. They are clear about their need for their pet and have difficulty understanding why the death may be "necessary." After all, to a child, the ability to end life seems merely the other side of the ability to prolong it. In fact, the ability to prolong life may exist, but may be financially impractical from an "adult" point of view. The attempt to convey to a child a balanced perspective on what is about to happen to his or her beloved pet has proved so difficult that parents often inform children only after the fact. In the short run this may be the easiest route, but some long-range consequences must be considered.

Our work with grief shows that sudden deaths are more difficult for the bereaved than those lingering deaths that provide an opportunity for anticipatory grief. Parents are able to benefit from anticipatory grief, but the child perceives the death as a sudden one indeed. This experience teaches children that they have little effect on their environment. Control over major events in their lives will rest outside of them; they are, in fact, "helpless." Children are often excluded from the decision to euthanatize a pet in an attempt to spare them the "guilt" of making such a choice. However, children feel guilt over their inability to help their pet, whether or not they are included in the decision-making process.

An example of the impact of a decision for euthanasia occurred recently in a New Jersey family. The family dog was elderly and subject to seizures. The family was leaving for an extended vacation and no one could be found to watch the dog during that time. The father had decided that they would keep the dog for as long as possible, but that they could not afford to board it again. Thus, the first day of vacation became "Brandy's death day." The entire vacation became a mourning period for the two children and their mother. Since that time, one child has refused to tolerate any mention of the deceased pet, and the younger child tells people that she hates her father for killing her friend. Surely there must have been a better way to deal with this event.

Might the death have been arranged to occur at a time when the family could have concentrated on each other's emotional needs? Could the children have been nearby when the pet died? Could they have been given an opportunity to say goodbye? Perhaps we should first ask whether or not the children would have wanted to do either. Students in the secondary-school level death-education class that I conduct describe their chief emotion toward the euthanatizing of a pet as anger. They were angry that their pet had to die, but in most cases, they have been able to accept that decision. They were still angry, however, that they were not told in advance, were deprived of a last goodbye, and were discouraged from mourning the pet's death.

When a person we love dies, the medical staff in many hospitals will now encourage the family to view the body. Family members have been increasingly involved by funeral-service personnel in preparing the body for burial. Since there is no parallel to a wake or funeral in most cases of animal euthanasia, would it be so far-fetched to allow family members a moment to view or even touch the dead pet? This is not "just" a dead animal. It has been a friend and, in some cases, a family member to the bereaved individuals.

**Secondary School Students' Responses To
Questions About Possible Euthanasia:**

A favorite pet of yours has a very bad (and very painful) disease.
Would you:

A. Let it die naturally, despite the pain?	5%
B. Let it die naturally, trying to control the pain with medication that could be costly?	65%
C. Have it put to sleep?	30%
D. Ask to have its body frozen in hope of a future medical breakthrough?	0%

[A starting point for additional discussion is then created by substituting the word "person" for "pet." The responses have not been essentially different.]
[Sample: 300 high school juniors and seniors, 1975-1982]

Just as the medical profession has changed many of its practices to acknowledge and provide for the needs of family members of the deceased, perhaps it is time that a similar accommodation be made for the bereaved family of a pet. This is not to say that such an attitude would be appropriate in all, or even most, cases. However, should not the needs of the family be considered along with the requirements of the veterinary facility when establishing routines?

Finally, what will happen after the pet is gone? A teacher in my school observed one young woman crying in the hall. He asked what was wrong, and she told him that she had just returned to school after her pet had been "put to sleep" that morning. She wanted to go to class, but she just couldn't concentrate. This educator told her to "stop being silly" and to go to class. Finally, some concerned friends gave her what she had come looking for. They talked of their feelings when their pets had died. Their statements gave the girl confirmation that she was not "silly" or unusual to have such strong feelings over a deceased pet. She cried for her lost loved one, and her friends joined her.

Children's literature observes this need for rituals and mourning in such books as *About Dying* (Stein 1974) and *The Tenth Good Thing About Barney* (Viorst 1971). A sudden or accidental death may affect subsequent mourning, but euthanasia is not, in most cases, sudden. We know that the coping skills we use as adults are learned early in life. The euthanatizing of a pet may have lasting consequences for a child. Shouldn't those involved in the procedure at every stage do all that they can to make those consequences positive ones?

Children will learn important lessons from the death of a pet. Discussion of the experience has a place in our schools. Such discussions are of value not because the death of a pet is "less threatening"; they are of value because to a child that death reaches into every area of his or her life, including school. For that reason, it is time for educators and veterinarians to begin jointly to investigate ways of helping young people to cope with this major event in their lives.

REFERENCES

Stein DB: About Dying. New York, Walker and Co, 1974
Viorst J: The Tenth Good Thing About Barney, New York: Atheneum, 1971

11

Helping Children and Adolescents Cope with the Euthanasia of a Pet

Carole E. Fudin and Susan Phillips Cohen

Human beings have interacted with other living creatures for thousands of years. Through the centuries, their relationship has evolved to include exchanges not only of food, raw materials, and protection, but of affectionate companionship as well. In modern North America, one significant bond is that between children and pets.

As do adults, children and adolescents form deep attachments to companion animals, who provide warmth, intimacy, stimulation, and nonjudgmental affection. Therefore, the loss of this special friend can be heartwrenching. When loss occurs as the result of euthanasia—the deliberate, peaceful ending of life—families face a valuable opportunity to teach a lesson in coping with the painful reality of death.

How children respond to this event depends on several variables. First, what did the pet mean to this child? Second, what is the child's developmental understanding of death? Third, how is the euthanasia of the pet presented and conducted? Carefully considered, the answers to these questions will guide families, veterinarians, and mental-health professionals to helping children and adolescents cope with the euthanasia of a pet and with other matters concerning death.

To illuminate these issues we will describe the physiological, psychological, and developmental components of pet–child relationships. Next, we will outline chronologically the child's level of understanding of death. Finally, we will outline practical suggestions to guide families and professionals in managing pet euthanasia.

CHILDHOOD DEVELOPMENT AND THE PET

At birth, infants are endowed with "innately fixed behavior patterns" (Levinson 1972) that cause them to respond favorably to soft, warm objects. They need nurturing and stimulating experiences that are affectionate and consistent. Babies orient themselves physically to the mother or mothering person, creating an active and interactive communication between the two. Such bodily communication stimulates the development of the child's nervous system. For a baby, the cat that rubs or the dog that licks is a delightful experience, providing the basic tactile pleasure. The consistency with which love and warmth are offered, particularly in times of distress, affects whether the infant will grow into a child who views the world with trust or with distrust.

Levinson made clinical observations of thumb-sucking among children raised with pets and those who were not, and noted that children raised with pets were less intensely involved in the need to comfort anxiety than the other children. He concluded that a calm, well-trained pet provided soft, cuddly succor and fulfilled the child's needs for consistency when there was a constant shifting of caretakers.

Between the ages of one and two, children begin to learn how to walk. The presence of an active pet to follow around encourages crawling, stimulates the use of muscles and the development of fine motor control, and makes learning to walk more fun. As children more actively explore their environment, they encounter some of its dangers. Pets frequently serve as companions and protectors, encouraging children to be more independent and active.

By the end of the second year of life, children have begun to experience themselves as individuals with desires and needs separate from their parents. This awakening is characterized by saying "no" and frequent battles of will with parental figures. Children also learn that they may not always receive parental approval or fulfill parental expectations. It is at this time that pets play the role of nonjudgmental friends and protectors who love them no matter what and provide trustworthy comfort when parents leave the children for short separations.

Children between the ages of two and seven years engage in magical thinking and believe that a wish constitutes an act. An angry child may wish the pet away, but when it does not go, the child can learn that hostile thoughts are not deeds. This insight allays fears of destructive impulses. Such impulses are often experienced in dreams or nighttime imaginings of fearsome creatures. In the bedroom, the meekest gerbil can constitute a first line of defense against under-the-bed boogie men.

According to Levinson (1972), children who are permitted early, gradual responsibility for pet care develop an enhanced self-image as authoritative persons. In addition, they accept authority more easily.

Caring for a pet allows children their first major, ongoing responsibility for a being other than themselves. Responsibility for a pet provides structure and teaches the importance of commitment. These lessons set the stage for later encounters with peers as well as for adult commitments such as a job and marriage.

By age six, the child has begun to relate more to classroom peers and to learn that significant relationships exist outside the family. Some children explore this new world of "other people" with anxiety and insecurity. This developmental step can be particularly painful if children's attempts are met with rebuffs.

As stand-in for buddy or best friend, a pet can be counted on to watch TV, play ultimate frisbee, or curl up near a child's sickbed. Pets offer children comfort by providing continued acceptance and a loving relationship in which children need not feel vulnerable. Knowing that their pet loves them helps to assuage hurts so that children are willing to reach out to peers once again.

Pets also serve as social lubricants, attracting other children and breaking conversational ice. Moreover, whether displayed or simply bragged about, an unusual, large, or attractive animal can raise a child's standing among peers and enhance his or her self-esteem.

A child between ages six and twelve is often given a great deal of independence. He or she begins to go to school alone or to run errands. The comforting companionship of a German shepherd with whom to parade down the street does wonders for a child's sense of personal safety outside. Returning to the home, contemporary America's latchkey children can be greeted and made comfortable by the noise and presence of the family pet. Left alone behind closed doors, even a barking chihuahua can be counted on to frighten away intruders. A child with a pet is never alone.

Children ages six to twelve may achieve enhanced mastery by providing care for animals that require special skill and knowledge. Ownership of a pet such as a horse encourages children to master facts, their environment, and themselves. Proper care of a horse goes beyond learning that it eats and providing it with a dry stall. Information on proper care is detailed and complicated, too much to be secured from a brief reading of a comic book, for example. Learning to curry a horse or teaching it to jump takes hours of practice. As a reward for this effort, the child will control one of nature's most powerful and beautiful creatures.

Children between ages six and twelve must accomplish many important developmental tasks. During this period, a sense of "identity" is established; children begin to accept themselves as male and female; they develop greater independence and consideration for others. Pets play an important part in helping the child learn to perceive himself or herself.

A perceptive child will notice if he is cruel, kind, or empathetic to another's feelings and needs by the way he relates to a pet. The child also can learn that there are limits to what he can do with himself or his pet. Appreciation for such limits strengthens the ego and affords greater reality testing. For example, even the most tolerant pet will eventually be bothered by nonstop petting and hugging.

Van Leeuwen (1981) noted that pet ownership helps children to learn more easily about male and female sexual behavior, about estrus, pregnancy, birth and the rearing of young. Children eagerly display curiosity and interest in this aspect of their pet's life, and if helped to understand in natural and healthy ways will unconsciously apply this information to themselves.

For children of this age group, a pet is a major source of physical affection. Children in this age group spend progressively less time at home, away from parental affection. In Western culture, pre-adolescent boys in particular are expected to outgrow their need for cuddling, which they can unashamedly enjoy from a pet.

As children move into adolescence, they look increasingly to the outside world and peers for love and friendship. This is a huge developmental step that children may find simultaneously exciting and frightening. The frequent struggles between adolescents and their parents often stem from a mutual need to "let go" and cling to each other at the same time. Animal companions help to ease the adolescent through this period by providing consistency, security and a chance to regress without being thought of as "babyish," when the world seems too frightening.

In summary, pets play a very important role in child development, encouraging deep attachments between children and their animal companions. When these attachments are severed, children may experience pain and emotional upset. While the death of the pet is distressing, it also provides positive critical experience in development: learning about and living through the loss of a loved relationship.

THE CHILD'S UNDERSTANDING OF DEATH

It is important to understand the significance of companion animals in the children's lives in order to help them cope with the death of a pet. While pet loss occurs for a variety of reasons, this chapter is primarily concerned with death from euthanasia. Children's responses to the euthanasia of a pet vary according to their age, personality, emotional development, degree of attachment to the animal, and the degree to which they understand and participate in the decision for euthanasia.

Before the age of five, children have a hard time understanding the significance of the euthanasia decision. They do not consider death to be a permanent state. Instead, they view it as a temporary condition that they equate with sleep. The dead person or animal is thought to return, particularly if it was "good." Children in this age group are accustomed to seeing cartoon characters blown to bits in one television show, only to return intact in the next one. They believe that those who die will continue to grow, sleep, and eat in death. They also believe that death is accidental rather than inevitable, and can be avoided if one is careful. At this developmental stage, death means, essentially, separation. Children know that death is special and unpleasant, even though they do not know what it is. At this point, they will miss the deceased animal primarily as a playmate. If the animal was relied on for physical and emotional stability and comfort, the loss will be still more profound, but the child's limited understanding, as well as any perceived lack of support from caregivers, will not permit easy, healthy integration of the event.

The common euphemism for euthanasia is the phrase "put to sleep." While this phrase may seem harmless, it can cause much misunderstanding and terror for children in this age group, because the children equate death with sleep. (This phrase should be avoided altogether, because it is misleading and belittles the significance of the event.)

Antelyes (1984) cited a case in which a child's pet had been euthanatized. The child was himself due to undergo surgery, and was told he would be "put to sleep" for the procedure. He became terrified because this is exactly what he had been told before his parents took his dog to the veterinarian, and the dog had never come home.

Children between the ages of five and nine understand that death is final. This is a crucial developmental step. During this age period, they also personify death (which means to assign human qualities to death, giving it the form of, say, Dracula or the Grim Reaper). At this age, children believe that one can avoid death if one is lucky or clever. By age nine, children understand that death is final, inevitable, and universal; they approach the adult conception. The awareness that every living thing must one day die, is often accompanied by a belief in an afterlife.

Because children younger than age six inaccurately conceptualize death, it is more important to provide support rather than detailed explanations when a pet is to be euthanized. Some basic explanations, however, may be offered. If a child is told that the pet is dying because it is very sick, and can be helped to die more easily, it should also be stressed that the animal is suffering from a very severe illness. Such emphasis is necessary to distinguish this illness from the minor ailments that befall people and animals. If this distinction is not made, the child can become frightened by minor conditions in himself or loved ones. The child should be reassured that although the pet must leave because it is so sick, mother and father will still be there.

After age six, children should be more informed of the details of the illness and the euthanasia procedure. If parents elect to witness the pro-
cedure, the child should be told and offered the option to do the same. It is important to encourage questions and provide honest answers. When explaining how and why a pet is to be ethanatized, always use clear, direct language that the child can comprehend.

Adolescents are, of course, old enough to understand fully the nature of disease and the considerations for the euthanasia decision. Adolescents often feel overwhelmed by physical and emotional changes, frequently experiencing life as beyond their control. It is therefore critical to include the adolescent fully in the decision to euthanatize a pet. The teenager may be the family member who is most attached to the animal and may need the most consideration regarding emotional readiness to "let go" of the pet.

Perhaps the most difficult part of helping any child through the euthanasia of a pet is dealing with anger, which may be misdirected at the parents or the veterinarian. It is important to understand that this anger is part of the grief process and not to take it personally (Link 1984). The child's anger may be especially intense if the decision for euthanasia was based on the family's inability or unwillingness to afford veterinary care, or if the animal had become unmanageably aggressive because of improper training. In these instances, parents should accept the child's rage and acknowledge their responsibility for the euthanasia.

HELPING THE CHILD TO COPE WITH PET EUTHANASIA

As a rule, all children should be informed of impending death as soon as possible, and with openness and honesty. If they are very young, do not overwhelm them with facts; offer basic, age-appropriate descriptions and remain available for questions. If the child is old enough to have cared for the well animal, he or she should be allowed to offer care and comfort to the animal until the time for euthanasia. The child who is old enough to participate actively in the sick animal's care is old enough to hear a detailed description of the euthanasia procedure. Children know their own capacities, and once advised of all they might see and hear during euthanasia, should be granted their request to be present.

Behavioral Indications of Bereavement Problems in Children

1) A radical change in behavior at home or school
2) Soiling (in young children who are toilet trained)
3) In very young children, nightmares and preoccupation about small hurts
4) In older children, frequent somatic complaints without actual physical

causation (Headaches and stomach aches are typical)
5) Increased separation anxiety

If such difficulties arise after a pet's death, the child and family would benefit from counseling and guidance from a mental-health professional.

Do's:

1. Encourage your child to participate in decision-making about the euthanasia.
2. Consider making final photographs of your pet and visiting special places you have shared with the pet.
3. Encourage your child to view the pet after it is dead. Seeing the dead pet reinforces the reality of death and makes it less mysterious and scary.
4. Help your child to plan and carry out a funeral or memorial service or some special ritual that family and friends can attend.
5. Look at pictures of your pet and talk about it with your child; doing so will help keep the pet's memory alive.
6. Encourage young children to write stories or draw pictures of the pet to stimulate their expression of grief.
7. Read children's books about the death of pets with your child.
8. Let your child know that grief is normal and necessary for healing.
9. Tell your child the truth, but at a level that he or she can understand.
10. Encourage the expression of all of your child's feelings, even if they seem silly or irrational. Never tell your child that he or she is "too big to cry."
11. Expect to answer the same questions over and over again.
12. If you are upset about your pet's death, share your feelings with your child. You caring strongly affirms the value of life.
13. Delay getting another pet. Replacing it too rapidly will inhibit healthful mourning and may lead the child to reject the new pet. Rapid replacement may also stimulate the unrealistic expectation and fear that everything can be replaced—including the child.
14. Acquire a new pet when your child is able to talk about the deceased pet without experiencing a great deal of pain, or when the child feels free to want a new one without feeling disloyal to the old one.
15. Thoroughly discuss the adoption of a new animal with all family members.
16. Make careful distinctions between a pet's medical condition and any conditions that the child may have. For example, if an elderly dog is euthanized after becoming incontinent, a child may fear wetting his or her bed.
17. Whenever possible, avoid euthanizing pets on holidays, birthdays, or at other special times. Having an animal euthanized at such a time not only increases the pain, but also ensures an annual reminder.

Don'ts:
1. Do not force a child to participate in any aspect of euthanasia or post-death activities.
2. Do not take the pet to the veterinarian for euthanasia without telling your child. If possible, do not conduct the procedure when the child is away; he or she may wish to say goodbye.
3. Never say that the pet ran away. Such evasion makes the child feel rejected and abandoned.
4. Never say that the pet was "put to sleep." This explanation often triggers sleep problems or intense anxiety about surgery and anesthesia. It is preferable to say that the pet was helped to die.
5. Avoid saying that "the pet is in heaven because God wants good creatures in heaven." This statement can result in behavior problems because the child will fear being separated from his or her parents for the same reason.
6. Never blame the veterinarian as the cause of a pet's death and do not make a scapegoat of the veterinarian, lest the child develop fear of caregivers.

REFERENCES

Antelyes J: When pet animals die. In Kay W, Nieburg H, Kutscher A, Grey R and Fudin C (eds): Pet Loss and Human Bereavement. Ames IA, Iowa State Univ Press, 1984

Levinson B: Pets and Human Development. Springfield IL, Charles C Thomas, 1972

Link M: Helping emotionally disturbed children cope with loss of a pet. In Kay W, Nieburg H, Kutscher A, Grey R, Fudin C (eds): Pet Loss and Human Bereaement. Ames IA, Iowa State Univ Press, 1984

Van Leeuwen J: A child psychiatrist's perspective on children and their companion animals. In Fogle B (ed): Interrelations between people and pets. Springfield IL, Charles C Thomas, 1981

ADDITIONAL READING

Anthony S: The Child's Discovery of Death. London, Routledge, 1940

Anthony S: The Discovery of Death in Childhood and After. New York, Basic Books, 1972

Havighurst R: Human Development and Education. New York, Longmans Green, 1953

Kastenbaum R: Death and development through the lifespan. In Feifil H (ed): New Meanings of Death, pp 17-45. New York, McGraw-Hill, 1977

Maurer A: The child's knowledge of non-existence. Journal of Existential Psychiatry 2:193-212, 1961

Nieburg H, Fischer A: Pet Loss: A Thoughtful Guide for Adults and Children. New York, Harper and Row, 1982

12

Goodbye, Kitty

Mary-Ellen Siegel

I was a full-time homemaker and mother when we accompanied our five-year-old daughter on her quest for the perfect little caged pet. We were thinking along the line of hamsters, guinea pigs, and birds, but they all lost their appeal the moment Betsy saw the white Persian kitten.

I couldn't resist him either. On the journey home, the little ball of white fluff curled up in Betsy's arms. She carried him into her room and put him on the little rug next to her bed. Her eighteen-month-old brother, Peter, had just awakened from his nap and he jumped up and down in his crib chanting, "kitty, kitty, kitty."

The name stuck, and soon Kitty became an integral member of the household. Two years later another little girl joined the family, and Kitty, now a full-grown cat, established his role of children's companion and caretaker.

He allowed himself to be fussed over like a doll baby, would play endless tag, and awaken a sleepy parent if a child cried out at night. He would lie quietly at the end of the bed of a sick or unhappy child, and if coaxed under the covers, remain there until "dismissed."

It wasn't until much later that I began college and then went to social-work school. At that time the only psychology I knew was gleaned from the popular media, but I knew that Kitty's effect on the family was profound. My marriage was fragile; the one object the children would always willingly share was the cat. Kitty was making us look, if not be, like the all-American family. Sometimes I would wonder: if something happened to Kitty, would we all come unglued?

My son was especially attached to Kitty. When his world was going all wrong, or if he had been reprimanded for some mischief, he would look up with his big blue eyes and say, "Nobody loves me. Just Kitty."

Kitty wasn't the only pet; we had our share of gerbils, hamsters, fish, parakeets, and even a rabbit. Kitty took it all in stride.

Peter wanted a dog, and Betsy, probably reacting to her own position in the family, worried that Kitty would be jealous. So Peter would say, "When Kitty gets used up, can we get a dog?" And in the next breath he would say, "You know what I mean about getting used up, don't you?" Then he would pause and ask, "How long do cats live?" and "Do you think Kitty will still be around when I go to college?"

The children were still young when I entered college, and then continued to graduate school. Kitty would sit on my long sewing table, now turned into a desk, and watch me work. I think he preferred my easy-listening radio station to their rock music.

The children grew up and Kitty grew old. He was no longer able to jump to the top of toy cabinets or play "cat and mouse," but he always knew when a teenager was lonely or overwhelmed.

Kitty, it seemed, never quite understood why the children went away to camp, and then, when his first mistress went away to college, he seemed completely bewildered. Whenever Betsy returned, she would rush into the house saving the first hug for Kitty.

"My wedding won't seem right without Kitty," said Betsy. So she was married at home, and our fifteen-year-old cat almost stole the limelight from the bride.

Often I would return home from work and find a note from Betsy, "Stopped by on my way home to see Kitty. Sorry I missed you," and then, as the months went by, "I washed out Kitty's dish. He hadn't eaten his food."

When I would get home from work, Kitty no longer was at the door with his usual greetings. Sometimes I would have to search for him.

The summer he was eighteen he began to show signs of renal failure and confusion. He wouldn't eat, would get lost in the house, and slept almost all the time. He was suffering, and we all knew it. We took him to the vet, who made suggestions. We tried everything. I took time off from work and so did the children. We tried not to leave Kitty alone for too long.

My marriage was ending. I had postponed the decision for so long, but now I could bring my professional know-how to the situation. We had once talked of family therapy. "Could Kitty come along too?" we had wondered.

"The family must be treated as a unit," the experts say.

"It is the interaction among family members that must be examined," they insist.

"Children should live in two-parent households," my parents' generation believed.

But they are not really children any more, I told myself. They will see their father whenever they want to, visit him, go out with him. Will I have to give him visitation rights for Kitty?

Could it be that a beautiful white cat had held a marriage together for so long? In those 18 years I couldn't remember an argument about the cat. Children, in-laws, a million other things could cause stress. But Kitty, never.

Kitty was failing. The prognosis was bleak, the veterinarian explained to the three young adults to whom I still referred collectively as "the children."

At the hospital where I worked, I regularly saw internists and oncologists too busy to listen to the numerous questions families posed regarding a parent or spouse. And I saw these professionals disappear as families tried to come to terms with a loved one's impending death. But not our veterinarian, Dr. Meisels. He suggested we come in after office hours. With warmth and respect he answered the children's questions and stood by as they made their own decisions.

I sat there numb. I thought back to the days when I wished I didn't have to clean out the litter pan. When I was pregnant and couldn't stand the smell of his food. When I worried—so needlessly—that Kitty would jump into a newborn's crib. And wondered if people would think we were a little nuts to have Kitty at the wedding. And over and over came the vision of the children loving their Kitty. And Kitty loving them right back.

The decision was made. Dr. Meisels took Kitty back into the examining room as we sat in the waiting room, each in our own private world.

When it was all over, he called us in. Betsy kissed Kitty. Peter's eyes filled. "Goodbye, Kitty," they said. And the veterinarian put his hands on each of their shoulders and said they must have taken very good care of Kitty for him to have lived such a long life.

We took the carrying case home. It still sits, rather forlornly, on a top shelf of the garage in my house. I have a new marriage and a new house where Kitty never was. And yet he is with us still. In pictures. In memories. In spirit. And in countless stories that no one else but us ever thinks is funny or special—except my four-year-old grandson. He likes to see pictures and hear about the Kitty who used to live with us all. "Someday, Mommy, could we get a Kitty?" he asks.

But it will never really be the same.

13

Equine Euthanasia and Client Grief

Harry V. Hagstad

Discussions of euthanasia in veterinary medicine, particularly con-cerning the human–companion animal bond, tend to focus almost exclusively on dogs and cats. Food animals represent an economic enterprise in which euthanasia is uncommon; when required, it is rarely associated with the type of bereavement experienced upon the loss of a beloved pet.

One animal, however, usually considered only in terms of rural settings, nevertheless fits the model of a companion animal: the horse. In the United States, approximately 3.2 million owners keep an estimated 8.25 million horses, 80% of which serve recreational purposes. More than 270,000 young people are engaged in 4H horse projects, an enrollment greater than the number of cattle and swine projects combined (American Horse Council 1980).

As a result of experience gained in the private practice of veterinary medicine, I became aware of the deep anguish felt by many clients upon the deaths of their horses. This reaction is particularly true of adolescent owners.

METHODS

In order to tap the experience of other veterinarians regarding the emotional impact associated with equine euthanasia, a questionnaire was sent to a randomly selected group of members of the American Association of Equine Practitioners (AAEP).

Questions were asked concerning the type of patients (pleasure horses vs. economically-based horses), numbers of horses euthanatized during the past year, reasons for performing euthanasia, and veterinarian preference regarding the presence of the owner at the time of performing euthanasia.

Fully completed questionnaires were received from 70 veterinarians (53% of those approached), representing all major regions of the United States. The total man-years of practice experience was 1,150. Responses were evaluated for statistical significance using the chi-square test.

RESULTS

Presence of owner during euthanasia

Respondents were asked to indicate their preference regarding the presence of the owner or other individual with the strongest emotional bond to the horse at the time of performing euthanasia. Owners were divided into four categories: adult males, adult females, adolescent males, and adolescent females.

When considering all clients, 41.4% of the veterinarians discouraged their presence during euthanasia, while only 13.2% encouraged it, a statistically significant difference ($p < .001$). The remainder indicated that the owner's presence during euthanasia was not an issue (Table 1). The preferences of the veterinarians were revealing when the clients were divided into the age and sex groups noted above. The presence of adult male owners was discourged by 24.3% of the respondents, but, at the other extreme, over twice as many (55.7%) discouraged the presence of adolescent female owners. Conversely, 24.3% encouraged the presence of adult males, while only 5.7% of the repondents encouraged the presence of adolescent females ($p < .001$).

TABLE 1
Distribution of veterinarians' preferences regarding presence of owners, by age and sex of owner, during euthanasia of horses.

Owner presence	Adult males		Adult females		Adolescent males		Adolescent females		Mean of all groups	
	#	%	#	%	#	%	#	%	#	%
Encouraged	17	24.3	10	14.3	6	8.6	4	5.7	37	13.2
Discouraged	17	24.3	26	37.1	34	48.6	39	55.7	116	41.4
Not an issue	36	51.4	34	48.6	30	42.8	27	38.6	127	45.4
	70	100.0	70	100.0	70	100.0	70	100.0	280	100.0

Pet Loss and Client Grief

Veterinarians' preferences concerning the presence of owners during euthanasia were influenced more by age than by sex. When all the total male sampling, regardless of age, was compared to the total of female sampling, the percentage of respondents discouraging owner presence during euthanasia was 36.4% for male owners and 46.4% for female owners—not a statistically significant difference. When all adults (male plus female) were compared to the total adolescent sample, the percentage of veterinarians discouraging owner presence was 30.7% for adults and 52.2% for adolescents—a statistically significant result ($p < .001$) (Tables 2 and 3).

TABLE 2

Distribution of veterinarians' preferences regarding presence of owner, by sex of owner, during euthanasia of horses.

	Sex of Owner			
	Males		Females	
Owner's presence	#	%	#	%
Encouraged	23	16.4	14	10.0
Discouraged	51	36.4	65	46.4
Not an issue	66	47.2	61	43.6
	140	100.0	140	100.0

TABLE 3

Distribution of veterinarians' preferences regarding presence of owner, by age of owner, during euthanasia of horses.

	Age groups of owners			
	Adults		Adolescents	
Owner's presence	#	%	#	%
Encouraged	27	19.3	10	7.1
Discouraged	43	30.7	73	52.2
Not an issue	70	50.0	57	40.7
	140	100.0	140	100.0

Since the veterinarian is often intimately involved with the grief experienced by the client, it seemed appropriate to analyze possible factors influencing the practitioners' reluctance or willingness to have the owner present during euthanasia.

Years of practice experience

Each respondent was asked to indicate his or her year of graduation from veterinary school. The practitioners were then divided into five groups, by decades, 1940s through 1980s.

The largest number of respondents was graduated in the 1970s (27). The next largest group was the 1960s graduates (18), followed by the 1980s and 1950s graduates (10 each). The 1940s were represented by five respondents.

The percentage of respondents who discouraged the presence of the owner at time of euthanasia tended to be in inverse proportion to the years of practice experience; i.e., a recent graduate was more apt to discourage the presence of an owner than was the practitioner with many years of experience (Table 4).

TABLE 4

Distribution of veterinarians' preferences regarding presence of owner during euthanasia of horses as a function of length of practice experience.

| | Decade of graduation | | | | | | | | | |
| | 1940s | | 1950s | | 1960s | | 1970s | | 1980s | |
Owner's presence	#	%	#	%	#	%	#	%	#	%
Encouraged	8	40.0	10	25.0	4	5.6	10	9.3	5	12.5
Discouraged	6	30.0	11	27.5	36	50.0	44	40.7	19	47.5
Not an issue	6	30.0	19	47.5	32	44.4	54	50.0	16	40.0
	20	100.0	40	100.0	72	100.0	108	100.0	40	100.0

Type of practice

On the premise that a stronger emotional bond might be experienced by the owner of a horse kept purely for pleasure than by one who maintained the animal for economic purposes (racehorses and work-horses), the respondents' preferences for owner presence during euthanasia was evaluated by type of practice. The percentage of veterinarians discouraging owner attendance at the time of euthanasia was essentially the same for all three types of practice; economically based horses, pleasure horses, and mixed (Table 5).

TABLE 5

Distribution of veterinarians' preferences regarding presence of owner during euthanasia of horses as a function of type of practice experience.

	Type of practice					
	Economically based horses		Pleasure horses		Mixed horses	
Owner's presence	#	%	#	%	#	%
Encouraged	5	6.6	13	14.8	19	16.4
Discouraged	32	42.1	35	39.8	49	42.2
Not an issue	39	51.3	40	45.4	48	41.4
	76	100.0	88	100.0	116	100.0

Number of euthanasias performed

Sometimes a procedure that is emotionally stressful when first performed becomes less so with repetition. To determine if this was a factor influencing the willingness of the veterinarian to allow the owner to be present at the time of euthanasia, respondents were divided into five groups based on the number of horses they had euthanatized during the past year. No correlation was shown between the number of horses euthanatized and the percentage of veterinarians discouraging the presence of owners during euthanasia (Table 6).

TABLE 6

Distribution of veterinarians' preferences regarding presence of owner during euthanasia of horses as a function of number of horses euthanatized during previous year.

	Number euthanatized during last year									
Owner's presence	None		1-5		6-10		11-20		Over 20	
	#	%	#	%	#	%	#	%	#	%
Encouraged	1	8.3	18	13.6	11	15.3	3	7.5	4	16.7
Discouraged	3	25.0	62	50.0	21	29.2	19	47.5	11	45.8
Not an issue	8	66.7	52	39.4	40	55.5	18	45.0	9	37.5
	12	100.0	132	100.0	72	100.0	40	100.0	24	100.0

Reasons for euthanasia

Finally, on the assumption that a serious injury with associated physical pain would make euthanasia more acceptable to the owner, the veterinarians surveyed were asked to indicate the most common reason for performing euthanasia in their practice. These data were then compared to their preferences regarding the presence of the owner during euthanasia.

Approximately half of the respondents reported that they discouraged the presence of the owner when the reason for euthanasia was severe injury or when euthanasia was performed because the useful life of the horse had ended, but only 25% discouraged owner attendance when the reason for euthanasia was a terminal illness (Table 7). The difference was statistically significant ($p < .001$).

TABLE 7

Distribution of veterinarians' preferences regarding presence of owner during euthanasia of horses as a function of reason for euthanasia.

Owner's presence	Reason for euthanasia					
	Injury		Terminal illness		Useful life ended	
Encouraged	21	15.4	15	22.0	0	0.0
Discouraged	65	47.8	17	25.0	16	57.1
Not an issue	50	36.8	36	53.0	12	42.9
	136	100.0	68	100.0	28	100.0

DISCUSSION

The choice of the "discouraged" category as the critical term regarding owner presence during euthanasia was based on the author's experience in private practice. "Encouraging" the presence of an owner would seem to be a definite action, preceded by a definite decision. Most owners, however, *do* want to be present when their horse or other companion animal is euthanatized, and encouragement is frequently not necessary. The "encouraged" category, in these instances, becomes difficult to separate from the "not an issue" group. "Discouraging" the presence of an owner, particularly since most owners do want to be present, is a clearly defined action and will rarely overlap with the "not an issue" response.

Technical competence is a basic requirement for any profession, but some fields require more. A successful veterinarian in private practice can be accurately decribed as part veterinarian, part pediatrician, and part psychologist. Veterinarians must, first of all, be competent in the technical skills of their profession. In addition, since their patients cannot verbalize their symptoms, veterinarians must, like pedtricians, depend on a third party for an accurate history. Finally, since the emotional bond between the owner and his or her companion animal is usually strong, sometimes as intense as that which exists between parents and their children, the veterinarian frequently becomes directly involved in a crisis situation and is called upon to assume a counseling role. Some professionals can handle these crises well; others cannot, and try to avoid them.

An attempt has been made in this study to equate the respondents' practice experience with their willingness to permit a horse owner to be present at the time of euthanasia—a situation of potentially severe emotional impact. What was not measured was the personality of the respondent, a factor which must, assuredly, influence the veterinarian's willingness or unwillingness to become involved.

Since the ability to handle the emotional crises of companion-animal owners effectively is part of a private practitioner's profession, it is appropriate to include preparation for this important role in the professional curriculum of veterinary students. An understanding of human behavior, particularly in the area of object relationships, and knowledge of child and adolescent development, will enable the practitioner to empathize with the client during a time of grief and to provide support; therefore, it is imperative that psychologists and sociologists become more deeply involved in the training of veterinary students.

REFERENCES

American Horse Council: Data on the United States Horse Industry. Washington DC, American Horse Council, 1980

14

The Pet With Cancer: Impact on the Family

E. Gregory MacEwen

Cancer is one of the most dreaded diseases known today. Just the word "cancer" incites fear and anxiety. One of the most difficult experiences a veterinarian must face is that of informing a family or pet owner that his beloved animal has an incurable disease. The purpose of this chapter is to share some of the experiences I have had with families of pets with cancer, and to relate the importance of understanding the profound psychological and emotional stress felt by these families.

The following excerpt from a letter written by an owner whose pet suffered from cancer emphasizes the emotional intensity of the relationship between an owner and his or her pet. This family's dog had undergone a stormy course of therapy, and therefore the entire experience was extremely unpleasant for everyone involved.

> Despite his fortitude, we knew the battle was nearing its end, as the wounds were becoming increasingly harder to bear. The hope, which had once been our comfort, was now our despair; and the stength, having once been our source of determination, was now our weakness. For as long as I live, I shall never be able to forget the desperation in his eyes. He'd always been so dependent on us for everything; we were his protectors, we shielded him, sheltered him, we nourished and cared for him—above all, we loved him! How could we make him understand that we were no longer able to secure him from harm or danger as we had in the past, for now another power had intervened.

With his head resting upon my lap, I began to explain to him why the time had come for him to leave us, and the emptiness within our hearts had already begun to pain since we would miss him terribly. Overwhelmed with guilt and remorse, I kept apologizing to him, confiding that we had never meant for him to suffer; and pledging, over and over how very dearly we loved him . . . and when he gazed up at me with that confused sort of expression, I felt as though we'd betrayed him. As if he understood, he mustered up the little bit of strength he had to raise his paw which searched feebly for the security of my hand. The tears streamed down my face as I gently kissed him goodbye, for somehow I knew I might never see him again.

The very next day, during a fleeting moment of courage, Mom took him to the hospital, where she remained close by his side, until the beat of his precious heart had sounded for the very last time.

No, I never saw him again!

There was a bond between us, a bond of faith, a bond of trust, a bond of devotion — a bond of love! Through this we derived all of our hope; when that had gone, our courage. And now, when the bond has been separated forever, our sorrow.

This letter exemplifies the type of relationship that frequently develops between an owner and his pet, and the strong ties of love and psychological dependence that are characteristic. It particularly expresses sentiments typical of an owner toward his sick or dying pet. Many owners experience overwhelming feelings of guilt and remorse. An owner may feel guilty because he thinks he has caused the disease, for not seeking medical attention sooner, for not doing everything possible, or for *doing* everything possible and thereby causing his innocent pet the pain and suffering associated with therapy. He may also carry guilt for electing euthanasia or for *not* electing euthanasia. A second important point is that the owner is ultimately responsible for all aspects of his pet's care — nourishment, shelter, health, and overall well-being. This can contribute to an owner's feeling responsible for his pet's sickness and death. Finally, this letter typifies the bond that develops between man and animal — a bond of faith, trust, devotion, and, especially, love.

Throughout the course of disease and treatment, the responses of the owner and family undergo characteristic stages. These responses are much the same as when the patient is a human being. The first major emotional stress a family must face is dealing with the reality that their pet has cancer. Typical reactions are denial and disbelief. At this point the owner may show anger toward the veterinarian; the veterinarian must anticipate this and not be personally offended. As stated earlier, guilt is another common reaction, since the pet is dependent on the owner for its livelihood. The pet is, in effect, an "innocent bystander." In human medicine, a person who develops cancer may feel responsible for his own disease, and guilt feelings are not uncommon. It is important for the veterinarian to be as supportive as possible during the first phase of the owner's emotional pain. In many instances the veterinarian is the only person who can help the owner understand his guilt.

The next stage is acceptance. Once the owner has accepted the reality of the situation, he must decide with the help of the veterinarian what action to take. The veterinarian is responsible for informing the owner of all treatment alternatives, and the pros and cons of each one. The veterinarian must also be familiar with the type of malignant process and extent of disease, so that he can give an accurate prognosis, both with and without treatment. The veterinarian must be cognizant not only of emotional needs and problems, but also of the reality of an owner's particular circumstances (e.g., time available, financial resourses). All these factors must be taken into account in deciding the best course of action.

One alternative is euthanasia, which of course constitutes one of the chief differences between human and veterinary medicine. Factors which influence the decision whether or not to elect euthanasia include the following:

1. General health of the animal
2. Overall prognosis and extent of disease
3. Effectiveness of available treatment
4. Financial resources
5. Time available to the owner
6. Emotional stability of the owner and/or family
7. Previous experience with another family member or another pet that was treated for cancer. ("We just can't go through it again.")
8. Ability to accept the fact that the pet cannot be cured. For some owners, one or two years of life is not acceptable, so they elect euthanasia.
9. Ability to accept the fact of euthanasia. In certain situations, particularly with elderly individuals and those living alone, there is such an intensely close relationship between owner and pet that euthanasia just cannot be considered. The owner may see no distinction between his pet's life and survival and his own.

In some cases euthanasia is clearly the best choice, but the owner will not allow it and pursues all alternative courses of therapy, regardless of cost, ineffectiveness, and adverse effects.

Having elected the course of therapy, the next stage that the owner or family goes through is one of optimism. A similar stage is experienced by human patients. Once a remission is achieved, the owner feels that his pet will "beat" this disease, and many keep raising the same issues or questions: "How long will he live?" and "What are his chances of being cured?" They keep expecting a change in prognosis because the pet is temporarily doing well: "How can he look so good when he has cancer?"

A major difference between veterinary medicine and human medicine is that when a person is ill, it is commonly the patient who accepts the major responsibility for his own care and treatment. With pets, all the responsibility naturally lies with the owner who makes the decisions, schedules the appointments, administers the medication, and must also keep track of the pet's eating, drinking, elimination, and sleeping habits. Any change must be brought to the veterinarian's attention. Inasmuch as owners have to take the responsibility for making all the decisions, they sometimes have to deal with the insensitive comments of others who have different opinions as to how the pet should be handled: "You are being cruel. Why don't you put him to sleep?" and "Why go through all that time and expense when he's only going to die?" Such comments can be extremely upsetting to an owner who has usually considered all of these factors and a hundred more many times over.

The final stage of emotional stress occurs when the pet has failed to respond to therapy, and relapse of the disease occurs. The owner becomes aware that the pet's death is inevitable. Again, the family needs support and help during this time. The owner may elect euthanasia, or may request therapeutic alternatives, no matter how unrealistic or unproven. When death does occur, there are often feelings of relief and emotional release as well as grief.

In conclusion, I would like to quote a portion of the same letter with which I began:

> I found it extremely difficult expressing what is truly in my heart, though I've come to realize that words could never really impart the sorrow that is felt when one loses his pet. It is a grief that could never be understood unless one has actually experienced it. But you can be assured that the loss of an animal is just as agonizing as the loss of a human, for certainly, if the pain were to be measured, they'd be equivalent. Perhaps even more severe, as the love you share with this animal is built around a special kind of innocence, and it is a bond that I doubt two people in this world today are capable of—because he is...the only absolutely unselfish friend that man can have in this selfish world.

15

Pet Loss and Separation: A Multifactorial Problem

Edward Baker

Loss of a pet and its attendant grief can be due to many causes other than death. All too often, family members are called upon to remove a perfectly healthy pet from a household for a variety of reasons, which may be beyond their control. The most common cause for separation brought to my attention as a veterinary allergist is the development of an allergy to the animal. Other common reasons include broken homes, nuisance and behavioral problems, and housing restrictions.

Such separation is often more jarring and traumatic than death. For death due to disease, age or even injury is understandable, even to young children. It can be prepared for, explained and, finally, ritualized as a last gesture of love and devotion. But separation from, or destruction of, a healthy animal is difficult to understand or rationalize.

People may react to an allergist's advice to remove a pet from a household in any of several ways, most commonly by non-compliance. A common scenario in my office involves an allergic client, or parent of an allergic child, telling me he has just been told that he must get rid of his pet. Most will candidly and frankly tell me that they have no intention of either removing the pet, or letting the allergist know they have not done so. This obviously creates an untenable situation for both the allergist and the patient. Although the allergist is rarely fooled, non-compliance does impair communication between physician and client, making the physician's job more difficult and the patient's response less satisfactory.

When a pet is removed from a household because of allergy, it is not uncommon for the family to develop a deep and abiding resentment against the allergic family member that may continually resurface for many years. Adults as well as children may exhibit this reaction.

Removal of a pet can create other psychological problems within allergic households. In a survey I conducted among allergists several years ago, I asked, "Have you observed guilt feelings, emotional reactions or psychological trauma following forced elimination of pets?" About 55% answered yes, and reported very similar reactions, including

- emotional reactions, psychological trauma and guilt feelings in the patient and other family members
- depression
- aggravation of the allergic state
- temporary feelings of deprivation of love and support, at least until medical benefit was evident
- resentment of the allergic child by siblings
- response as to the loss of a family member

Some families commented that they would rather "get rid of" the husband or wife than the family pet. Others said that they wouldn't give up their pet for a "million dollars." These are obviously gross distortions, but do indicate the degree of attachment some people have to their pets.

Divorce and broken homes are another frequent cause of separation from a pet. In the extreme, the pet may be used as a pawn, or bargaining chip, to extract an unfair advantage from an unhappy situation. As the ultimate act of cruelty, the pet may be euthanatized as a means of revenge by the supposedly aggrieved party. More frequently, the pet is parcelled out along with the rest of the property, and family members may find themselves permanently separated from the pet with whom a deep and abiding attachment has developed. In cases where euthanasia is requested as a result of family break-up, it is extremely important for the veterinarian to firmly establish ownership and understand the reason for the request. In this way it is possible for the veterinarian to prevent the needless destruction of a healthy animal.

Housing restrictions represent another area where permanent separation from an otherwise healthy pet can occur. With restrictive regulations in leases, pet owners, and particularly older people who are living in public housing, are finding themselves forced to give up a pet because of concerns about aggravating allergic conditions among other tenants. Proper planning and a little foresight, however, can prevent problems among the afflicted, while allowing the rest of the tenants to enjoy the salubrious benefits of pet ownership.

Housing, whether public or private, can present a serious problem to the pet owner. Lease restrictions frequently occur because the property owner has had a bad experience with a thoughtless or uncaring tenant. Yet the majority of pet owners, especially elders, do not permit their pets to be nuisances, curb their dogs, try to prevent unnecessary noise and, in general, try to be good pet-owning neighbors. It is sad to think that people must give up the affection, protection and therapeutic value of a pet because of misguided, unduly restrictive regulations.

When faced with the necessity of an irrevocable separation due to housing difficulties, some pet owners will try to find another place to live. Many others, however, will choose euthanasia, using such rationales as "She wouldn't be happy with anybody else," "Nobody else would understand him," or "I'm afraid someone else would abuse him or wouldn't take care of him the way I did." It is difficult to understand why people respond this way. It may be that they can't bear the thought of sharing something they have loved, and held dear, with someone else. Perhaps future psychological studies will provide answers.

In essence, then, the decision to euthanatize, or find a new home for a pet because of factors beyond one's control is different from and evidently more complex than the decision to euthanatize because of sickness or injury. Whatever the final decision, it would appear to involve a more intense emotional struggle with much longer-lasting consequences. I have often heard clients tell me that they gave up a pet once because of allergy, but they would never do it again. Many return to pet ownership in spite of their allergies. The progressive allergist has learned to recognize this special relationship between people and their pets and to work with the patient in developing a lifestyle suitable for patient and pet alike.

Not only veterinarians, but also physicians, social workers, and psychologists, should be mindful of, and prepared to cope with, the problems that can arise from the forced and permanent separation from a healthy pet.

16

Pet Loss: Veterinarians, Ministers and Owners Working Together to Resolve Grief

F. Ellen Netting, Cindy C. Wilson and John C. New, Jr.

This chapter presents four cases that examine the role of the clergy in helping people cope with pet loss. Although ministers — for convenience, we will use the term "minister" in this chapter to mean clergy generally — are automatically called in the event of human death, they are seldom notified when a beloved pet dies. It has been said that loss of a loved one is a wound to the spirit. Clergy are especially trained to deal with these wounds, and are a source of support when such trauma occurs. It is our purpose to suggest that the value of the minister as a resource in the event of pet loss has been overlooked.

Semi-structured, taped interviews were conducted with people who had recently lost pets. These people had either sought help from a minister or had been approached by a minister as they attempted to resolve their grief. Interviews were transcribed and the content was analyzed by a multidisciplinary team consisting of a social worker, a public-health educator, a minister, and a veterinarian.

CASE 1: EUTHANASIA

Ms. B, age 37, was a college-educated, married homemaker with three children. She had owned dogs all her life and described herself as a dog lover. On her daughter's second birthday she had given the child Problem, a mixed-breed dog. Because the entire family was allergic to dogs, Problem stayed outdoors. Since Ms. B worked in the yard a great deal, she spent a lot of time with Problem. When Problem developed cancer at age 12, Ms. B had to make the decision to euthanatize her.

Because euthanasia is a conscious choice, it can lead to feelings of guilt. A profound sadness may arise as one leaves the veterinarian's office without the cherished pet. The veterinarian and staff members must deal with these first grief reactions. When Ms. B brought Problem to be euthanatized, she found the veterinarian's attitude helpful.

> I think that he was very sweet and very understanding. He was. . .well, I almost want to say embarrassed because I could not keep from crying. He kind of was there. And he went out and got a box of Kleenex to hand me since I had used the 23 that I had in my purse! But he did not try to hug me or anything, which I really did not want him to do. But he was there. I knew he was there and feeling strongly for me.

Ms. B returned to an empty house. Her husband and children were away and not due back until late that afternoon. She tried to deal with her grief physically by scrubbing the house from top to bottom, crying the entire time.

A friend and member of the same church contacted Ms. B's minister, who called to check on her. Ms. B. said she would not have called him herself because she felt he had more important problems to handle. She admitted that she was severely grief-stricken and had cried for hours at a time.

CASE 2: EUTHANASIA

Ms. R, age 36, was unmarried and worked as a receptionist in a veterinarian's office. Within six months she lost both her dogs, who were old and had lived with her since puppyhood. One died of a lingering illness and the other had to be euthanatized after an illness. Working around other animals served as a constant reminder of her loss. Her major difficulty, however, was that when pet owners came to the office to have their companion animals euthanatized, she had no idea how to comfort them. Worse yet, she over-identified with them and usually left the office as upset as they were. The wounds from her own grief would start to heal, only to be reopened with each new euthanasia situation.

In Ms. R's case, she herself approached a minister who was one of the clients at the office. When Ms. R discovered he served as a hospital chaplain, she asked, "How do you work with people who encounter loss?"

She so empathized with the client's grief she explained, that she could be of little help to them.

CASE 3: PROLONGED ILLNESS

Ms. P, age 42, was single, never married, and without living relatives. A highly educated professional, she had always worked outside the home. Her parents had owned Fred, a Great Dane, and upon their deaths she had taken Fred to live with her. She readily admitted that Fred was her last living relative. Ms. P's attachment to Fred was unconventional in that the companion animal served as a substitute for a human relationship (Harris 1982). Ms. P stated, "Well, I always loved him. He was always a fine person to be with."

At age 9, Fred developed pancreatitis and died at home after a long illness. Although Ms. P had known that Fred was not doing well, she did not feel that she had been able to deal with her grief in an anticipatory fashion:

> I denied that [he was dying]. Mostly when he had had a bout with arthritis or pancreatitis the year before, I thought at that time I would have to have him put to sleep. I really put the doctor on the spot at that time and said to him, "When will I know when the time has come?" And he said that he would tell me. So I just had to depend on him to tell me. I knew that I would feel bad. Yes, I was surprised, because the grief was actually a lot worse than when Mother and Daddy had died.

Because Ms. P had felt such a close attachment to Fred, her minister, who knew them both, was well aware that this would be a difficult time for her. He made a special effort to be in contact with her during Fred's illness and, when Fred died, the minister contacted Ms. P. Ms. P's loneliness after Fred's death was tremendous.

> Fred's death was the first time that I had to cope with losing someone that I lived with. . . I could hardly bear to get in the car for a while because anytime that I got in the car he was with me. . . .

Because of her professional education, Ms. P was very much aware of Kübler-Ross' (1969) "stages of grief." She recounted her reactions:

Particularly [I went through] denial. Yeah, I did that right up
to the last minute. I bargained with the vet. What can I do to
keep him alive? And even maybe if we tried this and maybe if
we tried that. I did everything! Then I was really angry with the
new vet down there...on a couple of occasions when I felt like
he had not taken Fred's illness seriously.

CASE 4: SUDDEN DEATH

Ms. K, age 60, had been married 35 years, with no children. A school-
teacher most of her life, Ms. K had retired ten years earlier. Her husband
continued to work, leaving her at home during the day. Rollo was a small
mixed-breed dog that she "fell in love with." She primarily, was Rollo's
owner. At age seven, Rollo was hit by a truck and killed in front of Ms. K's
home while she was away. When she returned, her husband had found
Rollo and was preparing to bury him.

She recounted what she felt when her husand told her that Rollo was
dead:

> My first reaction was shock. My second reaction was anger
> because it was an unnecessary death...And I went down to
> where my husband put him in the box, and he had covered him
> up. I knelt down and touched him and he was getting cold. And
> my next reaction was guilt. I thought that if I had come home,
> he would not have been out there. He would have been with me,
> and I would have been in the house. Oh, I should have come
> home early. I was extremely guilty.

In the case of Rollo's death, Ms. K called upon her minister. She needed
to talk with someone about her feelings, and she considered him an
appropriate source of support. In dealing with her grief, Ms. K began
writing poetry for the first time in her life. An example follows.

> And we learned to communicate
> He with his eyes, and I
> with my voice.
> And we had long talks,
> And we took short walks,
> And every day our love for each other grew
> Until I was the center of his life and
> He was a great part of mine.

Ms. K stated that she never intended to write poetry again, but that she had written many poems to Rollo.

DISCUSSION

Loss takes many forms. The need to euthanatize a trusted and trusting animal can be heartbreaking. Loss by theft can be agonizing because of the accompanying uncertainty and anger. Death, whether sudden or prolonged, brings with it feelings of sadness, hopelessness, despair, guilt, and anger.

Case One described the euthanasia of an animal companion of many years. In such situations, owners may know that euthanasia is an option, and talking about feelings prior to the event, as well as after the pet's death, may expedite the healing process. A minister is one of several professionals whom an owner might approach for comfort. This role does not mean that the cleric equates the pet's life with that of a person. It means, rather, that the minister is equipped to deal with loss, and the management of grief is important regardless of the object of that grief.

Not only might ministers be viewed as resources when euthanasia is considered, but they might actually accompany a parishioner or friend to the veterinarian's office. Clerics are accustomed to being a part of rites of passage, special times, and difficult periods in people's lives. It would be logical, therefore, to include a minister in the decision-making process and in the trip to the veterinarian's office.

Case Two examined the "flip side" of Case One, demonstrating that people who staff the veterinarian's office often feel ill-equipped to deal with the grief experienced by their clients. Some people respond better to a minister than they would to a social worker or a psychologist when confronting grief. This in no way implies that clergy should replace secular helping professionals. Rather, the religious leader should provide an option. Veterinarians might establish communication with local clergy, so that appropriate referrals could be made when a client must have an animal euthanatized. These connections should be established in advance, so that the clergy will be aware that they might receive calls for help from local veterinarians.

Case Three deals with the prolonged illness of a pet. Ministers need not like animals to realize that owners are suffering during their pets' illnesses and hardships.

Again, it is not the object of the grief that counts. It is the fact that a person is having a hard time coping with stress. If ministers, say, could just call to check on owners who have seriously or terminally ill animals, it would mean a great deal. The pet owner's personal anxieties may be lessened by the initiation of contact by the minister. Instead of pretending "it's nothing," the owner would be allowed a safe outlet to express grief rather than repress these legitimate feelings. If veterinarians were connected with ministers, they might be able to call and say, "Ms. So-and-So has a pet that has just been injured. Thought you might like to know."

Case three is important because it examines a situation in which there was a person living alone. People who have no significant others or who have close, unconventional attachments to their animals may be very distressed by pet loss. The animal has become a true companion and a source of social interaction. Thus, these people may be particularly vulnerable when their companion animals die. Ministers should be trained to be sensitive to those vulnerabilities. Indeed, ministers would be especially helpful in assisting these pet owners in dealing with personal anxieties.

Case Four deals with sudden death, which is always hard to cope with because there is no chance for anticipatory grief. The owner may be in the denial stage of grief for several days. In Case Four, Ms. K sought her minister out so that she could discuss her grief. The suddenness of Rollo's death meant that Ms. K had had no opportunity to say goodbye. She went back several times to talk with the minister and to share her poetry. In cases like this, the minister has the opportunity to assist a person in working through her grief. Since Rollo died quickly, Ms. K did not have the chance to talk with a veterinarian and thus she had no professional with whom to interact. Being a determined person, she went to her minister. However, the minister might be aware that there will be people in his congregation who will not come to him, who will not have another professional to talk with, and who are suffering from the sudden death of a pet. In these cases, the minister should take the initiative and make a home visit to express concern.

The family situations varied in these four cases. Ms. B had a husband and three children. However, she was alone during the day and had become closer to Problem than did the other family members. Because of this closeness, Ms. B was dealing with an intense feeling of grief. Although the rest of the family were hurt and upset, their immediate reaction had been to ask for another dog. Ms. B was not as ready to take that step. Similarly, Ms. K was more closely bonded to Rollo than her husand was. Although he grieved, his reaction was not nearly as intense as Ms. B's. Ms. R and Ms. P lived alone. There were no immediate family members to share the grief. Ms. P was especially alone since she had no living relatives.

As an outside source of support, the minister may be helpful to families and to individuals. In the situation where owners have family in the same household, the "identified" owner may need additional assistance with his or her grief. For owners, who live alone, the minister may be a potential source of support in a sea of loneliness.

LINKAGES

There are numerous potential linkages between clergy and veterinarians in working with owners to facilitate grieving. The following might be explored:

1) When veterinarians are the first contact for a person who has lost a pet, it would be helpful for veterinarians to know who the local clergy are so that they can make appropriate referrals. One way to find this out would be to ask clients who their ministers are and to find out whether they would like to have their minister contacted.

2) Veterinarians might suggest to owners planning to come to the office to have an animal euthanatized that they bring someone with them. A minister might be suggested if the owner has no one else who can come.

3) Veterinarians might want to have their staff trained in dealing with grief. A logical source for training would be a minister or a hospital chaplain, who is trained and experienced in working with people going through crises related to the illness or death of significant others.

4) Connections could be made at the organizational level between local veterinary associations and ministerial associations. Most cities of any size have both types of organizations, and in rural areas there are regional associations. Communication could be facilitated by joint programming at meetings. For example, a discussion of the role of the minister in pet loss could be initiated as the program topic at a meeting of the veterinary association.

5) Workshops might be set up between local veterinarians and local clergy for numerous reasons such as discussing common issues, learning how to make referrals to one another, setting up foster homes for congregants' pets when temporary problems occur, etc. In short, such a workshop would create creative communication and facilitate other linkages.

6) When clients are trying to make the decision to euthanatize a companion animal, the minister might work with the veterinarian to facilitate the decision-making process.

7) Sometimes a decision to euthanatize a companion animal may be based on the fact that its owner can no longer care for it. This is particularly true when an older person dies and leaves an animal alone,

or when a person has to enter a living situation in which animals are not allowed. This type of euthanasia is particularly difficult since the animal may be quite healthy, although homeless. Ministers are often in positions to identify such situations and could work with veterinarians to develop options for owners who encounter this difficulty.

CONCLUSIONS

Research is needed on ways to deal with some of the issues raised in this chapter. First, studies should be undertaken to determine whether ministers are involved in pet-loss issues and to define their attitudes toward such intervention. Second, congregants might be surveyed to identify pet-related needs that they feel ministers might address. Third, research veterinarians and their staffs should be surveyed to identify the types of grief-related events in which they are involved and their methods of facilitating grief work. The clergy, like many other professionals, are involved in assisting people in crisis. The human/animal bonding issue has now begun to include the role of the minister in coping with grief associated with pet loss.

The authors express special appreciation to the Levi Strauss Foundation and the AETNA Life and Casualty Foundation for funding the PET PROJECT, one outcome of which was the present chapter.

REFERENCES

Alstine CV: Saying goodbye: helping clients face the loss of a pet. Calif Veterinarian 36:29-30, 1982

Barton CL, Beaver BV: Coping with the death of a pet: client grief. In Kirk RW (ed): Current Veterinary Therapy VII: Small Animal Practice, pp 72-74. Philadelphia, W. B. Saunders, 1983

Harris JM: A study of client grief responses to death to loss in a companion animal veterinary practice. Calif Veterinarian 36:17-17, 1982

Katcher AH, Beck AM (eds): New Perspectives on Our Lives with Companion Animals, pp 363-406. Philadelphia, Univ of Pennsylvania Press, 1982

Katcher AH, Rosenberg MA: Euthanasia and the management of the client's grief. Calif Veterinarian 36:31-37, 1982

Keddie KMB: Pathological mourning after the death of a domestic pet. Brit J Psychiatry 131:21-25, 1977

Maggitti P: The pet bereavement counselor. Dog Fancy 14(Sept):22-24, 1983

Nieburg HA, Fischer A: Pet Loss. New York, Harper & Row, 1983

SUGGESTED READING

Bustad LK: Animals, Aging, and the Aged. Minneapolis MN: Univ of Minnesota
    Press, 1980
Fogle B: Attachment-euthanasia-grieving. In Fogle B (ed): Interrelationships
    Between people and pets, pp 331-334. Springfield IL, Charles C Thomas, 1981
Harris M: Understanding amid death: bereavement, grief and euthanasia. In
    Anderson RK, Hart BL, Hart LA (eds): The Pet Connection: Its Influence on
    Our Health and Quality of Life, pp 261-275, Minneapolis MN: Center to Study
    Human / Animal Relationships and Environments, Univ of Minnesota, 1984
Nieburg HA, Fischer A: Pet Loss: A Thoughtful Guide for Adults and Children.
    New York, Harper & Row, 1982
Veterinary medical practice — pet loss and human emotion. Arch Foundation of
    Thanatology 9(2), 1982
Viorst J: The Tenth Good Thing About Barney. New York, Atheneum Press, 1971

Part 3
Perspectives on the Human/Companion Animal Bond

17

Grief and Mourning Following Human and Animal Death

Susan A. Iliff and Jack L. Albright

Much study and research has been devoted to the human mind and how it works; in recent years considerable effort has been made and much information published on human grief and bereavement behavior. Unfortunately, we cannot make this claim in the case of animals. It obviously is difficult to do research on and get conclusive results from animals because of the difficulty of direct communication with them. Before we proceed further, we must raise some questions concerning animal awareness: Are animals aware of and do they recognize themselves and others of their species? How do they view humans? Are they conscious of different feelings and desires? There are many ideas on this subject. K. R. Popper states ". . . Animals, although capable of feelings, sensations, memory and thus of consciousness, do not possess the full consciousness of self which is one of the results of human language. . ." (Popper, 1972). Donald Griffin, in *The Question of Animal Awareness* (1976), hypothesizes that animals' mental experiences include not only images and intentions but also feelings, desires, hopes, fears, and a wide range of sensations such as pain and hunger. Though it is conceded that animals may have subjective feelings as well as perceptions (sense-consciousness), for purposes of study we must concentrate on the animal's behavior toward objects and relationships in the outside world. Because relatively little is known about animal communication, most linguists and philosophers vacillate between denying to animals any significant mental experiences and grudgingly admitting the likelihood of simple ones but rejecting all others.

The greatest problem with this question is that it cannot be attacked and solved by scientific methods. What happens in the minds of animals may never be understood by humans. The mind of the dog is sometimes described as working in terms of "mind pictures." Most people are familiar with the dog's behavior during sleep. As he vocalizes and moves his limbs, we can imagine what the nature of his dream is.

One can easily imagine an animal angry, frightened, happy, unhappy, startled, and even hopeful. Yet many people will argue that to think animals have experiences, and to attribute to animals human-like emotions and needs, is unscientific and anthropomorphic. It requires ascribing human thoughts, expressions, and gestures to a nonhuman species. Despite the argument against anthropomorphism, few will have difficulty accepting the idea that injured animals feel pain, and starved animals feel hunger, just as humans do.

In addition to the general question of animal awareness, we must ask specifically about animals' awareness of death. What is death to the animal? Is it the loss of a companion animal or human companion? Is such an awareness innate or does it develop following emotional attachment? Is it the fact of death or just the absence of a companion, an object loss, which the animal recognizes? As yet, no definitive answers exist. The reader must decide for himself, based on personal knowledge and experience.

There is evidence to uphold theories of animal awareness of death. A widespread belief in many cultures is that the howling of a dog indicates coming death. In Taiwan, many people send for a priest when they hear a dog howl, anticipating the death of someone in the family. The Bible also states, "Dogs howling predict death" (Levinson, 1969). Dale Evans Rogers, in *Dearest Debbie*, speaks of happenings before her daughter's death. "Two weeks before the accident was the persistent wailing of our dog Bullet in the night. Previously, Robin's dog, Lana, had also cried in the night before her going away. . . ."

Although we cannot come to any firm conclusions regarding animal awareness, we will concede that animals do have or experience emotions, or what we will refer to as emotions, however different from those we know as human. Expression comes from emotion; thus, the more emotion felt, the more emission of sound or expressive activity.

Most social animals show emotion, especially between members of the same species. Attachment is of crucial importance in the development of the social animal species starting with the mother-infant relationship to sibling-family and finally to a male-female mate relationship. Animal friendships between species, like cats and dogs, can occur, as well as comradeship between dog and human, and so forth. Comradeship finds expression in a very strong affective reaction to cries of fear, warning, etc. It is not unusual for the sight of a dead individual of the same species to produce strong emotion and thus resultant behavior. For example, a farmer can keep ravens away from a field or fowl-run not only by using a scarecrow, but also by attaching a dead raven to it.

To understand the grief and mourning that occur after the death of an animal or human, one must understand the love, affection, and attachments that can develop and exist between animals and humans. Affection for pets is very great. Even today, Australian aborigine women breastfeed puppies and women in New Guinea suckle pigs.

Of all creatures, dogs form exceptionally close bonds with humans. "The Dog loves man with a love not born of consciousness and which never becomes conscious. It is an unreasonable love, a mysterious impulse, as strong and as imperative as all the primitive forces of Nature and Being" (Buytendijk, 1973). It is said that there is a very close relationship between knowing and loving which may be expressed in terms of understanding. Konrad Lorenz, famed ethologist, says, "The pleasure which I derive from my dog is closely akin to the joy accorded to me by the raven, the greylag goose, or other wild animals that enliven my walks thru the countryside; it seems like a reestablishment of the immediate bond with that unconscious omniscience that we call nature" (Lorenz, 1952). The value of the dog to man is purely psychological, except in a few utilitarian cases such as for sportsmen, policemen, and blind people.

SIGNS OF GRIEF AND MOURNING

There are two factors in grief: 1) awareness of the loss, and 2) appreciation of the value of that which is lost. In monkeys, it is not possible to distinguish the expression of pain, grief, or vexation, from moderate anger, except that grief is shown by weeping. Usually tears just collect in the animal's eyes, but a monkey from Borneo was seen to have tears rolling down her cheeks. Sufferers of grief initially show violent and frantic movements, then lapse into motionlessness and passivity. The facial muscles become flaccid, the head hanging downward. Breathing is typically slow and shallow, punctuated with deep sighs. Sadness in the dog is not uncommon, ranging from mild despondency to downright misery. Manifestations are seen in the woeful facial expression, with head and tail too heavy to raise, and a slow, slouching gait. Grief reactions can and do vary in degree and kind, depending on the nature of loss involved.

Grief and Mourning in Wild Animals

There are many recordings, both documented and undocumented, of grief, mourning, and resultant death-related behavior in wild animals. Wild animals, in this sense, means any animals not maintained as pets. From the monkey family, there is Cupid, a young male Macacus rhesus, who began self-mutilation following separation from Psyche, a female monkey, for whom he had formed a type of monogamous attachment. He went into a rage and ripped his body open in 20 different spots. Following a loss due not to death but only to separation, an animal strongly attached to a mate or companion can enter a state of apathy comparable to depression and mourning in man. This tends to uphold the theory that animal death appears as a type of object loss. There is the case of Cleo, a female orangutan at the Berlin Zoo, who after her first mate died became ill. Pregnant by her mate, she gave birth but treated the baby badly. After 1½ years of isolation, another male, Adam, was introduced. At first Cleo was afraid to approach Adam, yet it seemed as if she longed for him. This closely approximates human behavior in a similar situation (Fox, 1968).

As to behavior in birds, there is evidence of a Canada goose who died about two weeks following the death of its mate, having eaten no food thereafter. Death through a pining-type of grief can occur, as geese are known to be monogamous. Lorenz, an expert on greylag geese, has described the behavior: after its partner's disappearance, the goose attempts to find the partner. It moves restlessly day and night, flying great distances and looking all over, uttering its trisyllabic long-distance call. The search is continued over a wide range; and often the searching goose gets lost itself. From the moment the goose realizes its mate is gone, it loses all courage and flees from even the youngest and weakest geese, going to the bottom of the gaggle's ranking order. According to Lorenz, a grief-stricken expression can be seen in the goose's eyes. In the case of parrots and macaws, apathy states can last weeks and even months after the death of a mate.

A strange example involving foxes is thought valid, having been recorded in the *Journal of Mammalogy* (1947). A man driving between Flemington and Somerville, New Jersey, saw a fox standing by the roadside. It did not run away from the lights or the car. The driver stopped and found another fox lying dead beside the road; the live fox stood over it. The dead animal was wet all over. Since there were not wet spots nearby and no rain and the live fox was dry, it is assumed that the live fox had licked the dead one until it was wet. The motorist, Mr. William P. Comstock, took the dead fox by the tail to drag it down the embankment out of the way, but the live fox grabbed the dead fox's head in its mouth and a mild tug-of-war ensued. Finally, the dead fox was dragged out of the way, with the live fox following. Mr. Comstock then scratched the live fox behind the ear, to which the fox responded by a slight tail wag. Then Comstock left, not remaining to see what the fox did next.

Another episode, reported in the *Irish Times* newspaper, occurred when a man was driving along a road in Ireland. He saw something across the road and when he got closer he saw it was a procession of weasels. In front were four carrying the body of a dead weasel, and behind them were nearly 100 others, two by two. The man followed them as they crossed the road, climbed a fence, and entered a field, but he desisted when some of them began to hiss at him.

An authority on small mammals related the following tale. He saw by the side of the road two half-grown stoats (relative of the weasel) with the body of a third. One picked up the dead body at the nape of the neck and carried it a short distance. Then the other stoat took over. There are also well-documented accounts of badger funerals and burials, and of bears burying their dead. In addition, rats and grey squirrels have been seen carrying bodies of dead members of their own species, and elephants will drag a dead comrade through the jungle all night long (Burton, 1957). Baboons and other primates will sometimes carry a dead infant with them for days, until it is rotten beyond recognition. A mother moose will stand guard by her dead calf for periods ranging from a few hours to days.

A variety of explanations have been proposed for such behaviors. Whether these actions are genetically based or due to some environmental factor has not yet been determined. The next example illustrates this ambiguity. In September 1932, Major General Corrie Hudson saw a procession of about 30-40 langur monkeys. The first langurs were carrying a large dead one. The rest followed in a long thin line. After going down a hill and through a valley, they finally disappeared under a hanging cliff. There was a town cemetery nearby, and funeral processions were frequently seen on the road. Dwelling nearby, the langurs must have observed the funerals constantly. Major General Hudson said in a letter to Maurice Burton, "I do not think the langurs were imitating our funerals. I thought—and still think—they acted naturally to get rid of their dead (possibly) by concealment or burial, and the apparent mourners seem to me to be very like those people who join in to see something that's happening. I mentioned (in a previous letter) the fact of human funerals which the monkeys must constantly see just because it was a fact. Such human funerals are necessarily walking ones due [sic] to the narrow precipitous roads. The coffin is borne on a wheeled stretcher, the sympathizers more often precede the coffin in rickshaws or on horseback and await the coffin in the cemetery. I was not surprised because, as you say, one observes so many things that animals and birds do that appear completely human that surprise goes" (Burton, 1957).

There is a report of two dolphins swimming underneath a young dead dolphin; preventing it from sinking by supporting it on their backs, trying to keep it from being devoured by some predator fish. Grief and mourning behavior can apply to experimental research animals. Before beginning most experiments, time must be allowed for the animals to adjust to new surroundings. They may face losses of former cage-mates or companions in the wild, previous handlers, and so on. Any death- or separation-related behavior not accounted for could affect results of the experiment.

Grief and Mourning in Pet Animals

Accounts of pet animals and their mourning behavior are often documented. As with any anecdote, however, these stories can be exaggerated upon repeated tellings. Also, animal lovers typically overestimate their animals' powers and behavior, which often lessens the credibility of a story.

The Duchessa Vittoria di Sermoneta wrote of three of her women friends seeing a strange sight on the Piazza del Popolo in Rome. Alongside the road they saw a cat dragging a dead cat by the head. At least six more cats followed. All the cats hurriedly helped pull the dead cat off the street onto the pavement, as if afraid that a car would come by. Then again, taking turns, one pulled the carcass by the head with the others following. Although this continued, the observers grew tired of watching and left the scene so it is not known what the cats ultimately did with the body (Burton, 1957).

A family dog suddenly refused to eat and was no longer playful. The dog would wait by the front door, search the room, and was generally listless. These behaviors lasted for two weeks, and had begun 24 hours after the death of a tomcat which had grown up with the dog. The two had slept together in the same bed. The dog would defend the cat if it were chased by other dogs. A three-week change of locale with the owner, along with tranquilizer treatment, effected a complete recovery. This five-week period seems to be characteristic and typical of the acute mourning period in humans. Is it possibly the same in close animal relationships?

Other reports exist that lean more toward the psychic component of relationship between animals. One story involved two companion dogs. One was taken to the vet for euthanasia. The second remained at home but became hysterical and uncontrollable. A second example tells of a German shepherd and a Siamese cat who were companion pets. The German shepherd underwent surgery for a stomach torsion. The surgery was unsuccessful, and the dog died at 10:00 that day (the time was noted). What was later discovered was that the Siamese cat, who remained at home, became hysterical at exactly 10:00 (Fox, 1980). Do we call this a coincidence, or is there something deeper that we do not yet understand? The first story could be explained by the fact that the family would most likely be emotionally upset by having to euthanatize a loved pet. Animals, especially dogs, pick up cues from humans; thus, the dog remaining at home could have realized that something was going on and when his companion dog was taken away, and then gone into a frenzy as human emotions mounted to a peak. It is generally accepted that hysteria can be a reaction to grief and bereavement in humans, so is it not possible that this might be the case for animals?

There is also evidence against dogs' recognition and mourning of death of their companion dogs. The behaviorial account of eight Airedales being shot by their owner in the course of a domestic problem is repeated here. The dogs were gathered around a dish of food as the owner shot them in the head one by one. As they were shot, the others showed no fright, just kept on eating. None of them showed any curiosity or interest concerning their companions (Smythe, 1961). This story tends to uphold the theory that death to the animal is not death as we know it, but an object loss.

PETS AND SEPARATION

We have seen how some animals react to the death of a companion animal. As can be expected, animals may also react with grief and mourning behavior to the death of a human companion. To show just how much emotion a death could cause, consider how animals are affected by merely a temporary separation from a master or other human companion. The most common time for this to be seen is when owners go on vacation and leave their pets behind at the veterinarian's or a kennel. These pets often withdraw to a far corner of the cage or the run. They refuse to eat, causing onset of anorexia nervosa, which can persist until intravenous therapy is necessary. The animal is underactive, yet tense and constantly alert. Many symptoms, classified as both psychosomatic and somatopsychic, have been observed, including fever,

vomiting, diarrhea or absence of defecation, intestinal disorders including hemorrhagic enteritis, acute depression, reduced pain threshold,
hyperesthesia to handling (touch shyness), hyperpnea (abnormal breathing), and cardiac irregularities. Also pruritus and hive-like reactions
have been seen, as well as excessive eating, sympathy lameness, asthma-
like conditions, and convulsions.

Another type of loss-related behavior is called psi-trailing. There are
many accounts of this, with pets traveling great distances to eventual
reunion with their family. One illustration describes a family who
moved 500 miles away from their home, leaving their dog with neighbors, and their surprise when several months later the dog appeared on
their doorstep. No one knows how the dog could have known where to
go, never having been to the new home.

Mac, an Airedale, had been left at home while his master was away
and became despondent and depressed. With the caretaker's permission, some soldiers borrowed Mac, taking him to their camp to try and
cheer him up. By the route the dog travelled, the distance was over 55
miles but Mac made his way home within 48 hours of leaving the camp.
Dinah, a Red Setter bitch, was moved 25 miles by train when she was
pregnant. After arriving in the new place, she whelped and then disappeared with her five new puppies. Ten days later she arrived at home
with her five pups alive and healthy. Dinah's feet were raw and bleeding,
and she was extremely thin. In addition to the great number of miles
on foot, she had swum the River Blackwater, over 80 yards wide in the
narrowest part. The distance traveled was increased many times
because she must have had to leave four puppies in one spot and carry
one ahead, then go back and get another, over and over again.

This behavior has been scientifically tested to some extent. When
dogs have been moved from their home, often in a closed vehicle by a
circuitous route, then let loose, they can find their way home. At first,
they wander around vaguely for about ½ hour, then they distinguish (as
if through sudden inspiration) which direction is home and off they go
(Smythe, 1961).

HISTORY OF HUMAN ATTACHMENT TO PETS

There are many historical accounts of human attachment to and
mourning for pets. Records show that the Greeks had pets as early as
400 B.C. The ancient Hebrews had small house dogs; the ancient
Egyptians kept cats to guard their grain supplies from rats and mice.
Because of their great value, cats became sacred as well as part of the

household. The cat goddess Bastet was worshipped and had a holiday in her honor every year. Domesticated cats were revered as personifications of Bastet, dressed in jewels, and allowed to eat from the same dishes as their owners. Anyone who killed a cat or caused its death was put to death. Members of a household shaved their eyebrows and went into mourning upon the death of their cat. The master of the house put the body on a linen sheet, took it to a sacred house for embalming and anointing, and then a funeral was held. Cats were buried, some wrapped as mummies, in special vaults in cat cemeteries outside each city. The bereaved family would bury food with the dead cat and continue to make fish and milk offerings for many years (Rice 1968).

Dogs were also revered by the Egyptians, some say even more than cats were. They were buried in sacred dog cemeteries. When a cat died, members of a household shaved their eyebrows, but when a dog died, household members would shave their entire body, including their head.

In Hitler's Germany members of the Hitler Youth were each required to raise a pet dog from a puppy, and when it was grown and the children were emotionally attached to their pet, they had to kill their dog with their own hands. Yet Adolf Hitler, who had millions of humans murdered, was so attached to his dog Blondie that he risked his life for her. Many times during the last weeks of the war, he sacrificed his safety to let the dog run around outside for at least 15 minutes every day.

More recently, President Lyndon B. Johnson's public-relations staff attempted to increase his popularity with the American public. When LBJ's pet beagles, Him and Her, died, the public-relations office tried to give the impression of LBJ as a most bereaved pet owner. They succeeded in getting the press to shed tears. As a result of the publicity, a white collie, Blanco, was sent to LBJ by a young girl. Blanco thus became the new First Dog (Szasz, 1968).

PETS MOURNING HUMAN DEATH

Mourning behavior in animals following the death of a human companion is even more commonly observed. A German shepherd bitch owned by a couple from Boulogne was very affectionate with her master, Mr. B. After Mr. B's death, the shepherd underwent a period of anorexia and suffered epileptic seizures. She appeared to seek her master and was especially attentive to men's voices, as if listening for her master to speak.

Similar reactions have been seen in cats, despite the common belief that cats remain emotionally detached from their owners. After the death of their owner, shorthair cats have been observed to crawl into hiding places, refuse to eat for days, and show no interest in their surroundings; when handled, they showed either aggressiveness, stuporous apathy or escape attempts. They exhibited listlessness, dilated pupils, reduced body cleanliness and loss of social status among other cats.

There is evidence of pets dying of grief following the death of their master. The pattern is that of reactive depression and separation anxiety leading to stress, cachexia, and death. Such a psychophysiological response is in opposition to the drive for survival and self-preservation, and researchers do not really understand why animals are affected in this fashion. It is almost irresistible to conclude that the reason for a dog's refusal to eat following the death of a human companion is that the dog misses and is mourning for the departed loved one. A thoroughgoing behaviorist, however, unwilling to grant qualities of "mind" to the dog, might point out that the dog has been conditioned to eat in the presence of certain environmental signals, such as in his undisturbed home, or in the presence of the owner or a certain family member. When these signals are removed, the conditioned eating behavior will stop.

The most dramatic stories of animal loyalty to a human companion are told of dogs. An excerpt from a speech by Senator Vest to a jury in a trial for dog killing sums it up:

> . . . .And when the last scene of all comes, and death takes his master in its embrace and his body is laid away in the cold ground, no matter if all other friends pursue their way, there by his graveside will the noble dog be found, his head between his paws and his eyes sad, but open in alert watchfulness, faithful and true even to death (Szasz, 1968).

The most well-known tale is of Bobby, the famous dog who mourned his master for 14 years. The tombstone of Bobby read as follows:

> A tribute to the affectionate fidelity of Greyfriars Bobby. In 1858 this faithful dog followed the remains of his master to Greyfriars churchyard and lingered near the spot until his death in 1872 (Anderson, 1975).

William E. Campbell, dog trainer, states "I have seen fewer than two dozen cases of genuine psychic depression in dogs, i.e., cases that have not involved some environmental loss, such as death of an owner or another animal" (1979). This supports the position that dogs are relatively stable creatures but that when an extreme situation occurs, they can become very upset emotionally.

HUMANS MOURNING PET DEATH

Most people know someone who "went to pieces" over the death of a loved one. It often happens that this loved one is a pet. Pets can become members of the family, and many pet–owner attachments are very deep. They can approximate a parent–child or adult–child relationship. Deep understanding and love attachments can develop between a pet and owner. Indeed, such relationships can become so close as to cause problems, ranging from overdependence and simple behaviorial quirks to sexual complications. People living alone with a pet for years are often inconsolable upon their pet's death and can lapse into depression. In a study conducted by A. J. MacDonald, results show that 23 out of 31 parents reported that they had considered the possibility of significant emotional distress occurring either in themselves or their child if their dog were killed or otherwise permanently lost. It suggests that a certain amount of distress is anticipated by the public at the loss of a pet dog, and that mourning for dogs may be more widespread in the community than has been thought (MacDonald, 1978).

The loss of a pet can be very traumatic to a child, depending upon what role the pet played in the child's life—companion, friend, servant, admirer, confidante, toy, teammate, scapegoat, mirror, trustee, defender or master. This trauma can result in insecurity, anxiety, fear, distrust of the world, and even physical discomfort. For the child, a pet's death can raise questions of his parents dying and leaving him alone, uncared for, and unloved. If a family accepts the pet's death and mourns together for the loss, it will lessen the child's grief, anger, helplessness, hostility, and fear. The pet may be replaced and the child redirects his affection toward the new pet.

Not only children suffer trauma from the loss of a pet. Adult owners of pets that have died commonly undergo a period of mourning, and many cases have been reported of prolonged and pathological grief requiring professional counseling and treatment. The following three cases illustrate the psychiatric problems that may follow the death of a loved pet after many years of care (Keddie, 1977).

A 56-year-old married woman became distressed after the death of one of her 14-year-old Yorkshire terriers. Having an unsatisfactory marriage, she derived much support from her dogs. The terrier appeared to have died following an operation, but when it was brought back to the patient's house for burial; it surprisingly revived for several hours. Immediately after the dog's death the woman became depressed and tense. She had difficulty sleeping because of disturbing nightmares and attacks of sudden breathlessness. All tests proved normal except for a tendency to hyperventilation and the presence of sinus tachycardia. After threatening suicide, the patient was admitted to the short-stay unit of a psychiatric hospital. She was depressed and agitated upon admission. After two weeks of group therapy she was discharged. Her relationships with her husband and her dogs were resumed. One year later, no relapse was reported.

Another case involves a 55-year-old woman who had had symptoms for 18 months. The problems began following the sudden death of her 14-year-old poodle. She admitted to being dependent on the dog, whom she treated like a child. After the dog's death, she hadn't been able to bring herself to move its basket or bone. She also spent most of her waking moments thinking about the poodle. She was listless and had insomnia, as well as anorexia and its resultant weight loss. No physical dysfunctions were seen, but psychologically she was depressed and preoccupied with thoughts of her dog. She underwent outpatient psychotherapy and was discharged after four months. She was fully recovered then and planning to buy a new dog. Two years later, she was still well.

A 16-year-old girl became very upset after the death of her King Charles spaniel, whom she had cared for over a period of 13 years. She became depressed and weepy and within 24 hours developed an erythematous rash of the hands. Her doctor prescribed antihistamines, but she had to make 3 or 4 attempts to swallow each pill. Her difficulty in swallowing became more pronounced and 48 hours after the dog's death, she could not swallow either solids or fluids, though she had no discomfort or feeling of constriction in her throat. She was admitted to the short-stay unit of a psychiatric hospital. Superficially she was cheerful, though preoccupied with gloomy thoughts of her dog. She was restless and tended to play with her fingers. The patient was encouraged to talk about the distress she felt on losing her pet. She made rapid progress and left the hospital in one week. One month later, she was fine and planning on purchasing a new puppy. Her case was determined to be an acute hysterical conversion symptom in the form of hydrophobia.

Following the death of a beloved pet, one can sometimes observe phobic avoidance of persons, animals, places or things related to the deceased. Persons reacting in this fashion will usually not replace their lost pet with another one.

It is fairly well known that pets can be used for child therapy. Boris Levinson has written several authoritative books and articles on the subject. In his book *Pet-Oriented Child Psychotherapy* (1969), Levinson describes how pets have been used therapeutically by families both with and without conscious knowledge of it. In one schizophrenic family, a pattern was observed. When tensions and fears would rise, and sexual and aggressive drives become stronger, one family member would usually become ill. With a pet in the family, the pet became ill along with or instead of one of the family members. With such families, in some crises the pet may even die. The family then grieves over the pet's death and the mourning process serves to drive off intense destructive forces.

Data on bereavement reveal that a majority of grief-stricken people are women over 40. This information raises questions as to whether a middle-aged woman would be more susceptible to loss and thus more inclined to grieve, or whether it is due to some other factor. Studies could then be designed to determine whether the housewife is more often affected due to more frequent contact and thus presumably greater affection for the pet.

While most people are visibly upset by the death of a pet, one can only imagine, until put in the position, what it is like to decide whether to euthanatize one's own loved pet. One woman sums it up well, saying "Doctor, this is the hardest thing I've had to do in my whole life. Would you believe that even when I buried my husband, I didn't feel so bad?" (Antelyes, 1976). One other striking example occurred in England, where the people are known for their tradition of caring for animals. During an epidemic of hoof-and-mouth disease, many head and even complete herds of cattle had to be slaughtered. The total desolation of these farmers was due not only to the financial loss but also to the personal loss of the animals.

FUNERAL AND BURIAL FOR PETS

Pet owners need some way to deal with their emotions following a pet's death. In humans, the funeral service serves as an outlet for emotional energy. For animal owners, this possibility is increasingly being taken advantage of. A conspicuous example is that of Mr. G. L. Booth, a Madison, Georgia grocery store and service station manager who held a funeral for Sheila, his terrier. The service included scripture reading over the embalmed body, five dozen red rosebuds, four pallbearers, and a procession of several cars. The total cost was about $1000, but to those who would cry extravagance, Mr. Booth has asked,

"Who else in the world has found a million dollars worth of happiness for $1000?"

Most major cities now have a pet cemetery, though few lay claim to an animal funeral home. The first such establishment in the country is in Farmingdale, New York, and offers "complete arrangements for pets." Arrangements range from a $15.00 "minimal service" which includes pickup of the body, cleaning, disinfecting and grooming to prepare the body for viewing, and incineration after the viewing. "Preferred Service" can run into hundreds of dollars and includes casket selection, burial accessories and burial or cremation arrangements as well as the minimal service. William Hanson, director and manager, says the service has been extended to dogs, cats, birds, turtles, fish and rabbits. Caskets can cost from $18 to $210, depending on structural material and size.

Many of these pets are interred at the Bide-A-Wee Memorial Park in Wantagh, New York. It is a nine-acre cemetery with plots ranging in price from $40 to $150, depending on size and location. Animals buried here include dogs, cats, birds, monkeys, horses, goats, turtles, and a rat. The Hinsdale Pet Cemetery, near Chicago, has no space shortage, but some animal cemeteries are running out of room. This problem is lessened in one cemetery by a special section that has a 20-year turnover rate; after 20 years pass, the graves are dug up and the ground reused for burial.

Most cemeteries offer a choice of annual maintenance care, special care (seasonal flowers and Christmas decorations), perpetual maintenance (plastic flowers) or perpetual special care. Many people will visit and care for the gravesites themselves. Reportedly, one man waters the flowers on his dog's grave every week. Many visitors come on Memorial Day and have a picnic with other mourners. At the cemetery, when a pet is being interred, there is often much crying, occasional fainting, and other demonstrations of grief. S. Alfred Nash, former undertaker and supervisor of Aspin Hill, a pet cemetery outside Washington, D.C. stated, "I've seen more real sobbing here than in 40 years as a funeral director for humans. Don't forget—the law says you have to bury humans, but you bury a dog because you want to" (Rice, 1968). Sometimes people want to bury a dead pet with a deceased human. For example, a young girl was killed in an accident. Before her funeral took place, her pet rabbit died. The family wished to bury the rabbit with the girl in her casket.

Headstones carry a variety of inscriptions, some short and simple, others more complex. "Good Girl, Spotty...My Best Friend, Lady....Never Forgotten, Our Faithful Baby, Whitey....Ruby—The greatest. . . ." "Wait for us, darling, we too will be there, No matter how weary or late. Wave your paws and rend the air, to welcome us home at the gate" (Rice, 1968). "At the going down of the sun each day, dear one, we remember you." And as expressive as any other is "For the loved one." As well as epitaphs on tombstones, some people put announcements of their pet's death in the newspapers and animal magazines as a type of obitrary. One found in *Dog World* reads, "In loving memory of Lainesand's Red Cloud, 15 July 1963–16 January 1966, after Caesarian operation. God wanted one more angel to grace his heavenly throne, and so he took our Mandy, and bid us not to mourn. We wanted so to keep her, for she was to us given, but Jesus said it could not be, he wanted her in heaven. From your broken-hearted mum and all at Lainesand's Boxers" (Szasz, 1968).

Also developed recently are pension schemes or insurance plans for pets. The way one pension plan works is that after the owner's death, the pet can stay in a fully outfitted and supplied kennel in Westhampton, New York. At the time of writing, the cost was $300.00 per year. The Pet Insurance Agency of Philadelphia protects against sickness and death. An owner can collect $100 for the death of a pet and up to $500 on special policies.

Many wealthy pet owners leave the bulk of their estate to ther pet(s) when they die. In 1961, Mrs. Edna Avery Jones, of Atlanta, Georgia died and left $300,000 of her $420,000 estate as a trust fund to finance the care of her three dogs. The 80-year-old widow stated in her will that only when the dogs were dead, should the money go to her relatives.

CONCLUSION

Much of what is known about animal and human death and how they affect each other is inconclusive and hypothetical, and the entire topic is surrounded by controversy. There is little question, however, that people should be better informed so that when a death occurs, they will be better able to cope with the situation and to help others cope. Further research on communicating with animals may enable us to learn much that is valuable, not only about our pets but about ourselves.

It is fairly well known that pets can be used for child therapy. Boris Levinson has written several authoritative books and articles on the subject. In his book *Pet-Oriented Child Psychotherapy* (1969), Levinson describes how pets have been used therapeutically by families both with and without conscious knowledge of it. In one schizophrenic family, a pattern was observed. When tensions and fears would rise, and sexual and aggressive drives become stronger, one family member would usually become ill. With a pet in the family, the pet became ill along with or instead of one of the family members. With such families, in some crises the pet may even die. The family then grieves over the pet's death and the mourning process serves to drive off intense destructive forces.

Data on bereavement reveal that a majority of grief-stricken people are women over 40. This information raises questions as to whether a middle-aged woman would be more susceptible to loss and thus more inclined to grieve, or whether it is due to some other factor. Studies could then be designed to determine whether the housewife is more often affected due to more frequent contact and thus presumably greater affection for the pet.

While most people are visibly upset by the death of a pet, one can only imagine, until put in the position, what it is like to decide whether to euthanatize one's own loved pet. One woman sums it up well, saying "Doctor, this is the hardest thing I've had to do in my whole life. Would you believe that even when I buried my husband, I didn't feel so bad?" (Antelyes, 1976). One other striking example occurred in England, where the people are known for their tradition of caring for animals. During an epidemic of hoof-and-mouth disease, many head and even complete herds of cattle had to be slaughtered. The total desolation of these farmers was due not only to the financial loss but also to the personal loss of the animals.

BIBLIOGRAPHY

Albright JL, VanHof J: Animal Behavior. West Lafayette, Indiana, Purdue Univ Press, 1975

Alverdes F: The Psychology of Animals. London, Kegan Paul, Trench, Trubner, 1932

Anderson RS (ed): Pet Animals and Society. London, Bailliere Tindall, 1975

Antelyes J: A grave matter. Modern Veterinary Practice 57:407-412, 1976

Burton M: Animal Legends. New York, Coward-McCann, 1957

Buytendijk FJJ: The Mind of the Dog. New York, Arno Press, 1973

Campbell WE: Environmental stress in depression, Modern Veterinary Practice 58:788-790, 1977

Caplan, G: An Approach to Community Mental Health. New York, Grune & Stratton, 1961

Darwin C: The Expression of the Emotions in Man and Animals. Chicago, Univ of Chicago Press, 1965

Dimsdale JE: Emotional causes of sudden death, Am J Psychiatry, 134:1361-1366, 1977

Fox MW (ed): Abnornal Behavior in Animals. Philadelphia, W. B. Saunders, 1968

Fox MW: Canine Behavior. Springfield IL, Charles C. Thomas, 1965

Fox MW: Concepts in Ethology. Minneapolis MN, Univ of Minnesota Press, 1974

Griffin DR: The Question of Animal Awareness. New York, Rockefeller Univ Press, 1976

Hediger H: Man and Animal in the Zoo. New York, Delacorte Press, 1969

Higgins GL: Grief reactions. Practitioner 218:689-695, 1977

Hughes CW, Lynch JJ: A reconsideration of psychological precursors of sudden death in infrahuman animals. American Psychologist 33:419-429, 1978

Johnson CE (ed): Contemporary Readings in Behavior. New York, McGraw-Hill, 1970

Keddie KMG: Pathological mourning after the death of a pet. Brit J Psychiatry 131:21-25, 1977

Klinghammer E: personal communication, 1980

Levinson BM: The pet and the child's bereavement. Mental Hygiene 51:197-200, 1967

Levinson BM: Pet-Oriented Child Psychotherapy, Springfield, IL, Charles C. Thomas, 1969

Lieberman S: Nineteen cases of morbid grief. Brit J Psychiatry, 132:159;163, 1978

Lorenz KZ: King Solomon's Ring. New York, Thomas Y. Crowell Co., 1952

Lorenz KZ: Man Meets Dog. Baltimore, MD, Penguin Books, 1953

MacDonald AJ: Mourning after pets (letter). Brit J Psychiatry 133:551, 1978

Parkes CM: Recent bereavement as a cause of mental illness. Brit J Psychiatry, 110:198-204, 1964

Popper KR: Objective Knowledge, an Evolutionary Approach. London, Oxford Univ Press, 1972

Rice B: The Other End of the Leash. Boston, Little, Brown & Company, 1968

Rogers DE: Dearest Debbie. Westwood, NJ, Fleming H. Revell Co., 1965

Rynearson EK: Humans and pets and attachment. Brit J Psychiatry 133:550-555, 1978

Siltanen P: Life changes and sudden coronary death. Advances in Cardiology 25:47-60, 1978

Smythe RH: The Mind of the Dog. Springfield, IL, Charles C. Thomas, 1961

Stumpfe KD: Psychogenic death in animals. Deutsche Tieraerztliche Wochenschrift 85:400-403, 1978

Szasz K: Petishism, Pets and Their People in the Western World. New York, Holt, Rinehart & Winston, 1968

Tortora DF: Help! This Animal is Driving Me Crazy. Chicago, Playboy Press, 1977

Young PT: Emotion in Man and Animal. Huntington, NY, Robert E. Krieger Publishing Company, 1973

18

Attitudes Toward Animals and Effect on Veterinary Practice Management

Marvin L. Samuelson

A significant difference in attitudes toward animals is manifested by two major groups of people. Those who comprise the first group tend to think of animals as creatures with feelings and certain ethical rights. This attitude has been called humanistic or moralistic. The second major group regards animals as something owned, as personal property with some practical value or usefulness. The attitude of the second group is often called utilitarian or doministic. The two groups are generally antagonistic toward each other, or at least fail to understand or appreciate the other. The groups do not have an equal interest in pet loss and human emotion. A veterinary practitioner can expect difficulty in trying to serve and please both groups. Veterinarians' attitudes toward animals vary widely and are apt to be manifested in different styles of practice management or preference for a certain species. The veterinarian with the most inclusive view is likely to see animals as contributors to life quality for humans. Whether their role is for companionship, food, or service makes little difference.

Veterinary practice in the United States is for the most part conducted by private enterprise, with veterinarians capitalizing their own hospital facilities. A relatively small portion of practice is done by institutions and groups, both profit and non-profit.

All practices, profit and non-profit alike, must consider the marketing concept and costs of providing services. Attitudes toward animals and their appropriate care may be a stumbling block for both consumer-client and veterinary practitioner. A critical concern centers on the "fantasy of certainty" and reluctance to apply cost constraints and peer review. The burdens of "altruism," "free services," and over-indulgence in "good deeds for the day" can destroy a veterinary practice. Emotion must be controlled if the business is to be sustained.

The veterinarian who approaches practice with the idea of being solely concerned with rendering a professional service may soon experience defeat of this high ideal. The attitude that any concern for monetary reward is not in true keeping with the professional spirit may be admirable, but it ignores the reality that financial success is a vital prerequisite to professional success. Failure to plan for financial requirements leads to dissipation of the quality of service rendered. The animal patients and their owners may be the real losers.

The image of a veterinary medical practice held by clients, the community, and personnel in the practice is built on perceived quality of service and the personality of individuals associated with the practice. The veterinarian's satisfaction, self-esteem, and attitude towards a practice are likely to parallel the quality of service and ability to sustain appropriate levels of care. Good animal-health care is of little value if it is not marketable to people.

The human concern for, or attitude toward, animals is most important to veterinary practice managers. Animals do not seek veterinary care; they are brought to veterinarians by people. Animals don't make appointments or pay bills; their owners and friends do. Veterinarians are in the people business. Veterinary practice consistently deals with human attitudes toward animals. The triangle of animal, owner or agent, and the veterinary practice is always present.

An optimal approach for most veterinary practices might be embodied in a so-called professional attitude, which allows the practice of a combined art and science in an appropriate business setting. The professional attitude intends to provide space that enhances performance of the individual and the organization, yet fosters intimate patient care. The most effective veterinary practitioner relates well to people. The veterinarian with average scientific skills who relates favorably with other people is much more apt to succeed than a more learned colleague who has difficulty with human relations. Understanding and feeling the human/animal bond further enhances the doctor's usefulness.

A typology of attitudes toward animals was done by Dr. Stephen R. Kellert, School of Forestry and Environmental Studies, Yale University. This study was published in "Policy Implications of a National Study of American Attitudes and Behavioral Relations to Animals," September 1978 (available from Superintendent of Documents, U. S. Government Printing Office, Washington, D.C.).

Dr. Kellert describes nine different attitudes toward animals. All nine types are listed here as they might be seen by veterinary practice personnel.

1. *Humanistic* This type is distinguished by strong personal affection for individual animals. As clients, they are often referred to as companion-animal owners. Many types and species of animals may be seen. Pets are often thought of as members of the family. These clients tend to be anthropomorphic regarding their animals, but may vary widely in degree of psychological dependence. Such feelings of attachment may last a lifetime or change very suddenly. They are not apt to be highly concerned with general animal-welfare issues, but with individual animals' welfare. They are usually seen as highly desirable clients in a companion-animal practice, and appreciate kind treatment of their animals.

Persons with humanistic attitudes toward animals are usually but not necessarily affectionate with other humans, including any or all persons in the practice. Others, however, may show antisocial behavior or experience great difficulty with human relations. For them, the animal may be a link to society and a surrogate for human companionship.

2. *Moralistic* Great concern for the welfare of animals is the defining feature of this group. This attitude is typically more philosophic and less attached to individual animals. It is based on ethical principles opposing any perceived exploitation or infliction of harm, suffering, or death on animals. There is a tendency to promote a sense of kinship between humans and animals, but this may apply just to certain species of animals at the expense of others. As clients, they may make unreasonable demands on staff members. Many are lonely people attracted by a crusade or cause. They are inclined to judge people by association with animal activities. Receptionists especially would do well to understand the attitude and decline to become willing adversaries.

3. *Utilitarian* The primary characteristic of this attitude is the perception of animals in terms of practical or economic usefulness. Animals may be seen as stock or chattel. Utilitarians tend to be indifferent to matters of animal welfare or concerns which do not affect the animal's performance or practical value.

This attitude should not be viewed as lacking in affection or appreciation for animals. Most farmers and animal production-oriented persons share this view. Older, more traditional terms associated with the utilitarian type include *stockman, herdsman, animal husbandry, shepherd,* and *caretaker.* Kindness may be seen as a necessary, common-sense behavior supporting production or the desired response. This attitude may be applied to specific species, excluding certain others. For example, many food-animal producers own small pets and horses and enjoy significant emotional benefits. Indeed, there is increasing interest and demand for companion-animal care in rural areas.

4. *Doministic* A sense of superiority and a desire to master animals characterize this attitude. Animals are usually viewed as objects to control or dominate. There may be an association with skill in competition or an expression of prowess. This should not be mistaken as hostility toward animals. The ability to control may contribute to effective service, especially if combined with professionalism.

Considerable knowledge of and attachment to animals may be associated with the doministic attitude. These persons may be very effective animal trainers or handlers and be attracted by animal behavior-control methodologies. This attitude is often exhibited by veterinarians.

The doministic attitude may be applied at great variance with species and type of animal, depending on values assigned, for example the high percentage of rodeo cowboys who own pet dogs or a horse with which they develop special emotional attachment. Others may be fond of cats and shoot at birds. Range fighting over cattle and sheep is part of the American tradition.

Persons with high dominance levels toward other people are apt to experience conflict with any dominant subject. Clients with this attitude can make an unprepared receptionist or veterinarian very uncomfortable. A strong, dominant receptionist may alienate some sensitive clients, but be very effective with others. The well-prepared receptionist equipped with a knowledge of client relations can usually manage clients in a desirable manner. Such an individual is a special person in any practice.

5. *Negativistic or Neutral* People with this attitude toward animals generally have a desire to avoid them. Typical feelings expressed include fear, dislike, indifference, and superstition. This attitude is apt to be highly anthropocentric and alienated from the natural world and its ecosystems. Animal products may be consumed as food or clothing with little or no appreciation for their origin. Persons operating with this attitude may become so people-centered that positive aspects of the human/animal bond are not appreciated or may even be put down in defense. Veterinarians who have appeared before municipal zoning-control boards have usually observed some manifestation of this attitude.

To some extent, the negativistic attitude toward animals may be fostered by certain religious doctrines. For example, some persons may be very uncomfortable when human values are applied to animals or sensitivity is shown for non-human life forms. Any ethical humane concept may be very disconcerting for this type. Other ideologies embrace a much more holistic and sensitive attitude toward all living things and ecosystems.

6. *Aesthetic* People who hold this point of view are apt to hold up animals as objects of beauty and artistic appeal while remaining emotionally detached from individual animals. Persons so oriented may be attracted to sporting activities involving animals, like horse races, animal exhibitions, or showmanship. They tend to remain apart from the animals and enjoy being spectators. They may enjoy acting as critics of a veterinary practice, not always in a constructive spirit.

7. *Naturalistic* These people are generally interested in all animals, especially wildlife and the outdoors. They are not often recognized in a veterinary practice as they represent a very small group. Animals owned by these persons may have less meaning for them than do other animals in the wild. They are often non-owners.

8. *Ecologistic* This type, like the naturalistic, are oriented toward wildlife and the environment but are usually more intellectual and detached. They are more highly concerned with balancing ecosystems than with individual animals, but they do own animals. Veterinary clients with this attitude may be skeptical and usually require more detailed explanations of veterinary problems and procedures.

9. *Scientistic* This type of individual tends to be objective, intellectual, matter-of-fact, while viewing animals as physical objects for study and scientific gain. Scientistic people are able to remain emotionally detached yet curious, and usually are attached to an organization. They are not apt to be clients of a private practice.

An understanding of typology of attitudes toward animals is very helpful to personnel in a veterinary practice. It may be of real benefit to anyone engaged in activities where animal concerns are involved, especially to persons studying companion-animal loss and human emotion.

19

The Meanings of Loss: Human and Pet Death in the Lives of the Elderly

Joel S. Savishinsky

Aging in Western cultures is commonly perceived as a series of losses: strength, health, independence, sensory acuity, and financial security may all decline. Social losses add another dimension to this experience. Age mates of the elderly may enter institutions or take up residence in age-segregated housing complexes. Eventually, the contemporaries of older people start to die. By this time in the elderly person's life, younger family members may have moved away or, at the very least, established separate lives and residences of their own.

Aging, however, is not the exclusive province of the aged. It is a long-term process that begins, some would argue, at the beginning of the life cycle itself. A more culturally rooted view holds that we spend one quarter of our life growing up and three quarters of life growing old. Aging, seen in either biological or social terms, is thus a continuum. What old age does is to intensify and concentrate the losses and declines which have often been in process for years and decades.

Institutionalization is the fate of approximately 5% of the American population over 65 years of age (US Department of Health and Human Services, Federal Council on the Aging 1981:42). It is both a product of people's physical and cognitive impairments and an experience that can sometimes aggravate the consequences of these losses. Mobility, social contacts, tactile encounters, and other forms of sensory stimulation may all be diminished as a prelude to or a result of institutional life. Many of the therapeutic and recreational programs designed for the residents of geriatric facilities seek to redress these deficits.

The losses that elderly people have experienced lend shape to their speech, their bodies, and the attitudes they bring to bear on the social activities offered to them in nursing homes. A central issue in studies of aging people within such institutions is the meaning that they find in the losses they have experienced and the effect of these on their current behavior and morale. One way to investigate the phenomenon is to examine how the elderly respond to situations that precipitate recall and discussion of loss. Among the institutionalized elderly, such recreational activities as reminiscing groups, poetry classes, and life-history courses offer occasions where both memory and meaning may be crystallized. Another type of program that has recently been introduced to many geriatric and nursing institutions is pet therapy. Whereas the primary goal of most pet programs is to provide social and sensory stimulation for the elderly, several investigations have revealed that companion-animal visits also provide opportunities for reminiscing, life review, and discussions of loss (e.g., Bustad 1980; Corson and Corson 1980; Levinson 1972). This chapter is based on an anthropological study of a pet-therapy program conducted in four nursing homes in upstate New York, and focuses on the meaning that elderly participants find in the human and animal deaths they have experienced.

BACKGROUND AND METHODS

The pet organization under consideration is the Cornell Companion Animals Program (CCAP). It provides weekly pet visits to six geriatric institutions, as well as programs at several Headstart, day-care, and other educational facilities in the Ithaca, New York, area. The organization was founded in 1982 and is sponsored by the Department of Preventive Medicine at the New York State College of Veterinary Medicine. While CCAP maintains a paid, part-time director, it relies primarily on a corps of approximately sixty volunteers drawn from Ithaca College, Cornell University, and the general Ithaca community to staff its programs. Using their own or borrowed animals, the volunteers who visit the nursing homes spend an hour to an hour-and-a-half each week meeting institutional residents either in the privacy of their rooms or in lounge and recreation areas at the facilities.

Since December 1982, an anthropological study of the organization and human impact of the program has been carried out in several of the nursing homes it serves. The research has been conducted primarily by means of participant-observation in the institutions during the course of pet visits. Data are also being collected on the general operation of the geriatric facilities and the nature of the other recreational and therapeutic programs offered. In addition, life-history interviews with selected residents are conducted to develop a more detailed view of their backgrounds, personal losses, previous ties to animals, and adaptations to institutional life. These additional materials allow us to measure the significance of the pet sessions against the broader context of people's histories and their current living situations. Thus, while most clinical studies of pet programs conducted to date have centered on outcome and the measurement of individual changes resulting from such efforts, the value of this type of anthropological study is concentration on content, context and process.

FINDINGS

Companion-animal visits elicit a range of different responses from people. At each of the homes only some residents choose to relate to the pets and volunteers, but those who do frequently develop an expectation or desire for ongoing contacts with the same individuals and animals. In the course of visits, conversations, and the evolving relationships between regular volunteers and residents, the latter bring up a vast spectrum of topics and concerns. In many cases, the pets who have served to bring people together recede into the background after several sessions, and residents relate primarily to the staff members and visitors who accompany the animals. The issues that residents raise range from such mundane matters as the weather, recent holidays, and food, to more personal and philosophical ones such as family relations, medical problems, religious beliefs, and politics. Therefore, while we found that elderly participants often choose to talk during the sessions about the bonds and losses they have experienced with humans and animals, it should be noted that these are only two of the many topics they raise.

A number of significant patterns have emerged in the way residents talk and relate to volunteers, animals, and staff during pet sessions. Four of these patterns directly pertain to themes of loss, attachment, domestic life, and personal history, and their salient features may be summarized as follows.

1) Pet visits evoke memories from childhood and other life stages that contribute to the integrative process of reminiscing for the elderly. Anecdotes centering on animals frequently identify key features of people's natal families, the nature of their marriages, and of their ties to their own children. Since many nursing-home residents grew up and lived in rural areas, their histories are punctuated with stories of how

pets and working farm animals have figured in their lives. Familiarity with animal death as an aspect of farm life, however, does not diminish the poignancy of the particular ties and personal losses that they often recall. Since such reminiscing has been shown to be an important means for older people to construct a meaningful account of their lives, companion-animal sessions aid in the fulfillment of this task.

2) Animal visits help to counteract the decline of domesticity inherent in institutional life. Pets are symbolic and literal embodiments of the more complete domestic experiences that residents once enjoyed, and the staff members and companion-animal volunteers who accompany them during visits contribute to a family definition of the pet sessions. Just as many residents regard their former pets as having been "members of the family," some of them lay claim to volunteers and their animals as elements of a "new family." Volunteers reciprocate this definition of the situation, stressing that they want to be seen by patients "more like friends and family" than as institutional staff.

3) Residents often seek out and emphasize the physcial resemblances between visiting animals and the pets they once owned. Visiting pets are thereby associated with animals that patients have had to give up, as well as with the family members currently caring for them. Sessions thus provide opportunities for people to praise, criticize, and explore other domestic ties. Judgments and characterizations of relatives are often couched in terms of how these people have treated the residents' pets as well as the residents themselves.

4) People draw connections between human loss and pet loss, and it is through these connections that they commonly confront issues of mortality and morality. In regard to the latter point, residents take pride in, and sometimes credit for, the longevity of animals they have owned. Such lifespans are a positive element in the imagery and self-imagery of frail individuals who are contending with the imminence of their own death. In recalling pets from the past, at the very beginning of conversations, patients frequently discuss the circumstances of their animals' deaths. Details characterizing relationships usually follow. It is a common conversational sequence, then, for death to precede life in people's narratives. People often discuss such deaths, and the subsequent burials, in considerable detail. One person who described her backyard as a "pet cemetery," painted a picture in the air with her hands, telling how and where each animal had been laid to rest, and listing their names and the years of their deaths. Some residents diagnosed for diminished short-term memories proved quite capable of precise, graphic, and highly emotive renderings of animal losses that occurred several decades before.

People also project onto their pets, and onto the animals' deaths, some of the qualities of human kinship. Animals who are thought to have died of loneliness and grief, and littermates who died in relatively rapid succession, are believed to mirror the way in which people respond to the loss of family members. Discussion of such experiences with pets enables certain individuals to share their own grief or their fears of human loss. A married couple in one home spoke of how a pair of long-lived sibling cats that they once owned had died within a week of one another; later, in the same conversation, this man and woman observed how neither of them could contemplate living without the other.

One of the ways in which these confrontations with mortality are accomplished is that people move back and forth between human and animal deaths as they talk, or they alternate the recall of loss with the reassurance and momentary distraction of petting the animal at their feet or in their lap. The counterpoint of different memories or of talk and touch eases the sharing of painful episodes. For still other residents, humor softens the impact of loss. A woman whose two goldfish had died several months ago said: "I had a thought about what might have killed the ones that I lost last spring. You know I used to talk to them all the time. Not that they answered, but I liked to speak to them all the same. Well, I think I talked them to death."

Some people emphasize the finality of certain types of attachment and loss. They describe a relationship with a particular animal with which they were extremely close, and after whose death they were unable to take on another pet. As one resident said, "It's bad to get so attached to animals because those things happen to them and it's too hard to bear." At one of the homes, an elderly man who was very open to receiving human visitors asked that they not bring their pets into his room because they reminded him too much of the dogs and cats he used to have. In contrast to these experiences, other residents recalled that even after they had decided not to replace an "irreplaceable" pet, they eventually did so and were able to create a srong emotional bond with the new animal. In some cases, people compared this to their second marriage or to the slow, almost reluctant creation of friendships within the nursing home itself.

Deceased pets are also remembered and spoken of as sources of moral value. They are praised for giving and eliciting love, for demonstrating loyalty and trust, for teaching people how to care and be kind, and for offering opportunities to engage in life in a positive way. Human–animal companionship is portrayed at such times as a paradigm for caring, dedicted, and life–sustaining relationships among people. Some residents make a point of contrasting the moral meanings of pets with the values that characterize certain humans. Such individuals, in fact, measure or describe the moral stature of people they have known in terms of how these men or women treated animals. Some of the strongest castigations we heard were directed at people whom residents had known to abuse or neglect pets. Some of the warmest praise went to individuals who had shown exceptional concern or compassion for lost or injured animals. Residents praise family members who are caring for pets they had to give up on entering an institution, though some patients note, ironically, that certain relatives pay more attention to their pets than they do to their ailing kin. "They kept the dog and got rid of me," complained one woman. In the views and in the words of many residents, then, both the behavior of animals and the ways humans relate to them in life and in death are expressions of deeper moral meaning.

DISCUSSION AND SUMMARY

Various therapeutic programs now exist to help institutionalized elderly people cope with the social, physical, and emotional losses they have experienced. Companion-animal visits sponsored by community volunteers offer residents opportunities for conversation, sensory stimulation, tactile warmth, and ongoing relationships with others. The effectiveness of these visits derives, in part, from the symbolic meanings and the fears, hopes, values, and identities that people project onto pet animals in our own and other cultures (Savishinsky 1983).

An anthropological study of one such program in several nursing facilities in upstate New York (Savishinsky 1983-84) revealed that during the social interactions provided by pet sessions, some residents engage in a significant amount of reminiscing. The content of their conversations often turns from the pets that are present to memories of those they owned in the past. Such reminiscences are a vital part of people's reconstruction of their personal histories.

The elderly people in our study, as is true of most other pet owners, have had to deal at certain times in their lives with the death or loss of their animals. The grief and sadness that they recall reflect the fact that pet loss evokes some of the same responses in people as does the loss of human loved ones. This phenomenon has been noted by several researchers working with male and female, young and old individuals who have had to deal with such deaths (Cohen 1983; Fogle 1981; Keddie 1977; Nieburg and Fischer 1982; Quackenbush and Glickman 1983; Rynearson 1978; Stewart 1983; Van Leeuwen 1981). The fact that elderly people are often particularly attached to their animals because they have been deprived of many other meaningful relationships suggests that those dealing with old people need to be especially aware of their particular needs and responses to pet loss (Quackenbush 1984).

Of the many people who reacted to pet death and loss in our study, relatively few mentioned having to deal directly with a decision on euthanasia: an animal's death from accident, illness, or old age and an animal's loss through theft, a change of residence, or unexplained disappearances were more commonly cited. In one of the few critical comments about euthanasia, an elderly woman expressed her distrust of this process because she had never been sure that a veterinarian with whom she had left her dog had actually put the animal to sleep. "How do you know what they do with them once you hand them over?" she asked. Other people have had some positive experience with euthanasia at second hand: they recalled the relief they felt when a parent or one of their grown children took the responsibility for taking an ailing pet to the veterinarian to be "put down."

Our research has not brought us into contact with many situations of acute grief. Rather, we have been dealing either with people recalling pet loss that occurred in the past or with individuals commenting on their separation from pets who are still alive. These situations indicate both the long-term impact of deaths experienced earlier in life and the need for elderly people to deal with the ongoing significance of pets from whom they have been separated and through whom they remain connected to other family members. In such cases, acute grief is rarely the crucial issue. Instead, grieving has given way to reminiscing, and memory has yielded up new meanings.

Our study indicates that for some people, pets who are remembered in these ways are also a touchstone for reflection on the virtues and failings of humans and animals. The relations between people and pets are also seen as encapsulating lessons about mortality and moral value. Losses that occurred months, years, or decades ago continue to shape people's views of life, themselves, and others. In this process of recall and interpretation facilitated by visiting animals, residents are enabled to explore the existential experiences that Kierkegaard observed: the fact that "life is lived forward but understood backward" (cited in Geertz 1971:60). It is this moral and historical dimension provided by animals, not just their companionship, that enhances their stature as "significant others" in the lives of the elderly.

NOTES

The research centered on four geriatric institutions in Tompkins County, New York: Ithacare, Lakeside Nursing Home, Oak Hill Manor, and the Reconstruction Home. Lakeside has a maximum resident population of 260 individuals; the other three facilities can accommodate between 70 and 73 people. One hundred of the beds at Lakeside constitute a health-related facility and the other 160 are a skilled-nursing facility. Ithacare provides a domiciliary or supervised living situation for its residents, while Oak Hill and the Reconstruction Home are devoted entirely to skilled nursing care.

A number of undergraduate anthropology students at Ithaca College participated as researchers in the study: Nordica Holochuck, Susan Holochuck, Mari Kobayakawa, Rich Lathan, Andrea Nevins, Lisa Sahasrabudhe, and Tu Vu. Preliminary findings from the study are reported in Savishinsky, Lathan, Kobayakawa, and Nevins (1983), and Savishinsky (1983-84, 1984a, 1984b, 1985). A twenty-minute video documentary on the pet program, entitled "In Good Company," was made by Tu Vu and Joel Savishinsky in 1984.

I thank my students, the members of CCAP, and the residents and staff of the nursing homes, for their help and cooperation in the research. Members of the Ithaca College Faculty Seminar on Epistemology and Teaching made valuable suggestions on an early draft of this chapter.

REFERENCES

Bustad L: Animals, Aging, and the Aged. Minneapolis MN, Univ of Minnesota Press, 1980

Cohen S: Words of comfort. People-Animals-Environment 1(1):16-17, 1983

Corson S, Corson E: Pet animals and nonverbal communication mediators in psychotherapy in institutional settings. In Corson S, Corson E (eds): Ethology and Nonverbal Communication in Mental Health, pp 83-110. New York, Pergamon Press, 1980

Fogle B: Attachment-euthanasia-grieving. In Fogle B (ed): Interrelations Between People and Pets, pp 331-343. Springfield IL: Charles C. Thomas, 1981

Geertz C: Islam Observed: Religious Development in Morocco and Indonesia. Chicago, Univ of Chicago Press, 1971

Keddie KMG: Pathological mourning after the death of a domestic pet. Brit J Psychiatry 131:21-25, 1977

Levinson B: Pets and Human Development. Springfield IL, Charles C. Thomas, 1972

Nieburg H, Fischer A: Pet Loss: A Thoughtful Guide for Adults and Children. New York, Harper & Row, 1982

Quackenbush J: Pet bereavement in older owners. In Anderson RK, Hart BL, Hart LA (eds): The Pet Connection: Its Influence on Our Health and Quality of Life, pp 292-299, Minneapolis MN, Centre to Study Human-Animal Relationships and Environments, Univ of Minnesota, 1984

Quackenbush J, Glickman L: Social work services for bereaved pet owners: A retrospective case study in a veterinary teaching hospital. In Katcher AH, Beck AM (eds): New Perspectives on Our Lives with Companion Animals, pp 377-389, Philadelphia, Univ of Pennsylvania Press, 1983

Rynearson EK: Humans and pets and attachment. Brit J Psychiatry 133:550-555, 1978

Savishinsky JS: In the company of animals: An anthropological study of pets and people in three nursing homes. Latham Letter 5(1): 9, 10, 21, 22, 1983-84

Savishinsky JS: Pet ideas: The domestication of animals, human behavior, and human emotions. In Katcher AH, Beck AM (eds): New Perspectives on Our Lives with Companion Animals, pp 112-131. Philadelphia, Univ of Pennsylvania Press, 1983

Stewart M: Loss of a pet, loss of a person: A comparative study of bereavement. In Katcher AH, Beck AM (eds): New Perspectives on Our Lives with Companion Animals, pp 390-404. Philadelphia, Univ of Pennsylvania Press, 1983

US Department of Health and Human Services, Federal Council on the Aging: The Need for Long-Term Care: Information and Issues. Washington DC: Department of Health and Human Services, 1981

VanLeeuwen J: A child psychiatrist's perspective on children and their companion animals. In Fogle B (ed): Interrelations Between People and Pets, pp 175-194. Springfield IL, Charles C. Thomas, 1981

ADDITIONAL READING

Anderson RS (ed): Pet Animals and Society. London, Bailliere and Tindall, 1975

Arkow P: Pet therapy: A study of the use of companion animals in selected therapies, 2nd ed. Colorado Springs, CO: Humane Society of the Pikes Peak Region, 1982

Beck A, Katcher A: A new look at pet-facilitated therapy. J Am Vet Med Assoc 184(4):414-421

Brickel CM: A review of the roles of pet animals in psychotherapy and with the elderly. Int J Aging and Human Dev 12:191-198, 1980-81

Butler R: The life review: An interpretation of reminiscence in the aged. In Neugarten BL (ed): Middle Age and Aging, pp 486-496. Chicago, Univ of Chicago Press, 1968

Cusack O, Smith E: Pets and the Elderly: The Therapeutic Bond. New York, Haworth Press, 1984

Ebersole P: Establishing reminiscing groups. In Brusnwick I (ed): Working with the Elderly: Group Process and Techniques. North Scituate MA, Duxbury Press, 1978

Erikson E: Childhood and Society, 2nd ed. New York, WW Norton, 1963

McCulloch MJ: Animal facilitated therapy: Overview and future direction. Calif Veterinarian 36(8):13-24, 1982

McCulloch MJ: Pets in therapeutic programs for the aged. In Anderson RK, Hart BL, Hart LA (eds): The Pet Connection: Its Influence on Our Health and Quality of Life, pp 387-398. Minneapolis MN, Centre to Study Human-Animal Relationships and Environments, Univ of Minnesota, 1984

Messent PR: A review of recent developments in human-companion animal studies. Calif Veterinarian 37:26-31, 1983

Myerhoff B: Number Our Days. New York: Simon and Schuster, 1978

Savishinsky JS: What Cornell has discovered about volunteer experiences. People-Animal-Environment 2(1):14-18, 1984a

Savishinsky JS: Staying in Touch: A Report on Pet Therapy Programs in Four Geriatric Facilities. Ithaca NY: Department of Anthropology, Ithaca College, 1984b

Savishinsky JS: Pets and family relationships among nursing home residents. Marriage and Family Review 8(3-4):109-134, 1985

Savishinsky JS, Lathan, R, Kobayakawa, M, Nevins A: The Life of the Hour: A Study of People and Pets in Three Nursing Homes. Ithaca NY: Department of Anthropology, Ithaca College, 1983

Wilson C, Netting FE: Companion animals and the elderly: A state-of-the art summary. J Am Vet Med Assoc 183(12):1425-1429, 1983

20

Euthanasia of Pet Animals and the Death of Elderly Owners: Implications for Support of Community-Dwelling Elderly Pet Owners

Dan Lago and Catherine Kotch-Jantzer

With the recent growth of interest in the benefits of pet ownership for older people (Bustad 1980), organizations and programs have emerged that support pet ownership by members of this population. These include The People Pet Partnership, the San Francisco SPCA's "Old Friends" program, and People and Animals Coming Together (PACT). This chapter discusses the experience of PACT in coping with euthanasia, the unexpected death of pets, and the death of elderly pet owners.

PACT was established as a demonstration project and began placing pets with older owners in 1981. Earlier articles have described the planning process (Lago, Connell, and Knight 1982, 1983) and the impact of our operations (Lago, Knight, and Connell 1983; Lago, Connell, and Knight 1985). As part of an unusual evaluation procedure, a detailed longitudinal study is being conducted to compare participating PACT owners with other categories of pet owners. The articles mentioned above provide detailed information on the sample, research design, and early findings. This chapter focuses on data relating to the frequency with which elderly pet owners have their pets euthanatized, and the impact of the event on these owners.

BACKGROUND SURVEY DATA

In our initial survey of 137 elderly persons, conducted in 1981 to determine the feasibility of PACT, respondents were asked to comment on the disadvantages or problems associated with owning pets. Grief over the death of a pet was one of twelve coded responses. In that initial sample, a surprisingly low five percent of both current and former pet owners expressed concern over the death of pets. This concern ranked seventh, behind more day-to-day care concerns such as pet-sitting, health care expenses, property damage, the need to restrain pets, and so forth.

By the time of our 1983 survey, the sample included a subset of PACT clients (n=42), which had grown to a total of 294 current and former owners. Concern over grief at the death of a pet had risen to 11.7% of current owners and 11.3% among former owners. However, PACT owners were significantly more likely (29%) to be concerned with grief (X = −.001). However, concern over grief still ranked as the sixth or seventh greatest disadvantage for all groups. It should be noted that rates of concern for men and women were not significantly different: 10% for men, 12% for women.

Loss of a pet is, of course, a real possibility. Our 1983 survey documented an 11% rate of changes in ownership status changes for both current and former owners over one year. Tabulation of ownership changes in our 1984 survey indicated that 18% of former owners had acquired new pets (25 out of 139) and that 12% of current owners (20 out of 165) had lost pets in the preceding year. Of those 20 individuals who had lost pets, 53% (11 people) had had their pet euthanatized. In all but one case, when a young animal was severely injured, the pets were more than 10 years of age and the decision to euthanatize was made as a last step in humane care for aging pets. The 1983 data also showed that euthanasia was performed on 34% (48 of 140) of the pets last owned by former owners. Again, euthanasia was associated with advanced age of the pet in more than 70% of the 48 cases.

PACT CLIENTS SUMMARY TABULATIONS

As of January 1, 1984, PACT had made 60 animal placements; 12 of them (20%) were immediate post-euthanasia requests. Seven of the people were referred by their veterinarians; five were self-referred. The local veterinarians who made the referrals indicated that only a small percentage of their clients who had a pet euthanatized immediately expressed interest in or the need to obtain another pet. The veterinarians made referrals to us only when clients seemed particularly anxious, did not want to leave, or made remarks such as "What am I going to do without my pet?" Generally, veterinarians were unwilling to suggest another pet immediately, but encouraged people to contact them again if they had difficulty adjusting to the loss of the pet. Those interested in finding another pet immediately were very likely to become PACT clients.

Our overall program is heavily oriented toward women (84%), so it is not surprising that the immediate referrals are likely to be women, most of whom are either single or widowed. They are unusual as a group in that they insist on rapid selection of a pet. They are often committed to choosing animals that closely resemble their lost pet in both physical appearance and temperament or behavior. "Bonding" with the animal often appears to occur in the first moments of contact with an animal. Behaviors that are routinely observed in these women's approach to the animals include the use of high-pitched voices, crying, hugging and kissing the animal, and getting down on the floor to play with the animal. Such haste, emotion, and distress often result in poor discrimination in choosing a new pet, as shown by the following case.

A widow who had heard one of our group presentations telephoned, saying that the last of two wirehaired terriers her husband had bequeathed to her had died and that she needed a new dog immediately. She lived alone in an isolated area and was afraid to sleep at night without a dog in the house. She was distraught, and begged our volunteer to take her to the local animal shelter at once. The volunteer agreed, and escorted her to the shelter the next afternoon. As soon as she saw a small female Pekingese-terrier hybrid, the woman announced, "That's my new dog. Isn't she a dear? Let me hold her." The dog had just had a litter of pups removed from her and placed with owners. By the condition of her teeth and skin, it was known that the dog was fairly old, and she needed immediate health care. Although our volunteer stressed that the dog might not be appropriate and might not live very long, the client had already made up her mind. A negative evaluation by the participating veterinarian also failed to dissuade her.

The decision was made to acquiesce in the woman's preference, and we subsidized the necessary health care at a 50% rate. The owner is not bothered by the dog's sometimes aggressive behavior. She says it gives her pet character. The dog has nipped several members of her owner's extended family and our grooming and pet-sitting volunteers must approach her carefully. Her elderly owner says, "She's never bitten me, not seriously. You just need to learn how to get along with her. She's a dear, and needs me. I love her and you can never have her back." In the three years since the placement, the strong bond between owner and pet continues. The dog is gentler and has not experienced serious health problems, but most PACT volunteers still do not trust the dog and privately wish that her owner could have become attached to a more pleasant animal.

The immediate referrals have had a much higher rate of successful pet placement than has the overall PACT client group (83% as compared to 64%). This high success rate is a result of the intense motivation of these owners; they persist in managing the sort of behavior problems that terminate other placements. It is interesting that five of our most active senior volunteers (in nursing home visitation, public education, and public relations) have been recruited out of this set of "bereaved owner" placements.

Since PACT began placing pets with older persons, five pets have died before their owners. Only one dog was with a woman who was living alone; the other animals—a cat and three dogs—had been placed with married couples or sisters living together. The level of the owners' grief varied widely in these cases, from serious and prolonged to no noticeable grief. In two cases, the owners did not communicate with PACT. In one case, our volunteers learned of the animal's death several days after it had occurred. In one case, however, a routine innoculation-status check yielded the response, "Oh, he's dead—hit by a car several months ago. Sorry we forgot to tell you. It's just as well, since he was a lot of bother. No, we don't need any more pets." When asked how they were doing and how they felt at the time of the dog's death, the woman respondent laughed and said, "I'm doing fine; dogs die all the time. It didn't bother us much. It was more of a relief."

The other family that did not notify us had a long history of conflict over the pet. They had received numerous visits from their sponsor, from specialized animal training volunteers, and visitors who regularly took their dog, Dahlia, to a local nursing home as a visiting pet. The placement had been categorized as "maintained," not "successful." The dog died unattended in the garage during a winter night. Since the dog was over the age of twelve, the veterinarian could not rule out heart failure, but he thought that exposure to the cold was at least a contributing factor. The owners expressed no grief when they informed the nursing home visitor that the dog had died. Later, in discussion, they admitted to "feeling a little bad" at the way Dahla had died, but overall they were glad that the dog would no longer be a source of conflict. Neither they nor any of the other owners whose pets had died would consider having another pet.

A strong grief reaction to the one euthanasia of a PACT animal was observed. Two unmarried sisters in their middle eighties lived together and, with PACT's assistance, had adopted a pet, a large young adult male cat. The sisters had some conflict over the cat, but both became quite attached to it, particularly the nondominant sister. After only a few months, the cat developed severe cardiac problems, which caused convulsions and loss of consciousness. On several occasions, the PACT sponsor and the dominant sister rushed the cat to the veterinarian. When the veterinarian told them that this was a chronic, worsening condition, since the cat's heart could not support his body size, the dominant sister decided on euthanasia. The nondominant sister was taken to meet with the veterinarian, for him to confirm that the euthanasia was necessary to avoid continued pain for the cat. The sponsor, an age peer with strong knowledge of cats, had been giving the sisters anticipatory counseling about the possibility that the cat might not survive. She met regularly with the sisters in the weeks before the cat's death and continued to do so for months afterward. Several weeks after the cat's death, when this sister's grief had not diminished, the sponsor and the other sister encouraged her to see her family doctor, who prescribed tranquilizers. Over several months, the grief in the household receded and the nondominant sister reported that she was "over it." Nonetheless, the topic remains a sensitive one between the sisters and they have agreed not to risk pain again by taking a new pet. However, they still ask our sponsor to visit regularly.

Nine PACT animals have been bereaved by the unexpected death or institutionalization of seven owners. In four of the cases, surviving family members kept the pet. PACT placed two of the animals with other owners. Three of the animals were euthanatized by surviving family members.

Both animals that we relocated and three of the four pets kept by family members displayed symptoms of grief and behavior problems after the death of their owers. Refusal to eat, elimination in the home, loud or constant crying, aggressive behavior, anxious wandering, shyness, and fearful behavior were observed repeatedly. These symptoms varied in intensity and duration—one cat acted strangely for three months before accepting its new placement. The new owners of these pets needed and received calls of reassurance and consultations on behavior problems. They had to be encouraged to continue comforting their animal and to suspend judgment. During this period, both owners mentioned the possibility of returning the pet or having it euthanatized. Clearly the grief reactions of these PACT pets were compounded by the stresses of relocation.

Only four times has PACT been actively involved in considering euthanasia. The case that resulted in euthanasia for a cat with cardiac problems has already been described. In two instances in which the

PACT board was holding animals that had not been placed, it was difficult to accept euthanasia as an option. We embarked on an extended course of surgery and antibiotic treatment for one of these animals, a small hybrid terrier that had a persistent bladder stone and bladder infection. The treatment cost in excess of $350.00, but the dog's health was restored and she has become a regular nursing home visitor. In the other of these cases, a young male poodle had failed in three placements because of his hyperactivity, barking, and in-home elimination. Deciding Drifter's fate produced serious conflict in our board. Those who were frustrted by trying to work with this difficult animal felt tht he was harming our reputation and wasting our energies; others felt that it was immoral and contrary to our organization's purpose to kill a healthy animal. A deadline was set for the effort to find a suitable home for Drifter. If the effort had not succeeded by the deadline, he would be euthanatized. This decision galvanized one board member to find a young woman who is familiar with poodles, had kennel space, and agreed to work with Drifter. He was placed with her as an alternative to euthanasia.

In the final case, the owner was a sixty-seven-year-old woman whose daughter and infant granddaughter lived with her. Her large hybrid shepherd was routinely chained to the front porch as a security dog. The dog was twelve years old and appeared to be developing arthritic joint problems. The dog was never friendly and was becoming more aggressive. The daughter worried about the dog attacking her infant and encouraged euthanasia. We had previously provided financial aid for the dog's health care and now agreed to help cover the costs of euthanatizing the animal if the owner felt it was necessary. She met four times with our sponsor; two of the meetings included her daughter and other relatives. The owner's affections were torn, but she finally refused to have the dog euthanatized. Instead, she attempted to change routines in the home to provide more security for the child. Shortly thereafter, the owner died unexpectedly and her surviving family quickly had the dog euthanatized without contacting PACT, claiming that he had become upset and much more aggressive since his owner's death. The daughter kept a small, affectionate "inside dog" that her mother had owned. This dog continues to be an accepted part of the family.

DISCUSSION

The data reported at the beginning of this article support claims that a large percentage of PACT's older clients will have experience with pet euthanasia, either immediately before becoming clients or at some time after taking ownership of a PACT pet. Certainly, pet loss is a common occurrence, affecting approximately 10% of our current owner group per year. Over 50% of those who have lost pets have had them euthanatized.

Further, our data show a pattern of increasing concern over the death of a pet. This is not surprising in the PACT owners—a group self-selected for their affection for pets—but rates of concern have also more than doubled in the other samples. To some extent, it seems reasonable to suggest that growing national media attention to the benefits of companion animals and PACT's local publicity have influenced this rural sample to some extent.

One-fifth of our clients hope that a new pet will provide immediate aid in coping with the loss of a previous and highly valued pet. Our experience indicates that those who are willing to seek a new pet immediately find the strategy effective. It may be that pets meet the needs of these owners especially well. These clients appear to have a greater emotional investment in pets in general or in a particular breed of animal than in an individual animal. In such cases, others often exert pressure to delay taking a new pet until the person has recovered from the prior loss. As volunteers and service providers, we feel that we must avoid paternalism or value assumptions about appropriate grief responses and coping strategies. We help individuals to acquire pets as early as they wish, although we have become aware of the need to be more selective in screening animals before offering them as pets.

Our data and case reports also compel us to recognize that the motivations for pet ownership and responses to the death of pets vary widely. Consequently, we cannot assume that owners experience serious grief when a pet dies. Indeed, some owners report relief and some seem to have little feeling about euthanasia, believing that they have simply taken decisive action to rid themselves of a problem. Conclusions would be premature, since we have dealt with only one euthanasia and only four other sources of pet death, but it appears that euthanasia is more likely to be associated with a grief reaction by the owner.

Organizations such as PACT must be prepared to cope with the range of emotions and situations encountered because of pet death. Although great emphasis has been placed on the counseling and coping skills staff members need in euthanasia or pet-death situations, we feel that more emphasis should be placed on diagnostic skills in deciding just what responses are appropriate or necessary for our organization. Certainly, supportive counseling and factual information are helpful in some situations, and in severe cases it might be necessary to use professional referral networks and resources. We have usually found, however, that veterinarians and family members are confident and helpful in coping with normal grief reactions. In most cases, the issue is one of helping sponsors and volunteers to understand the owner's reaction accurately rather than to assume that grief counseling is needed. Training volunteers to listen and not to prejudge is probably as important as training them in the support of constructive grieving. Finally, our data indicate that the death of owners is often very stressful for pets and, in many cases, creates an increased risk of euthanasia for the pet.

RECOMMENDATIONS

PACT and similar groups must have knowledge of pet euthanasia and the grieving process. This knowledge must be translated into programmatic skills for volunteers, sponsors, and key referral resource persons. Most important, this knowledge must be applied on an individual, case-by-case basis; the organization must be flexible enough to respond to each client's actual needs, not to assumptions about those needs.

In our opinion, response to grief should be directed only toward individuals and families who are experiencing problems; it should not be promoted into a public education program with high visibility. Severe grief reactions are not common, and emphasizing them might not only increase their incidence among anxious owners, but could also provide a stereotypic target for those critical of close relationships with pets.

In terms of program planning, we can add little to the "best practice" guidelines emerging in the literatures (Katy et al 1984; Nieburg 1981; Quackenbush 1984). Sponsors are in a position to know earlier than veterinarians if an animal's health is failing. PACT and similar groups must develop a capacity for quickly assessing such situations and moving to support owners, families, and, in some cases, pets, with effective listening, accurate information, and good referral channels. We urge the active participation of sponsors—if owners express a need—in veterinary consultations, as well as their attendance and support during euthanasia and their help in developing meaningful rituals by which owners may mark the death of an animal. For example, funeral and memorial services may be helpful. Prompt social support, spending time with the owner immediately after euthanasia, and easing the owner's return to the empty house should be considered. PACT, as an organization, should send cards and clearly communicate condolences to bereaved owners, in addition to providing the personal involvement of the sponsor.

In addition, PACT and similar groups should employ referrals to the professional human service community in cases when severe grief is observed. In aging individuals, it is expected that life crises will interact with changes in physical or functional status to produce complex multiple conditions. To be effective in managing owners' grief, it is necessary to have a broad multidisciplinary assessment of their needs.

PACT's policy of always permitting the return of an animal after its owner's death is must useful and should be continued. Since interviewing surviving family members after a pet owner's death is difficult, we stress the need to gain the trust of family members (when they are present) as early as possible. Written agreements that family members will care for a pet after the owner's death have reassured some owners, who have added these documents to the family's legal papers.

Just as death is a common and accepted part of life for aging persons, loss of pets is a frequent fact of life. PACT must continue to recognize that reactions to such losses can be severe. Appropriately honoring the passage of a pet helps to communicate respect and acceptance of the eventual death of each of us. The death of pets is not a "disadvantage of owning pets" but another valuable demonstration of the inherent harmony of our relationships with companion animals.

REFERENCES

Bustad L: Animals, Aging, and the Aged. Minneapolis MN: Univ of Minnesota Press, 1980

Kay WJ, Nieburg H, Kutscher AH, Grey R, Fudin C (eds): Pet Loss and Human Bereavement. Ames, IA: Iowa State Univ Press, 1983

Lago D, Connell C, Knight BL: A companion animal program. In Smyer M, Gatz M (eds): Mental Health and Aging, pp 165-184. Beverly Hills CA: Sage, 1984

Lago D, Knight B, Connell C: Rural elderly relationships with companion animals: Feasibility study of a pet placement program. In Katcher AH, Beck A (eds): New Perspectives on Our Lives with Companion Animals. Philadelphia, Univ of Pennsylvania Press, 1983

Lago D, Knight B, Connell C: Placing companion animals in community settings. Organizational structure and operating policies in promoting health and well-being among elderly people. Proceedings of Pets in Society: The Social Importance of Pets in an Aging Society. Toronto: Pet Food Manufacturers Association, 1982

Lago D, Connell C, Knight C: The effects of animal companionship on older persons living at home. Proceedings of the International Conference on Human Animal Companionship in Honor of Konrad Lorenz's 80th Birthday, Oct. 26-28, 1983, pp 34-46. Vienna, Austria, 1985

Nieburg H: Pet Loss: A Thoughtful Guide for Adults and Children. New York: Harper & Row, 1982

Quackenbush JA: Pet bereavement in older owners. In Anderson RK, Hart B, Hart L (eds): The Pet Connection, pp 292-299. Univ of Minnesota Press, Center to Study Human-Animal Relationships and Environments, 1984

21

Euthanasia in Zoos:
Issues of Attachment and Separation

Bob Szita

Euthanasia touches the lives of zoo keepers in a deeply personal way. Keepers at the Staten Island Zoo, interviewed to discover their attitudes towards euthanasia, indicated from the very first that the issue was neither a simple academic question nor merely a controversial moral issue for animal caretakers. They revealed a variety of bonding experiences and a vast range of emotions that arise when those bonds are threatened or broken. For these caring individuals, the issue of euthanasia further complicates an already complex emotional experience.

During the interviews, the keepers could not discuss euthanasia and the accompanying feelings of loss and separation without first sharing and examining their feelings of attachment to animals. Without exception, all the keepers expressed attachments to at least some of the animals they cared for. The following are some of the ways in which they expressed their feelings:

"I think of them as friends."
"They're like pets."
"I look forward to being with them."
"It makes me happy to see them."
"They're fun to be with. It makes the day go nice."
"I love them."
"They are as close to me as a pet or even closer."
"I respect their smartness."

"I want to make them happy."
"It feels like love."
"I get attached to some animals the way I get attached to a pet dog."
"It's like friendship."
"They get into my heart."
"I get attached quicker and have stronger bonds with animals than with people."
"We have a mutually trusting relationship."

A variety of conditions fostered bonding, but two situations arose most often in the interviews. First, the keepers felt closest to the animals for whose care they were directly responsible, and thus with which they had the most contact. Over a period of months or years, they had the opportunity to develop a close relationship: "I deal with them every day. I like all the animals, but I get more attached to the ones I take care of." Second, the closeness of the relationship and level of attachment depend on the degree to which the animal responds in positive ways to the keeper. The keepers expressed concern for all animals, but acknowledged greater attachment to those that responded to their attentions. One keeper stated, "I take care of them equally, but I pay more attention to the ones that are friendly."

Some of the ways keepers described the reciprocal behavior of animals are:

"They eat from my hand."
"They follow me around when I clean their enclosure."
"The gibbon offers me his arm to groom and then picks through the hair on my arm."
"I know they trust me when they lick me."
"Some of the cats allow me to scratch their necks."
"They play with me."
"They reach out for affection by coming to me to be petted."
"It seems that some animals try to communicate with me."
"They recognize me as a friend. I can see it in their eyes and in the expression of their faces."
"When I talk to them they come to me or answer back in their own way."

Response to human contact in zoos varies among species and such responses of individual animals, directly affect a keeper's level of attachment. Snakes, for example, show minimal recognition of people. They typically shy away from large moving objects and are generally wary of anything touching them. They may recognize feeding time, but when they smell food they may strike at any moving object, including a keeper's hand. Such behavior discourages feelings of attachment.

Snakes that are highly defensive in the wild may become relatively docile after living in a zoo. However, their tame behavior is commonly viewed by keepers as indifference rather than a positive reaction to being cared for. When a snake sits peacefully in a keeper's hands, it is responding to physical support and body heat. The snake would show the same response to a warm rock. The reptile keepers commented, "Snakes cooperate if handled well, but do not show any interest in you"; "I'm fascinated with snakes as a group, but I don't get attached to any individual ones"; and, "I'd be more personally attached to birds and mammals. They recognize you more, need you more."

Reptile keepers said that they feel more attached to some lizards and turtles than to snakes. One commented about a lizard, "Monitors are intelligent and responsive. They look at you and like to be stroked." Another keeper described a favorite turtle. "She comes out to be sprayed whenever she hears the water hose." Some lizards and turtles can distinguish between their food and the hand that feeds them, and can safely be hand-fed. This kind of reciprocal behavior fosters feelings of attachment in animal caretakers.

Alligators and other crocodilians are unappreciative of human contact, and often respond aggressively. The keepers expressed respect and admiration for these animals, but no one felt a special attachment to them.

Birds and mammals are the animals to which the keepers acknowledge significant attachments. Here again, one of the main conditions for attachment is the level of reciprocal animal behavior. Many birds and mammals are highly social, and their social behaviors are frequently directed toward people. When such behaviors approximate human criteria for interpersonal contact, or when people can adjust their behavior to approximate the social behavior of the animals, strong bonds can form between keeper and the kept.

We are most familiar with this complementary and compatible behavior in the case of the family dog. Dogs relate to and respond to human families in much the same way that their wild counterpart, the wolf, relates to the wolf pack. Varying degrees of this compatible behavior obtains in other animals, too. In a zoo, chimpanzees and other primates will pick through a keeper's hair or beard and sit while the keeper returns the favor. Wolves will bound around playfully at the approach of a well-liked keeper, and the keeper may respond with various gestures to encourge the interplay. A trusted keeper may preen a parrot's feathers and the parrot will perform the same ritual on the keeper's hair. Even though the otters at the Staten Island Zoo are not handled, they will play with anyone at a distance by retrieving a coin tossed in the water and carrying it on their noses or their chests. One keeper is very clear about his reason for attachment: "I feel warm inside when an animal comes to me."

A variety of other explanations that accounted for keepers' feelings of attachment were offered during the interviews. Some keepers are attracted to the comical appearance or behavior of an animal. Beauty and intelligence were mentioned, too. Several keepers stated that they like certain animals because, "they have personality." Close attachment is encouraged in some cases by the uniqueness or novelty of an animal species unfamiliar to a keeper. The mere fact that an animal has lived at the zoo for a long time and is considered an "old timer" generates a certain amount of attachment as well.

One keeper suggested that a childhood experience similar to that of an animal being abandoned by its mother created his special feelings of attachment. Others observed that raising an animal from the time it is a baby makes it special to them: "She's like my baby. I would be devastated if she died"; "I raised her. She depends on me. It bothered me to leave her at the zoo. She no longer recognized me now that she is with her own kind. I like to remember her the way she was at home"; "She was born here. I hand-raised her. She recognizes me as a friend, the way a dog would recognize me."

As I listened to the keepers describe their relationships with the various animals they care for, it became apparent that parallels can be drawn with the relationships between people. As with animals, friendships are more likely to be closer when people see each other regularly. Just as the keepers express individual preferences for certain qualities and behaviors they perceive in animals, so people are attracted to each other for a variety of reasons. All relationships are reciprocal, whether or not animals are part of the relationship. An interdependence of needs, limitations, and preferances of both individuals must exist. The keepers gave some examples of this interaction: a male lion shows a definite preference for some keepers by offering his side to be scratched, but roars defensively at other keepers. Primates and wolves exhibit social needs that can be partially filled by human contact.

The keepers also made comparisons between people and animals:

> "I view animals as people. I respect their lives."
> "Judy (the chimpanzee) is smarter than some people."
> "They're like a part of my family."

"They're more fun to be with than some people."
"There's no game-playing with animals. It's a straightforward relationship."
"I attach human values to them."
"Some animals think they're people."
"There's lots of love energy toward people and people respond back."

Though each keeper's relationship with an animal is unique, they all share a similar emotional experience: the stronger their bond to an animal, the stronger their feelings of separation when the animal dies or is considered for euthanasia.

The emotional complexity of this issue makes it difficult to express feelings about euthanasia. All the keepers agreed, however, that euthanasia is an appropriate procedure under certain circumstances. One of the stronger rationales is that since zoos have assumed responsibility for the care and well-being of animals outside their natural habitat, the responsibility to ensure a good death is also theirs.

In a native setting, nature sustains life for the fit and healthy, killing the weak and old. A zoo, however, is like a nursing home in which the animals are sheltered from the strain of survival. Protected and nursed beyond their normal ability to survive, they often outlive their wild counterparts. A zoo's commitment to maintaining a high quality of life for an animal creates a paradox. In a zoo's artificial environment, an animal's physical life can be prolonged until the quality of life has deteriorated; at this time euthanasia is a rational choice. In this situation, the keepers agreed that an animal's life should be artificially ended.

It is one thing to endorse the practice of euthanasia in zoos, but quite another to decide exactly when the life of an animal should be ended. Ultimately, the zoo veterinarian makes the final decision, based on his own expertise and judgment as well as the recommendations of the zoo curator and input from the keepers. Even though the keepers do not have the last word in the decision-making process, they must carefully weigh for themselves the factors involved in order to deal with their own feelings of separation and to accept the decision. The degree of suffering by the animal is one of primary concern of the keepers when euthanasia is considered. All expressed sympathy for an animal in pain and most cited acute, chronic, and irreversible suffering as criteria for electing euthanasia.

Individual keepers, however, differed in their perception of suffering. They varied as to the level of suffering they would tolerate in an animal before recommending or accepting euthanasia. Some keepers believed they could accurately perceive when an animal was in pain, while others felt that in many cases an animal might suffer a great deal without showing it.

Prognosis was also a consideration in the keeper's readiness to accept euthanasia. How long should an animal continue to be treated when it shows no sign of improvement? Is there reasonable hope of recovery? If an animal recovers, what will be the quality of its life? For example, some birds seem to function quite well despite an amputated wing, but are severely handicapped by loss of a leg.

Some keepers thought that even though an arthritic animal showed signs of pain when it moved, it should be kept alive as long as it was able to walk, eat, and eliminate waste. They would recommend euthanasia only when it could no longer be encouraged to eat or when it could not rise to walk. Other keepers felt that aging animals with chronic arthritis should not be kept alive if they showed signs of pain by walking slowly or by limping. It is clear that individual keepers consider different factors when faced with the possibility of committing one of the animals in their care to be euthanatized.

Another factor to be considered is the level of attachment. Keepers recognize that their feelings of attachment for an animal have influenced their opinions as to whether or when euthanasia should be performed. One keeper might want to delay euthanasia longer than another who did not feel as attached. The opposite might also be true. Some keepers with stronger feelings of attachment might encourage euthanasia sooner because they are more uncomfortable with the animal's level of pain or lowered quality of life. The stronger the keeper's bond of attachment, the stronger his emotional reaction. Everyone involved in the decision was aware that personal feelings must be kept in perspective with the facts of the animal's condition and prognosis. With this in mind, the decision to euthanatize or not to euthanatize an animal can be made as objectively as possible.

After the euthanatization of an animal, the keepers described their feelings:

"I was very sad."
"I felt depressed."
"I felt terrible."
"I was upset."
"It was like mourning."
"I feel like crying but don't."
"I feel lonely, empty."
"I feel sorry for myself."
"I felt relieved."

Most of the keepers also expressed initial feelings of self-blame and needed to review their role in the care of the animal, even though in most cases the situation was beyond their control.

It was revealed during the interviews that the keepers talk very little among themselves about their feelings. Though some superficial talk occurs about missing an animal or about its empty cage, most keepers hold their feelings inside. Some said: "I mope around," "I keep busy," "I keep my mind off it," "I think about it a lot," "I try not to get too upset," "I try to remember the good times." Others talk to family or friends, and a few admitted to crying.

Several keepers remembered that they didn't feel too bad, if they thought the animal had had "a good long life," or "that its time had come." Their judgment that the animal had been happy in life and had come to the end of its natural lifespan made them more accepting of the death.

The keepers described a difference between their reaction to the unexpected death of an animal and their feelings about a planned euthanatization. After the intial shock of an unexpected death, keepers reviewed their personal responsibility: "Did I do anything to cause this?" "Could I have prevented it?" "Why didn't I notice anything wrong yesterday?" After an animal is euthanatized, a different process of self-examination ensues: "Did we make the right decision?" "Maybe it would have improved if we waited longer"; and "Did we let it go too long?"

Euthanasia is accepted and frequently practiced in zoos, veterinarians' offices, animal shelters, and humane societies, yet it remains a complex and controversial issue that demands further study. It is important to explore the relationship between zookeepers' feelings of attachment to the animals they care for and the influence of these feelings on their willingness to accept separation when an animal is considered for euthanasia.

During the past few years much work has been accomplished in the area of pet loss and human feelings. The writings of Nieburg and Quackenbush, among others, have contributed greatly to our understanding of bereavement after the loss of a pet. People who work in zoos would profit from knowing this work, since their feelings toward zoo animals are often similar or identical to feelings about pets.

I encourage further investigation into the bonding that takes place between zoo animals and their caretakers, especially the effect that this bonding exerts on decisions about euthanasia. New studies in this area might also benefit zookeepers in making better personal adjustments to the death of animals in their care and add to the growing body of knowledge of the human–companion animal bond.

22

The Bereaved Pet Owner and Social-Work Service Referral

Catherine A. Kotch and James E. Quackenbush

Companion animals have long functioned as an integral part of human society. The roles of pets today are almost as numerous as the breeds that have been developed. Often pets are retained to perform a specific task such as herding sheep or killing rodents; others are accepted as vital members of the family. Many pets are kept as a matter of course by casual owners who provide for the animals' basic needs without adding many frills or incorporating the pets into their lives. Sometimes pets are valued as symbols of their owners' status in society. Others are owned by enthusiasts who go to great lengths to prepare tasty, home cooked meals for their pets or ensure that the pets accompany them on vacation. Pets in our society may be loved as a child's friend, admired for leading the blind, or on the other hand, may be abused, abandoned, or used for sport.

Considering the wide range of roles played by pets, it is easy to anticipate an equally wide range of responses to a pet animal's death. One might hypothesize that a few owners would be affected very little by a pet's death; a very large percentage would be moderately affected; and a small percentage of owners would be severely affected. Although instances of the first group surely occur in the general population of pet owners, none were found in the present study because of a biased subject pool. The population for the study was selected from a group of pet owners whose pets had been euthanatized at the Veterinary Hospital of the University of Pennsylvania (VHUP). This facility is known for its excellence in pet health care and specialized medical services. Pet owners who are relatively unattached to their animals rarely invest the effort, time, and money necessary to take the animal to this hospital, wait to have the pet examined, and then pay the cost for services, medication, and tests. Many of the animals euthanatized at VHUP are euthanatized following an illness or injury that the owners had tried to treat.

Because some pet owners become upset when faced with the death of a pet, the hospital provides a social-work service designed to counsel pet owners who need assistance in making treatment or euthanasia decisions or in coping with the death of their companion animals. Clients are usually referred to the social worker by veterinarians, students, or other staff at the veterinary hospital.

This study examines the differences between the owners who are referred to the social-work service and those who are not, with the null hypothesis stating that no differences exist between the grief reactions of these two groups. Since this is a pilot study, the questionnaire that was completed during the telephone interviews included items that often indicate grief over human death. These items include the frequency and type of thoughts related to the deceased, guilt, crying, difficulty sleeping, and thinking that one has seen or heard the deceased since the death. Two questions were provided with Likert-scale responses so the owners could retrospectively rate their initial grief reactions on the same scale they had used to measure their grief at the time of the interview. The remainder of the questions concerned the people and pets in the owners' households, other stresses at the time of euthanasia, and the length of the owners' initial grief reactions.

Responses to the interview items by the social-work service clients (experimential group, $N=26$) were compared to responses by the group of owners who were not referred to the social worker (control group $N=24$). The social-work service clients were older, experienced longer initial grief, reported difficulty sleeping, and anticipated seeing the pet after its death. A more detailed explanation of these variables and those that were less significant can be found in the results and discussion sections of this chapter. Possible effects of the social-work service on the grief process are also addressed in these sections.

LITERATURE REVIEW

The literature dealing with grief upon the death or euthanasia of a pet animal must be examined carefully to differentiate hypotheses from actual findings. Stewart (1983) found no difference clinically between grief for a pet and other types of grief. Other authors have likened grief for a pet to grieve for a human (DeGroot 1983) or grief over any significant loss—such as that of an arm or leg (Nieburg 1980). Bereaved pet owners are expected to suffer the same symptoms as groups dealing with the above losses, but not necessarily to the same extent (Fischer 1980; Katcher 1979; Rowsell 1982). Guilt feelings, for example, may not be expressed as commonly after the death of a pet as after the death of a person (Cowles 1983). Crowe and Bennett reported from data-based research that many pet owners wept while speaking to a researcher of their pet's death a year after the death had occurred (cited in Rowsell 1982). More studies must be conducted in the field of bereavement for a pet so that the phenomenon can be better understood and differences in length of grieving time can be explained. Quackenbush (1982), among others, has emphasized that no culturally acceptable way of mourning a pet exists. Perhaps greater understanding of the grief experienced by pet owners will result in development of an acceptable mode of grieving and more effective counseling will be possible.

METHOD

Subjects A selection was made from a population of pet owners whose pets had been euthanatized at the Veterinary Hospital of the University of Pennsylvania during the month of August 1982 through August 1983. All of the social-work service clients who had been counseled during that time because their pets had been euthanatized were included in the research population. These owners were then matched by species of pet and date of euthanasia to owners who were not referred to the social worker. Twenty-eight owners were in each group. The telephones of three subjects had been disconnected and no current telephone numbers were made available. Two subjects failed to answer their telephones when the researcher called, despite repeated attempts. One respondent was excluded from the study because the person who brought the pet to the hospital at the time of euthanasia was not a member of the owner's household or family. No one who was contacted refused to participate in the study. Twenty-six (93%) of the social-work service subjects and 24 (86%) of the control group participated in the study. The social-work service group consisted of eight males and eighteen females, and the control group of ten males and fourteen females. The researcher asked to interview the person whose name appeared in the hospital files. If that person was not available, another member of the household who had also accompanied the pet when it was euthanatized was interviewed.

Instruments A questionnaire (see Appendix) including introductory and concluding paragraphs was developed to standardize the telephone interview. The introduction provided information about the researcher and the purpose of the study, and explained that participation in the study was voluntary. The questionnaire was designed to assess the incidence and extent of grief symptoms the owner experienced after euthanasia of the pet. This measure was pretested and demonstrated face validity, but no information on internal validity or reliability was available. The conclusion thanked the participant and provided the social worker's name and telephone number, so that any subjects suffering unresolved grief could call following the interview.

Procedure

1. The social worker recorded on individual index cards information concerning all social-work service clients who had been counseled following euthanasia of their pets between August 1982 and August 1983. The cards listed the owner's name, address, and telephone number, plus the pet's name, birthdate, and date of euthanasia. Each card was assigned an identification number, which was recorded on a master list.

2. The social-work service cases were matched by species of pet and date of euthanasia to owners who had not counseled with the social worker. The matching was facilitated by a computer printout obtained from the medical records department, which provided a list of all euthanasia cases, the pets' species, and the date of euthanasia. The file was then traced by the hospital case number, which also appeared on the printout. If a match to the same date as the social-work service case was unavailable, the next closest date listing a euthanatized pet of the same species was used. All pets in the study were cats and dogs. Information for each case was recorded in the same format used for the social-work service clients, and the identification numbers were again entered on a master list.

3. The cards, free of discernible group identifiers, were then presented to the researcher who was "blind" to the respondents' group classifications.

4. Telephone calls were placed by the researcher at varying times of day and evening, in no particular order. The researcher responded empathetically when the subject expressed feelings about the pet, the euthanasia experience, or the veterinary hospital. All questionnaire reponses were recorded on raw data sheets, and calls continued until most of the subjects had been contacted and interviewed. Non-contact rates were also recorded.

RESULTS

A chi-square analysis was calculated for each variable and for both the experimental and control groups, in order to determine any differences between the two populations. Table 1 shows the grief symptoms and the self-ratings of grief (see questions 1-10 in Appendix B for the complete items). Two variables were significant at the .05 level: anticipating seeing the animal (.0461) and difficulty in sleeping (.0481). The variable of being initially affected by the death for two months or longer was significant at the .025 level of analysis. Examining Table 1, it becomes apparent that although most of the variables are not significantly different between the two groups, social-work service clients reported a higher incidence of grief symptoms. These variables include thinking sad thoughts of the pet; feeling guilty; recent crying over the pet; thinking that one has heard the animal since its death; and rating initial and later grief as very severe or extremely upsetting.

Table 2 shows demographic information for both groups of subjects. If the groups were identical except for the experience of having spoken with the social worker, all of these variables would be expected to indicate nonsignificant differences. The variable of age, however, is significantly different at the .025 level. Other variables, such as additional stress, fewer people in the household, having no other pets, and being the person who was most upset at the pet's death also imply a pattern that possibly predisposed the social-work service clients to react more strongly to the death of their pets. Acquiring, or considering acquisition of a new pet does not create a difference between the two groups, and respondent gender accounts for only slight variation.

In addition to describing differences between the owners of euthanatized pets who spoke with the social worker and those who did not, this study examined the frequency with which grief symptoms were experienced by bereaved owners. Even owners whose pets had died 14 months previously reported that they had thought of their pets in the last two days. Guilt was also experienced, but not as frequently as might be expected (36% of all owners). Forty-four percent of all pet owners who were surveyed had not cried since the month following their pet's death, but 36% of the same group had cried during the week of the telephone interview. (The remaining 20% cried sometime in between these two periods.)

Of the subgroups of eighteen pet owners who reported that they had cried within a week of the interview, twelve were social-work service clients and six were from the control group. Eighty-three percent of the control group cried during the interview, while only 33% of the social-work service clients cried at that time (see Table 3).

DISCUSSION AND IMPLICATIONS

The demographic profile of the owners who spoke with the social workers was similar to that of the control group. The social-work service clients were significantly older than the other subjects. These clients also reported anticipating seeing the animal and having difficulty sleeping with significantly greater frequency than the control group. Finally, these clients were initially affected by the pet's death for a longer time than were the owners who had not spoken with the social worker.

A comparison of the results of the interview reveals a consistent trend. Although these differences between the groups are not statistically significant, the social-work service clients experienced other stresses at the time of the death, owned no other pets, lived with fewer people in the household, and were the most upset people in their households as a result of the pet's death. Future studies should interview the individuals from both groups who were most attached to their pets before the euthanasia.

A consistent, although not statistically significant pattern also occurred with grief symptoms. The social-work service clients reported a higher incidence of thinking sad throughts, feeling guilty, recent crying over the pet, and thinking they had heard the pet since its death. These clients also rated their initial and later grief as very severe or extremely upsetting more often than did the control subjects. If a larger sample were available for a follow-up of this study, these trends might prove statistically significant as the sample size increased.

Of all the pet owners who were interviewed, most reported thinking about the pet during the two days prior to the interviewer's call. Less than half were thinking sad thoughts, and more than one-third felt guilty. Half of the owners anticipated seeing their pets in a familiar place; one-third had cried in the last week while thinking of their pets; slightly less than one-third had difficulty sleeping; and one-fourth thought they had heard the pet. Care must be taken to avoid generalizing these results to all pet owners. Veterinary hospital owners are more likely to be committed to their pets than are "typical" pet owners and thus may react more strongly to the deaths of their pets.

When a pet is euthanatized, information should be gathered about the people comprising its household. Demographic identifiers, such as the age of the owner, should be examined in order to determine which pet owners might be more at risk for long periods of grief. The questionnaire used has been tested in a telephone interview format and could be repeated to obtain a longitudinal perspective of the pet owner's grief process and how it relates to social-work service referral. Despite the

	Thought of pet in last 2 days		Type of thought		Guilt		Cried		"Saw" pet*		"Heard" pet		Difficulty sleeping		Initially affected*		Initial grief		Later grief		Other stress	
	yes		sad		yes		in past week		yes		yes		yes		2 + mo.		5		4-5		yes	
	Freq.	%	Freq.	%	Freq.	%	Freq.	%	Freq.	%	Freq.	%	Freq.	%	Freq.	%	Freq.	%	Freq.	%	Freq.	%
SWS Clients	24	92	11	22	12	46	16	62	12	46	8	31	11	42	18	69	13	50	9	35	13	50
Owners Not Referred	20	83	8	16	6	25	6	25	8	33	5	21	4	17	9	37	5	21	5	21	9	37
X^2	.952		.427		2.424		2.424		3.978		.640		3.907		5.058		3.429		1.175		.791	

Table 1. Grief symptoms in pet owners who had a pet euthanatized: A comparison of social work service clients with owners not referred for social work services.

* significant statistically with $p < .05$, dF = 1, chi-square test

	Age*		Number of other people in household		Person most upset		Other pets owned at time of euthanasia		Acquired new pet		Considered new pet		Owner gender	
	40 + yrs.		0-1		Self		No		Yes		Yes		Female	
	Freq.	%	Freq.	%	Freq.	%	Freq.	%	Freq.	%	Freq.	%	Freq.	%
SWS Clients	18	69	15	58	18	69	18	69	14	54	8	67	18	69
Owners Not Referred	9	37	8	33	12	50	11	46	14	58	6	60	14	58
X^2	5.058		2.98		1.92		2.805		.102		.104		.643	

* significant statistically with $p<.05$, $dF=1$, chi-square test

Table 2. Demographic information on pet owners.

	Freq.	%	Average number of months since euthanasia	Range (months) since euthanasia
SWS Clients	12	46	6.8	2-14
Owners not referred	6	25	7.8	3-11

Table 3A. Pet owners who cried within one week of the telephone interview

	Freq.	%	Average number of months since euthanasia	Range (months) since euthanasia
SWS Clients	4	15	8.5	3-12
Owners not referred	5	21	7.8	3-11

Table 3B. Pet owners who cried during the telephone interview

sensitive nature of the interview, all owners agreed to participate in the study. This attitude may be a reflection of this facility's reputation or may indicate that owners find increased attention to their grief so important that they are willing to experience a little more pain so that they or others may benefit later.

The telephone interview for this study provided a unique stimulus to these bereaved pet owners. They remembered a time and event that was difficult for many of them, and 18% of the total group cried while they spoke to the researcher (whom they had never met). It is interesting that 83% of the subjects who had not seen the social worker and who had cried in the week of the interview also cried during the interview (see Table 3). This behavior indicates a need in these people to speak with someone about the euthanasia and implies that some pet owners who might benefit from the social-work service are not being referred. Some veterinarians are hesitant to refer owners to the social worker and express the opinion that the social worker is a resource of "abnormal" clients only. This error might be eliminted by issuing an awareness-education memo to the veterinarians, students, and clerical/support staff (all valuable sources of referral). Another productive approach might be to notify the social-work service of each euthanasia case, so that a human-services worker could add his or her evaluation of the owner's reaction to the veterinarian's judgment. This study could be improved by interviewing owners near the time of the pets' euthanasia to obtain a measure of initial grief. A comparison of that response to a retrospective response expressed during the later interview would indicate changes in response to various items measured. This procedure would help control for recall error on that item.

APPENDIX: TELEPHONE INTERVIEW

Introduction

Hello, this is *(interviewer name)* calling from the University of Pennsylvania. May I speak with *(owner name)*, please?

I'm conducting a study for the veterinary hospital at Penn on owner reactions to the death of a pet. This call will take about five minutes; is this a convenient time for us to talk or should I call back later?

I'd like to ask you some questions about your pet *(pet name)*, who was euthanatized here in *(month)*. Did you happen to be the one who brought *(pet name)* to the hospital then?

I know this may be a difficult conversation for you, but your participation is greatly appreciated because it is very important for us to know if we are meeting the needs of our clients. If you do not wish to answer any of these questions, just let me know and we will either skip that question or end the interview, whichever you wish. Participation in this study is completely voluntary and all of your answers will be anonymous and confidential. May we begin now?

Questionnaire

1. In the last two days (prior to this phone call), have you thought about _____?
2. When you do think about your pet, what sort of things do you think about?
3. Have you experienced guilt because your pet was euthanatized?
4. When was the last time you cried when you thought about this pet?
5. Since _____ died, have you ever anticipated seeing it in a familiar place?
6. Since _____ died, have you ever thought that you heard it?
7. Have you had any trouble sleeping since your pet died that you did not have before?
8. How long were you initially affected by your pet's death?
9. On a scale of 1–5, how would you rate your grief reaction during that time?
   1 — not affected, life as normal
   2 — a little sad, angry, or depressed
   3 — somewhat sad, angry, or depressed
   4 — very sad, angry or depressed
   5 — extremely affected, almost every part of life disrupted
10. On the same scale, how would you rate your grief feelings now?
11. At the time that your pet was euthanatized, were you experiencing any other stresses in your life (unemployment, divorce, moving)?
12. What year were you born?
13. When your pet died, how many other people were living in the household?
14. In your opinion, who was most upset by _____'s death?
15. Did you own any other pets at the time _____ died?
16. Have you gotten any other pets since then?
17. Have you considered getting another pet?

Conclusion

On behalf of the veterinary hospital, I want to thank you for talking with me and helping us improve our services. If you ever want to discuss anything with the social worker here at Penn, please feel free

to call. I'll give you his phone number so you can jot it down. It's
_____ , and the social worker's name is _____ _____ . Thanks
again! Goodbye.

REFERENCES

Cowles KV: Adult human responses to the death of a pet: a qualitative study.
In Abstracts Selected for Presentation at the Conference on the Human-
Animal Bond. Symposium conducted at the Univ of Minnesota and the Univ
of California, 1983

DeGroot A: Euthanasia–animal death–human grief: Is the veterinarian educa-
tionally prepared to cope? In Abstracts Selected for Presentation at the Conference on the Human-Animal Bond. Symposium conducted at the Univ of
Minnesota and the Univ of California, 1983

Fischer A: Mourning the loss of a pet. American Kennel Club Gazette (Octo-
ber), 1980

Katcher AH, Rosenberg MA: Euthanasia and the management of the client's
grief. Compendium on Continuing Education for the Practicing Veterinarian
1(12):887-891, 1979

Nieburg HA: Pathologic grief in response to pet loss. In Kay WJ, Nieburg H,
Kutscher AH, Grey R, Fudin C (eds): Pet Loss and Bereavement. Ames, IA:
Iowa State Univ Press, 1980

Quackenbush JE: The social context of pet loss. Continuing Education
3(6):333-338, 1982

Rowsell H: Anguish and grief: helping the aged to cope with the loss of a pet.
In proceedings of Pets in Society: The Social Importance of Pets in an Aging
Society, pp 61-70. Toronto: Pet Food Manufacturers Association, 1982

Stewart M: Loss of a pet–loss of a person: a comparative study of bereavement.
In Katcher AH, Beck AM (eds): New Perspectives on Our Lives with Companion Animals, pp. 390-409. Philadelphia, PA, Univ of Pennsylvania Press, 1983

Part 4

Euthanasia in Veterinary Practice and Laboratory Animal Medicine

23

Holism, Euthanasia, and Veterinary Medical Practice

Roger A. Caras

The imperative I seek to establish here is that of holism as applied to euthanasia in veterinary medical practice. The issue goes beyond how someone handles the death of his beloved pet, and involves much broader sociological and psychological phenomena.

It is never easy for someone to lose a pet or a companion animal; nor is it a simple matter to perform killing on demand. If it were easy, the companion animal concept would not have come into being and lasted for several centuries, as it has. Small wonder that the dog is such a companion animal, for he is descended from a social animal, the wolf—and the wolf, since he adheres to a highly structured, hierarchical society of alpha and beta animals, was ideally suited to engender a new species that would learn to lie at our feet and lick our hands. What we have not considered is how ideal a species humans might prove as companion to the dog—or to any other species that might acknowledge man as lord and master.

Humans have evolved to need companion animals just as the species we selected evolved to fill their role. If this were not so, I doubt very much whether medical science would be currently investigating the effect of pets on human heart attacks, ulcers, and hypertension as well as the contribution of animals to psychological well-being. In a sense, we have been selectively bred by our pets to need them—while all along we imagined that it was the other way around: that we were breeding them to have an expressive tail, to have no white marks except on the chest, to display herding instincts or territorial instincts, or the desire to sit on a silk cushion and eat bonbons.

The point is that people and their animals have become one over the millenia, inextricably interlocked. We constitute a team—or millions of small teams—and to shatter a team creates highly emotional crises in people. Some seem to endure stoically the loss of a pet, possibly because they are ashamed to cry, but others cannot assume such a brave face.

Let us look at the spectrum of these different reactions in a holistic context. For generations, humans have isolated themselves from the unpleasant realities, the terrible truths resulting from the injuries they themselves have perpetrated upon their planet and its other inhabitants. We live in an era of rude awakenings and considerable confusion, and matters will probably worsen as more truths are thrust upon us. There is no longer any place to hide. Consider man's management of wildlife.

As a young man, I began to hear murmurings about American wildlife being subjected to unendurable pressures. I was born just a quarter of a century after the American bison was snatched back from the brink of extinction by the American Bison Society; thirteen years and eight months after Martha, the world's last known passenger pigeon, died in Cincinnati; and just ten years after the last Carolina parakeet had died. The last of the heath hens had just recently disappeared from Martha's Vineyard. Just as I was beginning to grow and find myself, a new truth was emerging: certain animals were rapidly becoming extinct. Although not many people seemed to care deeply, the crisis had come to light.

Ultimately, we learned that our wolves were almost extinct in the contiguous forty-eight states; then, our grizzly bears were nearly gone; and finally, we found out about the disappearance of whales. Our sacred bald eagle, as well as the brown pelican, were nearly eliminated by DDT, and by 1941 only fourteen whooping cranes survived in the world. The California condor all but disappeared, with only two dozen remaining today. The cheetah vanished from Asia in 1952, and the Asian lion was down to one hundred sixty-two specimens. The black rhino is now on the way out.

There is no excuse for ignorance of this appalling situation, and no denial of our culpability as a species.

A sort of desperation seems evident today in the way people love their pets—as if to compensate for past carelessness of animal and other natural resources that now seem doomed to extinction. Other changes are also occurring. An eye-blink ago, as time is measured on this planet, virtually the entire human race pursued hunting for a livelihood. If someone in the family did not hunt, no one ate, which meant death by starvation. Today, less than one percent of the world's population regards hunting as having any economic significance at all. Do these figures imply a softening of attitudes—a warming, if you will, of humans toward other life forms?

Although we still live with the unpleasant reality of the slaughterhouse, most of us regard that necessity as operating on a different level of existence—one irrelevant to the average steak-eater. Moreover, a new phenomenon has arisen: many restaurants suddenly are offering vegetarian meals on their regular menus, and the number is constantly increasing. The trend may be inspired somewhat by health considerations, but a great many vegetarians are of that persuasion, at least in part, on moral grounds.

There may be growing guilt over the way in which we have treated members of the animal kingdom. We have assigned new "jobs" to animals within the human community and regard them in a more sentimental light. We regret the harm done to them in the past. Our first guilt applies to the injustices done to the species, our second guilt to wrongs against individual creatures. Both forms function in the person who arrives at the veterinarian's office with his cocker spaniel in his arms. He is not logical or pragmatic about his pet.

The current concern over vivisection, sometimes bordering on hysteria, has generated a wave of vigilantism and strident debate in which science and education are on the defensive. The public demands a cure for cancer, muscular dystrophy, AIDS, herpes, birth defects, and impotence. Everyone wants better techniques for dealing with trauma. Yet some anti-vivisectionists label the researchers who try to answer these demands as monsters. Night raiders have broken into laboratories and issued wildly conflicting statements about what had transpired there, creating guilt and confusion. Those who protest the implant of a baboon heart in a human baby as a dangerous precedent are clearly unaware that pig-heart valves have routinely been used to replace human heart valves for fourteen years; that in the early 60s baboon and chimpanzee kidneys were placed in human beings; that burn victims are wrapped in pigskin to protect them until they can tolerate skin grafts; that diabetes sufferers use insulin that still is largely derived from the pancreas of pigs or cows; that people with occluded leg arteries benefit by installation of shunts that prevent gangrene and amputation, and that these shunts often are made from the carotid arteries of cows. These facts emerge while protesters march, while fund raisers and vigilantes break the law and defy logic. It is not an easy time to be a human animal, particularly if one's personal link to the animal kingdom, one's pet, may be in dire trouble.

We also face the ultimate confusion of extraordinary reproductive physiology techniques and bioengineering developed through the use of animals: artificial insemination, about as new as the butter churn; embryo transfer; DNA surgery using enzymes as surgical instruments; daily refinements so exquisite that the men and women doing the work barely believe what they have wrought. The news media relay accounts of interspecific embryo transfer. In Cincinnati an eland carries a bongo zygote to term; in Louisville a horse gives birth to a zebra; zygotes are frozen, then thawed to be implanted and grow to term. What follows is the absolute certainty that all of these techniques now are available, or will be shortly, for man and woman. At the time of writing, mice and cattle are being cloned in Ft. Collins, Colorado; if you can clone one mammal, you can clone any mammal.

Progress in technology now occurs with "dizzying" speed. The rate of progress now increases exponentially every five years.

There is, however, a catch. We have the technology, but we seem to lack the ethics, the morality, the philosophy, or religion to guide us. The new technology has totally outstripped traditional morality. In plain truth, there no longer seems to be a consensus on what is right or wrong. Cloning, frozen embryos, and DNA manipulation are devoid of moral guidelines. Not one of the Ten Commandments comes close to touching any of these issues. We are adrift.

So when a client walks in with his terminally ill pet, more than a pet owner confronts the veterinarian. Here is a person who lives in a time when no one knows how to feel about a great many things; who feels guilty to some degree, perhaps, over our historic treatment of individual animals, whole species, and entire habitats full of extraordinarily diverse fauna and flora. Given such confusion, how can that pet owner achieve perspective? What once was right is so no longer. What was wrong may be worse than wrong now. Added to that is the fact that today's pet owner is seldom able to express grief just because a pet animal has died or is about to die. We still subscribe to that Victorian stiff upper lip; we still live at a distance from our emotions. The owner of the sick cocker spaniel is loaded with all manner of guilt, confused by shifts in societal wordly attitude, and beset by the moral systems of others.

We should remember, too, a few things we have failed to perform as a society. We still must determine if animals (our pets, perhaps, foremost) may claim any rights. We certainly have taken the trouble to define our own, but we have not yet, as a society, acknowledged theirs. We also have failed to define "property." A lawn mower is property, and so is an empty beer can—and so is an animal, once we have acquired it. But is there a difference? No one seems to know, least of all the owner of a pet that is in trouble. We must consider animal owners within this expanded, holistic context.

24

Breaking the News: The Problems and Some Answers

Andrew T. B. Edney

Our job as veterinarians dealing with people's companion animals is to diagnose and treat all manner of disorders. Where treatment is clearly doomed to be ineffective, or has become so, we must end that animal's life in the most practically humane way possible: that is, by euthanasia. We are thus privileged to spare our animals all the unpleasantness of distressing terminal illness.

Such a situation is difficult enough to handle in "ordinary" circumstances, and is all the more so when the death or the indication for it is unexpected, or premature. Suggestions on how to manage these events in our clients' lives have been offered in a number of publications (Edney 1979; Katcher and Rosenberg 1979).

We have been concerned for much of the time with the disturbing effects of euthanasia on the clients. What I want to explore here are the problems engendered in ourselves.

Why is it so difficult to tell people the worst? It is plainly not just because we do not like to make people unhappy. No one finds it easy to break bad news. Can we make it easier for ourselves and, consequently, for the animals in our care and their owners? We all know that no treatment can be guaranteed and that some failures will occur, no matter how competent we are. Why do we blame ourselves, then, when such events happen? Why do we fear being blamed? Simply accepting that such things occur and recognizing that they create feelings of guilt in those in charge of cases goes a long way to making it easier to handle the situation.

Paradoxically, it seems to be the most highly competent clinicians who take on large measure of blame from their clients' setbacks with recalcitrant cases.

Buckman (1984) identified two sets of fears that may be obstacles to breaking bad news: those fears and anxieties we all experience as clinicians wanting to succeed; and those factors that drive us into taking responsibility for the disease itself. Buckman suggests that the first makes it difficult to begin the dialogue with an owner, and the second makes it difficult to continue communication.

A prime fear of clinicians, particularly those newly qualified, is that the owner will blame the veterinarian for the animal's illness. This attitude is not confined to veterinarians or to our medical colleagues. All bearers of bad tidings are resented to some extent. The reaction seems quite irrational when the communicator has very little or no control over the events. Some people grow angry with weather forecasters for announcing rain (or the lack of rain). In Britain, weather forecasters become comedians to protect themselves. In antiquity, the bearers of bad news were said to have been disposed of even more severely.

Transferring adverse reactions to the bearer of bad news is not aberrant behavior, however distasteful it might seem to be on the receiving end. The price of borrowing from the library may go up, but it is little use berating the person who issues the books, any more than it is to complain to the gas station attendant when the inevitable round of price increases occurs. They have no influence over these nuisances; yet we all tend to identify any agent as the one to blame. Buckman suggests that the more authority we assume, the more we become targets.

If we understand that blaming the professional is a normal reaction, veterinarians can learn not to take the reaction personally. Veterinary students are not offered much guidance in the management of euthanasia, although some schools now include the subject at least as a small part of the curriculum. Graduates of longer standing have usually learned from (sometimes harrowing) experience, or from close observation of other veterinarians how to deal with extremely delicate situations. Carrying out procedures in which some training has been provided is difficult enough for the new graduate, but someone with very little or no training, moves in an unknown area full of pitfalls. Before we have gained some experience, most of us feel insecure. At such times the client is most sensitive to mishandling. With greater experience, we learn to cope where we have been trained, but we may feel even more awkward in cases where we have not had instruction. Most of us feel very uncomfortable indeed when a client reacts emotionally to our diagnoses. Such emotions as dismay and despair, particularly if accompanied by weeping, are avoided by most British people. They will (unconsciously perhaps) put off revealing facts and opinions which might precipitate a dramatic reaction, not only to avoid seeing others in a distressed state, but also because they feel guilt about being the triggering influence. Problems are compounded in a busy clinic, where overt expressions of grief or explosive angry outbursts are less private than we would like them to be.

Veterinarians who spend a good deal of effort in developing a manner of calm, efficient authority may have difficulty appearing sympathetic. To pet owners, they may seem unfeeling. Clearly, as clinicians they cannot be involved emotionally in all the serious cases they see. But an aloof, uncaring approach will not generate any comfort, no matter how efficient and otherwise "correct" it is.

Expressions of sympathy sometimes even backfire. A veterinarian's sorrow can be interpreted as sympathy, or it may appear to the owner to be an acknowledgement of blame. Suppose one tells the owner of a dog that was opened up to discover the cause of its difficulties, "Sorry, it's a very invasive tumor that is inoperable." The statement is open to misunderstanding. Buckman believes the knack of expressing sympathy clearly without accepting undue responsibility is difficult, and must be taught by demonstration for the best results.

Saying, "sorry," in an inappropriate way often invites the owner—who is usually looking for someone to blame—to blame us. Consider the situation when someone telephones when you are alone in the house taking a bath: you stand by the phone, dripping wet, explaining why it took longer than usual to answer. The caller says, "Oh, I'm terribly sorry." Why should he be sorry unless he knew the exact timing of your bath arrangements? In no way could he have prevented the inconvenience. What he is really saying is, "I'm sorry this has happened to you," but that is not how it sounds.

Buckman (1984) identifies another snare for the inexperienced: fear of not knowing all the answers. He pinpoints the paradox that one must be very experienced indeed before he can safely say he simply does not know the answer. The clinician who is dogmatic about what will happen is asking for trouble, even though the owner's attitude is that he is not paying for doubts but for certainties. If, in response to the owner's question, you say a particular dog's condition is definitely curable (or incurable) or that it has about four weeks to live, you are likely to be just as wrong. The truth may well be quite unavailable to any mortal. We should not feel any burden of guilt over unanswered questions. Yet many of us attempt to answer the unanswerable.

Our own fears of illness and death should be as much considered as the feelings of our clients about the terminal situation of their animals. Much thought on the subject of death is hard to accept, and the need to deal with death as a part of life is suppressed in much of Western society. It is important to acknowledge that the longest-lived of our common small companion animals will usually survive only a fraction of our own lives, if we live a reasonable length of time. Yet many people resent the reality that their animal has reached the end of a (comparatively) long life; they may become quite hostile when you draw their attention to the fact. Their overreaction often engenders an unreasonable level of guilt in the unfortunate clinician.

In my experience, most veterinarians do not engage in the very risky business of shielding clients from the truth that their animals are dying of some intractable terminal illness. The situation certainly occurs in human medicine, and I suspect that doctors try to shield themselves from some of the problems already described, as much as to spare the patient. Anyone who withholds such important information from an owner is surely inviting a much higher level of hostility when the truth becomes obvious. Confidence in a clinician's diagnostic skill can only be undermined by such a strategy. If the veterinarian reveals at the end that he knew all along that it was (say) a malignant neoplasm that would inevitably mean an early death, then confidence in his honesty will be rightly questioned too. And yet these evasions are common in human medicine. Not every awful detail need be spelled out, but raising false hopes of recovery can be equally disastrous. Buckman (1984) identifies a strong temptation for clinicians to take credit for remissions of clinical signs. Patients may then be shielded from anxiety by the overconfident dismissal of possible recurrence, particularly after tumor removal. Subsequent relapses, which are bound to occur from time to time, then become a matter of personal failure. Not only can the practitioner's error become very public (owners who have been let down are seldom reticent about it), but the result can be demoralizing for the clinician.

It is obviously essential to train undergraduates in the skills of those who are accomplished at communicating with the owners of dying companion animals.

I conducted a small survey of veterinary schools in Europe and North America to try to determine how such matters are taught. My findings seem to indicate that very little attention is given to the formal teaching of euthanasia management. Most schools rely on clinic situations rather than actual instruction. With a few impressive exceptions, little actual lecture time is allotted to the issue. Only a few schools, so far, have indicated use of video or role-play techniques. Surely the subject is ideal for that? It does at least merit more serious attention.

Veterinarians encounter the additional problem of making the decision to end an animal's life. The desires of the owner are often difficult to identify. Nonetheless, the final decision is indeed the owner's. Owners do not always appreciate that fact. There are ways of putting pressure on owners to influence their decision, but in most cases an owner who wants his animal destroyed has a right to that. If he does not want it killed, he has that right too, in most cases. What he does not have is the right to cause needless suffering, whether or not that is felt as actual pain. Any form of distress or misery is unacceptable. I have kept animals in a state of oblivion for quite a long time because of an owner's refusal to accept that its reasonable lifespan had ended.

What many owners do want is for their veterinarian to take the initiative and make the decision for them. One soon learns to identify the signals and to act accordingly. Owners frequently feel they are acting as executioners and would prefer us to "sign the death warrant." By doing so, they are able to transfer a little of the guilt with which they feel burdened. Rather than assume more blame for the situation, we really need to explain carefully that it would be selfish to allow an animal's misery to continue, and that it is a kindness to spare it further misery and allow a peaceful ending.

REFERENCES

Buckman T: Breaking bad news: Why is it still so difficult? Brit Medical J 28(8):1597-1599, 1984

Edney ATB: The management of euthanasia in small animal practice. J American Animal Hosp Assoc 15:645-649, 1979

Katcher AH, Rosenberg MA: Euthanasia and the management of the client's grief. Compendium on Continuing Education for the Practicing Veterinarian 1(12):887-891, 1979

25

Euthanasia and Bereavement: A Study of Clients and Veterinarians

Sharon McMahon

The following recommendations to help manage euthanasia and pet death were developed from a study of 55 clients, including 10 men and 45 women ranging in age from 14 to 95 years, and a group of 25 veterinarians, including 20 men and five women, in the Windsor–Essex County area of Ontario, Canada. Personal interviews (X–4 hr), an extensive 300-item "Human Survivor" questionnaire, imagery activity, and a 30-item veterinarian instrument were used to gather data.

The human survivors' imagery (gestalt) activity of drawing the deceased animal from memory was used to "measure" closure and resolution of the pet's death. The Hurt Index was devised as a personalized reflective measure to assess the intensity of emotion that the pet's death caused the survivor. Demographic variables have not been correlated for this article; rather, a global picture is presented.

Contemporary veterinary practice involves triangles of interaction, process, responsibility, and communication. The first triangle (Fig. 1) incorporates the participants: the human, the animal companion, and the companion care-givers. As one thinks of the variations of interaction among these participants, the complexity of the social dynamic (interspecies and intraspecies) becomes self-evident. One must add to this factor the "intra"actor components of spirit, body, and mind. For each participant, the relative weight of these components will vary according to natural biological endowments. Questions arise from time to time about the "spirit" and the mental activities of the animal participant. We cannot, however, ignore the spirit of such heroic, symbolic, and real-life animals as Lassie and Man-O-War, to name only two contemporary symbols. Storytelling and myths continually demonstrate animal devotion, intelligence, and long duration of "love," and recollection by the human survivors of their animals' "spirit," as well as the variety and intensity of the bond between humans and companion animals.

Figure 1 shows how the participants in this bond interact with one another. Focused energy is reflected in the stronger emotional content communication, both verbal and nonverbal. The death (euthanasia) of a pet concludes the future-oriented, stable or growth-oriented interaction. The congruence of the shared "heart" of the diagram is thus broken. The survivors experience tension and distress for variable lengths of time.

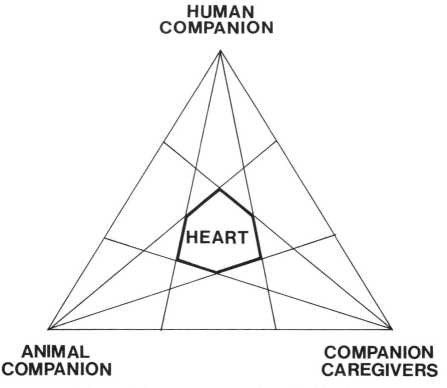

Figure 1. The human—companion animal bond.

An individual participant's role in the animal-bond relationship has a direct effect on his adaptation to the death of the animal. Even at a great distance (whether defined in terms of time, space, difference in intellectual and emotional capacity, reality orientation, and degree of attachment), the death of an animal still evokes individual responses in each survivor. In grieving the death of a long-lived, lone "significant other" animal, human survivors may either experience an extremely stressful and agonizing reaction or else pass through a well-prepared, less stressful one. Others who were more distantly attached to the relationship might be expected to demonstrate less personalized, more objective responses and coping behaviors.

The meaning and impact of the animal's death (as well as the method or cause) influence survivors' responses and adjustment. Figure 2 shows time-and-distance variables and their interaction during life and death experiences. Survivors' experiences with death may be better understood when they acknowledge their own moral and ethical precepts, philosophy of life and death, religious-cultural beliefs, and other values and can share them with others, including the veterinarian.

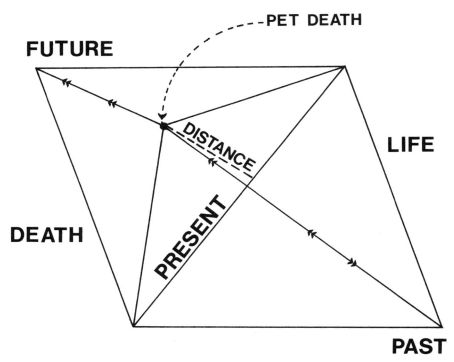

Figure 2. Time-and-distance variables associated with pet death.

Veterinarians deal with planned and unexpected pet death daily. Each year millions of animals, many of which have been pets, are euthanatized in private and humane-society clinics and in research facilities. Thousands more die in traumatic and unknown ways. Some die as "sacrificial" animals, while still others provide food for humans and for animals. Many animals who die leave behind human companions who must adjust to the severance of special bonds. Others die alone, uncomforted victims of abuse or trauma. These animals are often neglected and unknown. Veterinarians and humane societies can help in some of these situations; the averge pet owner cannot. Their personal responsibilities focus on their animal dependents, their own companions.

Just as the death of a pet exerts an impact on the immediate human survivor, so it does on the family and community associated with the animals. Many factors—including values, relationships, interpretations, and perceptions of all those who have been associated with the deceased animal, will influence the stages or trajectory of bereavement and the outcomes of adjustment to the animal's death. The veterinarian is often concerned about these variables when euthanasia is discussed as an option or, indeed, as the only "right" course.

People's responses to death can be expressed verbally and nonverbally. Changes in behavior, language, mood, lifestyle, and patterns of daily activity may occur. Thoughts of the deceased may overwhelm other thoughts and preoccupy communication and emotional energy. Veterinarians' bereaved clients may make time for the beginning of grieving in the office or at work, but veterinarians typically can find little time for grieving. Grieving can be influenced by the many pressures on all participants. The stages of preparation and anticipatory grief; the existence of a mutual, positive, trusting relationship; and the possession of an accurate, realistic base of information are all helpful elements for the people involved in this life experience.

Research findings from the study samples revealed that positive closure of grief for all of those associated with the death of a pet, whether or not by euthanasia, is enhanced by

1) discussion of the pet's condition and prognosis, expected costs of care, and expected cause of death without euthanasia
2) understanding of the method, reason for, and cause of death
3) expected behaviors and feelings during euthanasia
4) decision made by the animal's owner (alone, with family, or supported by significant others)
5) provision for time to prepare for the animal's death
6) assurance that death was or will be peaceful

7) some control by the animal's owner of the final hours and minutes with the animal and the way the animal will die or be assisted to die

8) reassurance that it's all right to cry, and time to regain composure before leaving the office, clinic (by a private exit), or graveside

9) a realistic understanding of the pet's life cycle

10) freedom from guilt for acts of omission or commission

11) willingness on the part of support groups (such as classmates or co-workers) to allow bereavement activities in keeping with owner's degree of attachment to the pet

12) knowledge that the veterinarian has done what is possible considering the animal's condition, the quality of life possible for the animal after intervention, the ability of the client to care for the animal afterward, and to bear the cost of treatment

13) purposeful remembrance and recognition (by phone call, card, or note) by the veterinarian, staff, family, and others about the deceased pet

14) knowledge that counseling will be available for survivors if the client, veterinarian, or others think that help with completing grief work is needed.

The final point indicates that although grieving is purposeful and time-limited for some people, for others it is more difficult and open-ended. The difficult pattern of adaptation is often the one more publicized because of the "high-risk," pathognomonic reaction of survivors. The risks include (1) illness; (2) emotional distress; (3) breaks with reality; (4) preoccupation with death; (5) suicidal behaviors; (6) guilt-laden and hopeless–helpless reactions; (7) denial of the pet's death; (8) inability to "image" (draw, visualize, verbalize, and symbolize) the dead animal; (9) inability to re-establish human and animal relationships; and (10) difficulties with work or daily routine.

For veterinarians, the question arises about who needs follow-up help with adjustment and grief, and who does not. The risks to human survival that accompany difficult and unresolved grieving demand intervention by other professionals. It is therefore important for care-givers in particular to achieve insight into the dynamics of the human–companion animal relationship as experienced by some people. Care should be taken to avoid brusque, judgmental statements and behaviors concerning the responses of human survivors.

The groups studied suggest that it may be helpful for those assisting human survivors to tabulate the risk factors involved. The more risk factors checked off by the veterinarian, client, or allied professional, the more urgent is the need for therapeutic guidance and intervention. The risk factors identified are as follows:

1) anger (without reconciliation)
2) denial of events related to the pet's death, of outcome, or of ability to love a pet again
3) isolation from significant others or "distant" persons
4) physical weakness, loss of orientation to time or place, loss of coordination
5) extreme youth or age and loss of first or previous pet
6) lack of a support group that understands the shock of pet death
7) intense and longstanding relationship with the deceased animal
8) lack of preparation for the event
9) past unresolved death experiences
10) recent death of a relative, close friend, or another pet
11) Hurt Index of less than 50 (when compared to 100 as ultimate pleasure)
12) unrealistic expectations of the veterinarian's curative skills
13) lack of opportunity for verbal preparation about the nature of the trauma, mutilation, or accidental injury that led to the animal's death
14) inability to have participated in the decision-making process about euthanasia
15) inability to have one's personal wishes fulfilled regarding the decision about euthanasia and its administration and about disposal of the corpse
16) lack of experience with death
17) guilt about the circumstances of the pet's death
18) predisposing physical problems (e.g., cardiac, gastric, neurologic, or metabolic disorders), especially if these problems are similar to those of the deceased pet
19) lack of control or perception of lack of control; helpless and hopeless feelings
20) dissatisfaction or unresolved, incomplete feelings preventing closure (resolution) and "moving-on" activities.

As the animal-health professional, the veterinarian's primary responsibilities are animal-focused. However, the triangles of the human–companion animal bond must be recalled and the client must be considered at the time of an animal's death, when the animal–doctor relationship is ending or has ended. Veterinarians may share their concern about and responsibility for their bereaved clients by making or suggesting referrals to other professionals such as doctors, nurses, clergy, psychologists, teachers, and social workers. This sharing will help reinforce the reality factors and provide support for grief work, as well as for conciliatory or clarifying activities related to any issues of contention that may have arisen between client and veterinarian (or the veterinary staff). The sharing can also give veterinarians a "recouping time" for the restoration of their own psychic energy after the planned euthanasia or the traumatic, unexpected death of "special" patients. Veterinarians must remember that they are not alone in the responsibility, accountability, and experience—or "gift"—of performing euthanasia. All veterinarians share this responsibility, skill, and ability. Many clients expect this of their animal's doctor.

To cope with this pressure, it can be helpful to remember that euthanasia is controllable. One can determine a right time and place. In most circumstances, euthanasia need not be rushed. When an unusual circumstance arises, reaching out to other colleagues; informing the client in the most immediate, accurate way; and feeling comfortable and accepting of the client's decision about the termination or extension of a pet's life can all help relieve the stress and aloneness that is sometimes associated with this work. Sharing responsibility can help relieve the decision-making dilemma of whether to try to effect a cure, to prolong life at any cost, or to facilitate a peaceful death for one or many animals.

The giving of emotional and physical touch, of verbal and nonverbal expressions of support to colleagues or clients can help them accept, adapt to, and resolve the normal psychic and somatic tensions experienced by all those who share in the death of animals, especially companion animals. Active listening, empathic responses, reflective replies, hugs (with permission), and personal means of communication can help others experience the potential good offered by ethically performed, well planned, artful euthanasia.

The research findings also indicate that veterinarians have expectations of themselves and their clients at the time of a pet's death. Veterinarians expressed the wish for a network of ongoing support that would allow technical discussions and motivate the sharing of concerns and coping strategies. All of the veterinarians surveyed wished for more preparation time to spend with geriatric patients and their human companions. Over 85% of the veterinarians wished that animals, especially favorite patients, would die in their sleep, naturally and without pain. All felt that pet owners should be educated about the life expectancy of pets, the euthanasia option and process, and how to assure that their pet's remains would be handled with respect and in the way the owners had planned and hoped for. Leisurely, deliberate, documented preparation for the death of a pet seemed to eliminate detrimental surprise elements for all concerned, thereby helping all participants to be mutually supportive and effective in their respective roles when the animal's death did occur.

All of the veterinarians hoped that in the near future all pet owners would become "parent-like" and "adult-like" by assuming decision-making responsibilities and by becoming aware that they have a responsibility to assure their animal companions a dignified, peaceful end. The final hope of the veterinarians was that the survivors would be receptive to the idea of referral to other professionals if they need help in resolving their grief.

BIBLIOGRAPHY

Allan J, Clark H: Directed art counseling. Elementary School Guidance and Counseling 19(2):116-124, 1984
Anderson RK, Hart BL, Hart LA: The Pet Connection: Its Influence on Our Health and Quality of Life. Minneapolis MN, Center to Study Human–Animal Relationships and Environments, Univ of Minnesota, 1984
Guidano VF, Liotti, G: Cognitive Processes and Emotional Disorders. New York, Guilford Press, 1983
Stevens JO (ed): Gestalt Institute. Moab UT, Real People Press, 1975

26

A Veterinarian Confronts Pet Loss and Client Grief

Alton F. Hopkins

When a family pet dies or must be destroyed, there is usually a period of sadness, the degree of which varies from family to family. In most families, the response is a good cry by the children and some sniffles and tears by the parents—the parents reacting partly to the loss of the pet and partly to their children's grief. A sizeable minority, however, will deviate from this pattern. Trying to anticipate, understand, and react to these exceptions can be a challenging but personally rewarding endeavor for a veterinarian.

The exceptions usually fall into any of four categories:

1. An unexpected family member is the primary griever.
2. An unexpected degree of emotion (either more or less) is shown by one or more members of the family.
3. An atypical relationship exists between family members.
4. Unexpected interference comes from outside the family.

By way of definition, the "family" we're talking about here is the group of people and animals living together and encompasses everything from a one-person-one-pet situation to a multiple-person-multiple-pet household.

Let me catalog some of the common grief situations seen in a busy small-animal practice and how I try to handle them. With few exceptions, these cases involve the death of a pet.

Let us begin with the relationship between the stereotypical hunter and his dog. For 15 years this person will be the picture of indifference towards his "no account, rabbit-chasing, quail-eating, covey-bustin' S.O.B." But when the end of life comes for old "Bud" you can bet the macho bit will come to an end. The astute veterinarian will expect a very emotional scene. There is a relationship between a man and his dog that develops through many weekends in the field or hundreds of hours in a duck blind—a relationship perhaps beyond the understanding of anyone who has not experienced it. For some reason the other members of the family usually fail to perceive the real need old Bud has filled in Papa's life. And so his display of grief is a surprise and puzzlement to them. Having experienced this kind of relationship myself, I sometimes have to share the Kleenex box with these men, and I suspect my display of empathy helps to put "Mr. Macho" at ease to express his grief.

We are only beginning to understand the role of pets in the development of a child's personality, but one thing is for sure: when a child's pet dies, the situation must be treated with sensitivity and the child's grief must be respected. An oft-repeated scenario in my office goes something like this: Mother, Father, and 12-year-old John Jr. have just been told that the family dog, age 13, has terminal cancer and must be put to sleep. Silent tears well up in the boy's eyes when he realizes his companion for as long as he can remember is gone. I seldom intervene in this kind of grief, except to quietly express genuine condolences to the child and try to let him know I understand his loss. If another family member behaves dismissively, I will find a way to communicate that the way the child feels is normal, healthy, and appropriate.

A related situation occurs when the 10-to-12-year-old child shows no emotion but the parents both begin to weep, each patting the inert child on the shoulder as if consoling *him*—finally looking at each other, becoming embarrassed and fumbling for an apology for acting so foolishly. This has happened dozens of times and I never know quite how to react. To the adults I offer a box of Kleenex, a friendly smile and assure them there is no need to apologize. But the child in this case puzzles me. Is he glad the dog is gone? Does he not understand the dog is really gone? Is he only in control enough to save his tears for later in his room? Is he perhaps stupid? My instincts tell me this child has a problem, but the same instincts stop short of telling me how to react in any kind of helpful way.

Here's one I've seen many times: The owner (usually the husband) just breaks down and sobs in a most unexpected way. This is not Mr. Macho and his hunting dog but rather Mr. Average, and the animal was always considered to be the wife's or children's pet. In these cases, the other family members seem to forget their own grief and turn their attention to the sobber. My recollections of these encounters are that the family members invariably reach out and touch, hold, hug, pat, stroke the sobbing one. His grief seems to become the focus for their grief and then their reassurance. Again my magic Kleenex box seems to come to the rescue, usually provoking comment—even laughter through the tears—about having to be fussed over like this, and the family end up in control of themselves. I suspect but can't prove that this demonstration represents an emotional flashback to a similar situation which occurred during childhood. One thing this episode is sure to produce is a most sincere letter of gratitude a few days later from the non-sobbing spouse, commending my understanding and tactful handling of the whole encounter.

Another category of people deserves mention here. They are the people who accept the death of their pet as so routine, so matter-of-fact, that you have to wonder whether something is lacking in their emotional makeup. I have known people who seemed very attached to a pet—to the extent that I was prepared to expect an emotional outburst when I announced that their pet was not going to make it and probably should be helped to die. To my utter surprise, such people respond to my pronouncement like this: "OK, will you please dispose of the body?" Not even "How will you dispose of the body?" "May I see her one more time?" Just "OK, if you'll dispose of her, I'll pay my bill on the way out. Appreciate all you did. We'll see you when we get another one. Bye now." I have more of a problem coming up with an appropriate response to that kind of reaction than to any other. I'm afraid to respond in kind with the same "matter-of-factness" for fear that it will be interpreted as callousness or indifference. At the same time I feel foolish expressing concern at the loss when that loss seems of no concern to the client.

There are in any veterinary practice a number of clients who have multiple-animal households. Veterinarians generally recognize these owners as requiring a slightly different approach in all encounters but particularly in death or euthanasia situations. These people have an amazing empathy with their pets. They will go to any expense, bear any inconvenience, tolerate any kind of mess or odor, to prolong the life of one of their pets. Unbelievable self-sacrifice! Because most of these people don't have the money to indulge their emotions this way. Yet, typically, they cannot bear for the animal to experience pain. If that pet shows signs of pain, especially whimpering or whining, they start talking euthanasia fast. Sometimes, if the procedure necessary to cure the animal's ailment is perceived as being painful, they will either insist on euthanasia or else take the animal home to be nursed and fussed over until it dies. When death finally comes, they tend to handle it with little apparent emotion. The pet will be buried somewhere with the critters that have gone on before, and life goes on in the household as if nothing had happened. Any veterinarian hearing this would insist that I observe one exception to this generality—these people always have *one* pet out of 10 or 20 or 30 or 60 that is very special, and the loss of that pet will engender a more emotional grief reaction, sometimes to extremes.

There is a kind of grief over the loss of an animal that happens more frequently than its counterpart in the loss of a human loved one. This involves the extreme feeling of guilt when the individual has actually caused the animal's death in a way that could easily have been prevented. When this occurs, there is really no way to gloss the matter over because the owner really truly did cause the animal's death by doing something grossly stupid or careless. At any rate, the family member who caused the death usually grieves for several weeks longer than if the death had been from some cause outside his realm of control. There's not much for me to say to an individual like this, so I seldom express anything other than genuine condolences—the one exception being when the perpetrator of the fatal act is a child. The self-centered world of a child should not, in my opinion, be burdened with this kind of guilt. Leaving the gate open for Rover to be hit by a truck should be a learning experience certainly, but not in a crippling way to a developing personality. If I perceive a parent or older sibling becoming overbearingly accusatory, I generally take the youngster away alone and offer some reassurance that although what has happened is terrible, it can't be undone, and the main thing is to let it be a lesson to be more careful in the future—and by the way, don't take the rantings of your big brother too seriously. He is really just relieved that Rover didn't get killed when *he* inadvertently let him out.

Old people, especially those living alone, are very special when they lose their companion animal. My experience has been that a person in this situation seldom cries, at least in my presence. A resigned blank stare and shaky voice give away their true feelings, however. This quiet grief can continue for many weeks. Even a month later when they are returning unused medicine, it is evident to me that they still feel the pain of loss. A gentle hug or a firm handshake is enough to convey that I understand. The joker in this situation is some well-meaning relative who takes it upon himself to purchase another pet (usually as much like the old one as possible) and appear at the bereaved's doorstep with the new bundle. Boy, talk about the wrong thing to do! The elderly person, not wishing to offend the obviously well-intentioned relative or friend, accepts the new pet with graciousness. But soon I am called with these questions:

"What am I going to do with this thing? I don't like it. I don't want it. How can I get rid of it? I never intended to get another pet and besides, as you well know, nothing can ever replace Sparky."

Actually many of these people do get another pet *in time*. But not while they are feeling the grief of loss of a living creature with whom they were perhaps closer than anyone in their family. To a person who has never felt that way about an animal, this is very difficult to explain. One analogy I have used successfully to help persuade a well-meaning relative to pick up and return the replacement pet is to imagine her father passing away and then two weeks later, while her mother is still grieving, someone brings some old man to Mama to live there and keep her company.

In summary, the death of a pet of any age belonging to a person of any age is an emotional event that almost always invokes a grief reaction of some degree for a period of time. As evidence of this, I need look no further than my letter file. In 25 years of practice I have been involved in the birth of thousands of animals. I have made many difficult diagnoses and effected (at least in my own mind) some near-miraculous cures. I have performed surgical operations, some of them very difficult and demanding. I have pioneered a few techniques that have saved a lot of animal suffering. To this date I have not one letter of gratitude, not even a thank-you note for any of these accomplishments. What I have received are hundreds and hundreds of calls and letters and gifts expressing extreme gratitude and deep affection for my words, actions, attitude, concern and understanding at the time of a pet's death. What this says about the human/companion-animal bond I'm not sure, but it seems to me to say something like this:

The feelings of love, acceptance, dependence, empathy, sympathy, anger, fear, suspicion, and concern are readily accepted as normal by our culture, in a relationship with a pet animal. But the sudden surge of grief over loss of a pet comes as a total surprise to many of those experiencing it, and they don't really know how to handle it. I'm sure they are embarrassed by their actions but at the same time they realize their reaction was spontaneous and real. So the expressions of gratitude to me are really their way of saying "Gee, Doc, I felt like a fool acting that way over an animal—until your attitude told me that what I felt and did was OK and not so weird after all."

27

Death and Euthanasia: Attitudes of Students and Faculty at a Veterinary Teaching Hospital

S. L. Crowell-Davis, D. T. Crowe, and D. L. Levine

A survey was carried out at the University of Georgia College of Veterinary Medicine concerning the attitudes of students and faculty toward animal and human death, especially as it relates to veterinary practice and selection of a career in veterinary medicine. Twenty-nine freshmen, twenty-six sophomores, twenty-eight juniors, seventeen seniors, and thirty veterinarians anonymously filled out a questionnaire.

Forty-six seniors and veterinarians who had euthanatized an animal and had experienced the death of an animal they had been trying to save reported their reactions, which are summarized in Table 1.

Of the 130 veterinary students and veterinarians answering the questionnaire, 78% believed that nonhuman animals are sentient (conscious of their own identity); 42% believed that nonhuman animals have souls; 74% believed in an afterlife for humans; and 34% believed in an afterlife for nonhuman animals.

One hundred and thirteen of the students and faculty remembered the death of a family member. Of these, seven (6%) felt that this had affected their selection of a career in veterinary medicine. One hundred twenty-five of the students and faculty remembered the death of an animal with which they had had a personal relationship. Of these, 33% believed this relationship exerted an effect on their selection of a career in veterinary medicine. Twenty-eight veterinarians answered questions

Reaction	After euthanasia	After natural death
Sense of relief	65%	43%
Sleep disturbance	13%	24%
Sense of failure or inadequacy	41%	78%
Episode of loss of temper	7%	13%
Feeling of "lump in throat"	61%	63%
Crying	46%	46%
Need for solitude	35%	41%
Need for alcoholic drink	9%	11%
Having an alcoholic drink	9%	9%
Depression	57%	67%
Anger	48%	43%

Table 1. Reactions of veterinarians and senior students to animal euthanasia vs. natural death (sample = 46).

regarding how the death of such an animal affected them as veterinarians. Of these, 40% felt that their history affected how they practiced veterinary medicine; 30% felt this affected how they cared for critically ill or injured patients; and 37% felt this affected their attitude toward critically ill or injured patients. Of those who had experienced the death of an animal with which they had had a personal relationship, 95% had experienced a short-term emotional effect and 43% had experienced a long-term emotional effect.

Veterinarians were aware of the following events having occurred in at least one of their previous cases: 79% had observed a severe short-term emotional effect following the death of an animal they had been trying to save; 18% had observed severe long-term emotional effects following euthanasia; 23% had observed severe long-term emotional effects following the death of an animal they had been trying to save.

Twenty-nine percent of the seniors and 60% of the veterinarians reported that they would euthanatize a healthy animal at the owner's request. Eighty-eight percent of seniors and 90% of veterinarians said they would euthanatize an animal that was severely injured but could be saved if the owner requested euthanasia.

Of 16 seniors who had at some time performed euthanasia on a client's pet, six (38%) had at some time wished they had not done so. Of the 30 veterinarians, 18 (60%) had at some time wished they had not euthanatized a client's pet.

Of 119 persons answering the question, 84% believed that the machine maintaining the life of a 21-year-old person with a flat electroencephalogram and almost no hope of recovery should be unplugged. Of 123 persons answering the question, 78% believed in capital punishment for first-degree murder.

PET LOSS AND HUMAN EMOTION STUDY

Dear _____:

The following set of questions is part of a study of the attitudes and reactions of practicing veterinarians and veterinary students towards human death, animal death, patient death, and euthanasia.

Completion of this questionnaire is voluntary. By its completion, you will be contributing to the understanding of the veterinarians' attitude towards grieving and patient death. Through studies like this, it is hoped that we will learn how to better support the grieving client and cope with our own reaction towards death. Your help is greatly appreciated.

Please answer all questions to the best of your ability. In describing real incidents, do not use real names: i.e., refer to Mrs. X, Mr. Y, the Z Veterinary Hospital. Do not sign your own name. If necessary, complete comments selections on the reverse sides of pages.

Abbreviations used in the questionnaire are as follows:

    Y=Yes   N=No   NA=Not applicable (e.g., cannot give opinion
                                        because have never euthanatized an animal).

Thank you for your time and co-operation.

Please return to:
Dr. S. Crowell-Davis, Anatomy and Radiology
or
Dr. T. Crowe, Small Animal Clinic

Thank you.

QUESTIONNAIRE

Following is a set of questions for evaluation of veterinarians' and students' reactions to death, animal death, patient death, and euthanasia. Please answer all questions to the best of your ability.

I. 1. Age: _____ yrs.
    2. Sex: F(1) _____ M(2) _____
    3. Marital status: *
        (1) single (never married) _____
        (2) married   _____
        (3) divorced   _____
        (4) widowed/widowered _____

* Check current status. If you are currently married but have previously lost or been separated from a spouse, note number of times on appropriate line.

4. Race (check one):
   (1) Caucasian_____   (4) American Indian_____
   (2) Black   _____   (5) Oriental   _____
   (3) Hispanic _____   (6) Other (Specify)   _____

5. Socioeconomic status of home in which you grew up: (check one):
   (1) below average _____
   (2) average   _____
   (3) above average _____

6. Current status in veterinary profession: (check one):
   (1) Pre-vet   _____
   (2) Freshman   _____
   (3) Sophomore   _____
   (4) Junior   _____
   (5) Senior   _____
   (6) Intern or 1st year in practice   _____
   (7) Resident or 2nd to 4th years of practice   _____
   (8) 5 to 10 years of practice   _____
   (9) 10 to 20 years of practice   _____
   (10) Over 20 years of practice   _____

7. Please answer 7A if you have not graduated from veterinary school and 7B if you have graduated.
   A) What type of work do you hope to enter (check one)?
      (1) mixed practice   _____
      (2) small animal practice   _____
      (3) large animal practice   _____
      (4) meat animal and/or dairy practice   _____
      (5) companion animal practice (small animal and equine) _____
      (6) equine practice   _____
      (7) other (specify)   _____
      (8) don't know   _____
   B) What type of work do you do (check one)?
      (9) mixed practice   _____
      (10) small animal practice   _____
      (11) large animal practice   _____
      (12) meat animal and/or dairy practice   _____
      (13) companion animal practice   _____
      (14) equine practice   _____
      (15) other (specify)   _____

8. If you are a graduated veterinarian in a specialty or training in a speciality, please check the appropriate speciality. Otherwise check NA.
      (1) NA   _____
      (2) Anesthesiology   _____
      (3) Critical Care (Emergency Care)   _____

(4) Surgery _____
(5) Internal Medicine _____
(6) Pathology _____
(7) Other (specify) _____

9. How many brothers did you grow up with? _____
10. How many sisters did you grow up with? _____
11. Majority of life has been spent in (check one).
    Rural Setting
    (1) Meat Animal Farm _____   (6) Other (Specify) _____
    (2) Horse Farm _____   (7)**Suburban**
    (3) Dairy Farm _____   Setting _____
    (4) Crop Growing Farm _____   (8) **Urban** _____
    (5) Hobby Farm _____   (9) Other (Specify) _____
12. Religion (check one):
    (1) Catholic _____   (6) Moslem _____
    (2) Protestant _____   (7) Agnostic _____
    (3) Jewish _____   (8) Atheist _____
    (4) Hindu _____   (9) Other (Specify) _____
    (5) Buddhist _____
13. Which of the following animals have you or your immediate
    family (in the same residence) owned? (Check as many as apply):
    (1) dog _____   (7) bird _____   (13) gerbil _____
    (2) cat _____   (8) fish _____   (14) hamster _____
    (3) horse _____   (9) snake _____   (15) guinea pig _____
    (4) cow _____   (10) frog _____   (16) Other (Specify) _____
    (5) goat _____   (11) turtle _____   (17) Other (Specify) _____
    (6) pig _____   (12) rabbit _____   (18) Other (Specify) _____
14. Which of the following animals have you had as pets that you had
    or have a close relationship with? (check as many as apply):
    (1) dog _____   (7) bird _____   (13) gerbil _____
    (2) cat _____   (8) fish _____   (14) hamster _____
    (3) horse _____   (9) snake _____   (15) guinea pig _____
    (4) cow _____   (10) frog _____   (16) Other (Specify) _____
    (5) goat _____   (11) turtle _____   (17) Other (Specify) _____
    (6) pig _____   (12) rabbit _____   (18) Other (Specify) _____
15. Which of the following animals have you had a close relationship
    with that you did not own?
    (1) dog _____   (7) bird _____   (13) gerbil _____
    (2) cat _____   (8) fish _____   (14) hamster _____
    (3) horse _____   (9) snake _____   (15) guinea pig _____
    (4) cow _____   (10) frog _____   (16) Other (Specify) _____
    (5) goat _____   (11) turtle _____   (17) Other (Specify) _____
    (6) pig _____   (12) rabbit _____   (18) Other (Specify) _____
16. Do you believe nonhuman animals are sentient? (conscious of
    their own identity)
    Y(1) _____   N(2) _____

17. Do you believe nonhuman animals have souls?
    Y(1)_____   N(2)_____
18. Do you believe in an afterlife for humans?
    Y(1)_____   N(2)_____
19. Do you believe in an afterlife for nonhuman animals?
    Y(1)_____   N(2)_____

II.   1. Do you remember the death of a member of your family?
    Y(1)_____   N(2)_____
2. If yes to 1, was it Mother (1)_____
                            Father (2)_____
                            Brother (3)_____
                            Sister (4)_____
                            Spouse (5)_____
                            Child (6)_____
                            Other (7)_____
    Comments: (your age, their age, cause of death, effect on you, effect on other members of the family)

3. If yes to 1., do you feel this had any effect on your selection of a career in veterinary medicine?
    Y(1)_____   N(2)_____
4. Do you remember the death of an animal you had a personal relationship with?
    Y(1)_____   N(2)_____
5. If yes to 4., did this have any short-term emotional effects on you?
    Y(1)_____   N(2)_____
    Comments:
6 If yes to 4., did this have any long-term emotional effects on you?
    Y(1)_____   N(2)_____
    Comments:

7. If yes to 4., do you feel this had any effect on your selection of career in veterinary medicine?
    Y(1)_____   N(2)_____
    If yes to 4., and you are a veterinarian, do you feel this (8-10):
8. affects how you practice veterinary medicine?
    Y(1)_____   N(2)_____
9. affects *how you care* for critically ill or injured patients?
    Y(1)_____   N(2)_____
    If yes, how?
10. affects *your attitude* towards critically ill or injured patients?
    Y(1)_____   N(2)_____
    If yes, how?

11. Do you remember the death of an animal you did not have a close emotional relationship with (e.g., a dog that had been hit by a car, a baby bird in the woods)?

    Y(1) _____   N(2) _____

    Briefly describe:

12. If yes to 11, did this have any short-term emotional effects on you?

    Y(1) _____   N(2) _____

    Comments:

13. If yes to 11, did this have any long-term emotional effects on you?

    Y(1) _____   N(2) _____

    Comments:

14. If yes to 11, do you feel this had any effect on your selection of a career in veterinary medicine?

    Y(1) _____   N(2) _____

    If yes to 11, and you are a veterinarian, do you feel this (15 to 17):

15. affects how you practice veterinary medicine?

    Y(1) _____   N(2) _____

    If yes, how?

16. affects how you care for critically ill or injured patients?

    Y(1) _____   N(2) _____

    If yes, how?

17. affects your attitude towards critically ill or injured patients?

    Y(1) _____   N(2) _____

    If yes, how?

18. A 21-year-old person is in the intensive care unit with his or her life being sustained by machine. The EEG is flat. Doctors give almost no hope for recovery.

    Should this machine be unplugged?

    Y(1) _____   N(2) _____

19. Do you believe capital punishment should be administered for first-degree murder?

    Y(1) _____   N(2) _____

20. Have you had any formal training in how best to explain to a client that a pet is terminally or critically ill?

    Y(1) _____   N(2) _____

21. Do you feel such training has been or would be useful in practice?

    Y(1) _____   N(2) _____

22. Please describe how you feel about death, in general.

23. Please describe how you feel about death in animals.

III. Refer to the following scenario to answer questions 1 to 3.

   An animal is presented to you that has a good to fair chance for recovery with intensive, extensive care (at least 4-6 hours of your time, immediately). The owner can afford to pay for it. Without your immediate care, the animal will most likely die.

1. Would you care for this animal if it came in at 8:00 a.m.?
   Y(1) _____   N(2) _____
2. Would you care for this animal if it came in at 5:00 p.m.?
   Y(1) _____   N(2) _____
3. Would you care for this animal if it came in at 1:00 a.m.?
   Y(1) _____   N(2) _____
   Comments: How would this affect you, your practice, your other services, and your other patients?

4. Have you ever wished you had not euthanatized a client's pet?
   Y(1) _____   N(2) _____
   Comments:

5. Has your euthanasia of a client's pet ever led to severe short-term emotional effects on that client or the client's family that you are aware of?
   Y(1) _____   N(2) _____
   If yes, please describe.
6. Has your euthanasia of a client's pet ever led to severe long-term emotional effects on that client or the client's family that you are aware of?
   Y(1) _____   N(2) _____
   If yes, please describe.

7. Has the death of an animal you were trying to save ever led to severe short-term emotional effects on the animal's owner or the owner's family that you are aware of?
   Y(1) _____   N(2) _____
   If yes, please describe.

8. Has the death of an animal you were trying to save ever led to severe long-term emotional effects on the animal's owner or the owner's family that you are aware of?
   Y(1) _____   N(2) _____
   If yes, please describe.

9. Would you euthanatize a healthy animal if the owner requested it?
   Y(1) _____   N(2) _____
10. Would you euthanatize a severely injured or terminally ill animal that was in pain without the owner's permission?
    Y(1) _____   N(2) _____
11. Would you euthanatize an animal that was severely injured but could be saved if the owner requested euthanasia?
    Y(1) _____   N(2) _____
12. Have you ever euthanatized an animal?
    Y(1) _____   N(2) _____
    If yes, check appropriate boxes in column A.

13. Have you ever had a patient die that you had been trying to save?
    Y(1) _____   N(2) _____
    If yes, check appropriate boxes in column B.

	A. after euthanatizing an animal	**B.** after an animal you have been trying to save has died
Have you ever		
felt a lump in your throat	14.	15.
cried	16.	17.
felt a need to be alone	18.	19.
had difficulty sleeping	20.	21.
yelled at someone	22.	23.
felt a need for an alcoholic drink	24.	25.
had an alcoholic drink	26.	27.
been depressed	28.	29.
felt angry	30.	31.
felt a sense of failure or inadequacy	32.	33.
felt a sense of relief	34.	35.

Comments:

28

Client Grief Following Pet Loss: Implications for Veterinary School Education

Walter E. Weirich

Veterinary schools have so far done little in their clinics to help people cope with the death of a pet, and are not routinely training new veterinarians in methods of dealing with the problem. In fact, most veterinarians actively avoid involvement with people at this difficult time. However, the way the veterinarian presents the information that the pet will die or should be euthanatized can profoundly affect how successfully the client will be able to work through this painful period.

The degree of attachment people feel for their pets has been appreciated by mental-health care providers only within the past decade. Pet owners and veterinarians now realize that a strong bond develops between certain people and their pets. When that bond is broken by the death of the pet, the owner's grief may be as intense as it would be if a human member of the family had died.

THE STUDY

This study was devised to determine what a group of clients whose pets had died or been euthanatized at the Small Animal Clinic at Purdue University felt about the way they were treated by the staff when the pet's death occurred.

One hundred people whose pets had died or been euthanatized within the past 12 months were sent a questionnaire. A copy of the cover letter and questionnaire are included as Appendices A and B. No selection was made other than to identify the most recent 100 hospital deaths prior to the date of the study.

The study was designed to collect anecdotal information and required the respondents to provide their answers in narrative form. It was hoped that this approach would least constrain the respondents and encourage them to express their thoughts in their own words. No statistical studies were done.

PURPOSE

The study was conducted to provide material for a new block of instruction currently being planned for fourth-year veterinary medical students. Information was sought to gain insight into what actions were most helpful to clients. If the activities of particular clinicians were identified as constructive, they might be studied and serve as role models for student emulation.

RESULTS AND INTERPRETATIONS

Thirty-five of 100 people returned the questionnaire for evaluation. Several causes might account for nonparticipation in the study. Some, perhaps worthy of consideration, are

1. Some people do not grieve intensely for their pets.
2. People still in the anger phase of grief might elect not to respond.
3. Some did not receive, lost, or did not have time to return the questionnaire.

Whatever the reason, 65 of the questionnaires were not returned.

The responses received revealed the following information:

1. Guilt is prevalent. Clients feel a great deal of guilt whenever their pet dies. Guilt appears to intensify with euthanasia because owners feel they are signing a death warrant. Many reported nagging questions in the form of "what if": "What if I had noticed the pet was sick earlier?" "What if I had taken the pet to the veterinarian earlier?" "What if I had asked for a second opinion earlier?" Most sought some kind of reassurance that they had done everything they could have done.

2. Clients wanted to be told the facts. They wanted to know what tests could be performed to define their pet's problems. Did these tests cause the animal discomfort or add to the morbidity? If they were informed by telephone that their animal had a fatal illness and would die, they wanted to talk rather than be alone with their own thoughts.

3. Several people stated that they appreciated a caring attitude on the part of the clinicians and students. They also thought the hospital rules had been suspended for them when they were allowed to visit their pet in the intensive care unit. Several people mentioned that students who had nothing to do with their pet seemed to know what was going on and stopped to call their pet by name and to talk.

4. Several people mentioned that they appreciated being informed of what was happening to their pet during its final illness.

5. Some clinicians and students created false hopes in the minds of their clients, making the death or the decision for euthanasia more difficult.

6. Clinicians were often mentioned as being helpful for two reasons: (1) they were very good at dealing with people and (2) they have had experience with cases in which the pets often die. These clinicians preferred to talk to people face-to-face, and spent 20 to 45 minutes explaining to clients that their pets should be euthanatized or would soon die. They demonstrated very clearly to the clients that they cared about the pet and about the owners.

APPENDIX A: COVER LETTER

Dear

Only recently has the significance of the human/companion-animal bond been appreciated by mental health authorities. People become very attached to their pets, a situation yielding many health benefits. But, when a pet dies or must be euthanatized (mercy killing), pet owners endure the same stages of grief that they would for a human member of their family.

It is now known that adults suffer grief over the loss of a pet that is as deep as that felt for the loss of a child. The example of the tough outdoorsman who loses a loyal and dedicated hunting companion is a case in point; the "tough guy" image is not shattered if he demonstrates his grief. It only means that he is a sensitive, caring, normal human being.

Practicing veterinarians have recognized for a long time the emotional trauma that people experience with the loss of a pet. Many veterinarians handle these situations very well; others are less well equipped psychologically to be of much help to their clients. Few schools of veterinary medicine offer any instruction to prepare their students to deal with this delicate and very human situation.

Your name was selected because your pet was seen at the Small Animal Clinic at Purdue University. Your pet died or was euthanatized at the clinic. Please forgive this intrusion into your private thoughts, but if the veterinary profession is to be helpful to our clients, we must know what they are going through. Attached is a questionnaire designed to obtain information on the grief you experienced with the loss of your pet; how the personnel at Purdue dealt with you at that time; and if they were helpful or not. This information will be used with other data to formulate specific blocks of instruction to help our students aid their clients through this difficult time.

I realize that what I am asking is not easy for you, but I hope you will fill out the questionnaire and return it in the envelope provided. You need not identify yourself. Thank you for your consideration of this important matter.

Sincerely yours,

(Signed)
Walter E. Weirich, D.V.M., Ph.D.
Director

APPENDIX B: QUESTIONNAIRE

1. How were you told of your pet's fatal illness and that your pet would die in a short time?
2. Did the manner in which you were told help you through the shock of hearing this bad news?
3. What could or should the veterinarian have done or said that would have helped you through this difficult time?
4. What was your immediate reaction?

5. Describe how your feelings changed later as attempts were made to keep your pet comfortable and prolong its life.
6. If you reached a decision for euthanasia (mercy killing), what did the Purdue veterinarians do that was helpful to you in reaching this difficult decision?
7. How could this situation have been handled better?
8. When your pet actually died or was euthanatized, how would you describe your feelings?
9. How did your feelings change and over what period of time did they change?
10. How did other members of your family who had a close relationship with the pet react?
11. What comments would you make that might be helpful to us but were not expressed in other parts of the questionnaire?

If you would prefer to discuss this with me on the telephone or see me personally, I would be pleased to talk with you. You may call me collect at _____.

29

Euthanasia in Laboratory Animal Medicine

Donald H. Clifford

Euthanasia of laboratory animals is a subject so charged with emotion as to make open and objective discussion difficult. In advocating "animal rights," certain organizations have taken a position that animals should not be used at all for teaching and research, or should be so used only as a last resort. One may accept the view that animals should not be used for teaching and research, but it logically follows that the individual who holds that opinion should also object to killing animals for food, clothing, and medical purposes, or using them for personal pleasure or sport.

DOUBLE STANDARDS

A double standard for euthanasia exists in much of society and in the laboratory setting. Restraint and exsanguination of animals (i.e., kosher killing) is accepted for religious purposes but taboo for laboratory research. Generally, minimal restrictions apply to the physical method of killing animals for food. Game wardens and zoo personnel face the problem of whether to kill injured or surplus animals by physical means for food, or by parenteral methods such as the injection of barbiturates, which may render the carcass inedible. A game warden may kill an injured deer, using a lethal dose of succinylcholine, which does not render the meat inedible. Both the culling of pups by drowning ("bucketing") by dog breeders and the wounding of wild animals in the

213

woods by hunters are tolerated with minimal protest, but these methods are prohibited in the laboratory.

New regulations have necessitated review and re-evaluation of many old and current techniques used to induce euthanasia. For example, physiologists have used potassium chloride to arrest anesthetized dogs' hearts in diastole. This chemical causes contraction of smooth, striated, and cardiac muscle. Many people view the resultant stiffening of the animal as unacceptable. The thought that euthanasia by potassium chloride causes pain, and should therefore be discontinued is untenable; the animals are already under anesthesia. A consensus maintains, however, that this technique should be reserved for situations in which it is specifically needed. The administration of a muscle relaxant prior to the lethal injection of potassium chloride is a different issue. In paralyzed animals, death should be produced by a more acceptable drug such as sodium pentobarbital.

CHANGING RULES

As in society generally, attitudes towards euthanasia among veterinarians, animal-care personnel, and investigators are changing. The everyday euthanatizing or killing animals for food takes place below society's threshold of awareness, while companion animals are commonly equated with children. Veterinarians and other personnel who are engaged in the care of animals in the laboratory, and who are required to euthanatize or kill animals, are frequently viewed with disfavor. Such attitudes produce stress, making work with animals in teaching and research institutions seem less desirable. In fact, laboratory-animal personnel may find themselves in quadruple jeopardy. They are: (1) criticized by humane groups for supporting teaching and conducting research with animals; (2) monitored by federal, state, private, and public agencies and organizations for the drugs and techniques they use and the care they provide; (3) reluctantly accepted by some administrators who view their efforts as a potential source of bad public relations and increasing cost; and (4) seen by many teachers and investigators as institutional vigilantes who are constantly trying to limit or change the use of animals in teaching and research. Thus, the traditional role of veterinarians and animal-care personnel as advisors to investigators, helpers, and spokespersons for animals is changing. The guilt and stress involved in euthanatizing animals are bearable only if society is honest, truthful, rational, and accepts the premise that a human life is more important than a nonhuman life. Support people and groups consisting of sociologists, psychologists, psychiatrists, and ministers are available to console and support grieving pet owners, but this need has not been well recognized for animal-care personnel who operate in the laboratory.

CRITERIA FOR EUTHANASIA

There is universal agreement that all animals that must be killed should be euthanatized or killed in a humane manner. Criteria for euthanasia of laboratory animals dictate that the process should be:

1. humane and unassociated with pain, fright, struggling, vocalization, or other signs of discomfort on the part of the animal
2. safe for the attending personnel
3. easy to perform
4. rapid
5. appropriate for the age, species, health, and number of the animals
6. esthetically acceptable to attending personnel
7. reliable and reproducible
8. irreversible
9. nonpolluting, or without an adverse environmental impact
10. without a great potential for drug abuse by associated personnel
11. economical
12. devoid of chemical changes in the tissues
13. without histopathological changes that would interfere with subsequent investigational studies
14. free of chemical deposits (*Guide for the Care and Use of Laboratory Animals* 1978) or burden on the animal.

Euthanasia should be performed by trained persons in accordance with institutional policies and applicable laws. The choice of method depends on the species of animal and the project at hand or the use of the animal. The method of inducing euthanasia should not interefere with postmortem examinations or other procedures. Approved procedures for euthanasia should follow guidelines recommended by the American Veterinary Medical Association (AVMA) Panel on Euthanasia (see page 235).

Animals of most species can be killed quickly and humanely by intravenous or intraperitoneal injection of a concentrated barbiturate solution. Mice, rats, and hamsters can be killed by cervical dislocation or

Table 1. Euthanasia methods. (1)

Category of Animal	Physical Methods												Parenteral Methods (1)										Inhalant Methods							
	Cervical Concussion(s)	Cervical Dislocation	Cranial Concussion	Decapitation	Decompression	Electrical Stunning	Electrocution	Exsanguination	Hypothermia	Pithing	Shooting-Bolt	Shooting-Bullet	Chloral Hydrate (4,5)	Chlorbutanol	Ketamine	Pentobarbital(6)	Potassium Chloride	Procaine	Succinylcholine(7)	T-61 (ml·kg)	Tricaine:MS 222	Urethane	Air	Carbon Dioxide	Carbon Monoxide	Ether	Exhaust-Motor	Halothane	Methoxyflurane	Nitrogen
A. Amphib. Fish Reptiles	Plus or minus other methods *	*	*					With other methods	*				*		IP 60 IT *		IP 0.5			PC 1-3 gm/l *	PC 1-2%		Chamber		*		*	*		
B. Birds	*	*	Objectionable to some people				With other methods		*						IP 100								Chamber		CO₂ is safer *		CO₂ is safer *	CO₂ is safer *		
C. Cats Dogs	Physical means are avoided unless preceded by anesthesia.													With other methods *	IP IV IT IC 90-100	Preceded by anesthesia		with other methods	IP IV IT IC 0.3 *				Chamber	Dangerous		Dangerous	*	*		
D. Ferrets Foxes Mink															IP 100								Chamber	Dangerous		Used on ranches			*	

(1) Adapted from Fox JG, Cohen BJ, Loew FM: *Laboratory Animal Medicine*, (Academic Press, 1984).

(2) Per cutaneous, PC; per orem, PO; subcutaneous, SC; Intralymphatic, IL; Intramuscular, IM; Intravenous, IV; Intracardiac, IC; and Intraspinal, IS; Intrathoracic, IT.

(3) Recommended and/or commonly used agents are capitalized.

(4) Maleate, hydrochloloride, sodium, etc. are omitted for clarity.

(5) Doses are in mg/kg unless designated otherwise.

(6) Barbiturates are considered collective under pentobarbital.

(7) Succinylcholine represents muscle relaxants.

* Consult Laboratory Animal Medicine for details.

N.B. Many agents are used in combination.

Table 1. (Continued)

CATEGORY OF ANIMAL	Physical Methods												Parenteral Methods (1)										Inhalant Methods							
	CERVICAL CONCUSSION(3)	CERVICAL DISLOCATION	CRANIAL CONCUSSION	DECAPITATION	Decompression	Electrical Stunning	Electrocution	Exsanguination	Hypothermia	Pithing	SHOOTING-BOLT	Shooting-bullet	Chloral Hydrate (4,5)	Chlorbutanol	Ketamine	PENTOBARBITAL(6)	Potassium Chloride	Procaine	Succinylcholine(7)	T-61 (ml-kg)	TRICAINE-MS 222	Urethane	Air	CARBON DIOXIDE	Carbon Monoxide	Ether	Exhaust-Motor	HALOTHANE	METHOXYFLURANE	Nitrogen
E. Non-Human Primates	Plus or minus other methods *	Plus or minus other methods *	Plus or minus other methods	Plus or minus other methods *	Physical means are avoided unless preceded by anesthesia.								IM SC. With other methods		IP IV 100							IV IV 5-50 ml/kg After anesthesia						Plus or minus other methods *	Plus or minus other methods *	
F. Rabbits	*		*					With other methods							IP IV IC 100								Chamber		*			*	*	
G. Rodents															IP IV IT IC 150–200								Chamber		*					
H. Ruminants					*	*		* With other methods		*	*				IP IV IT IC 100													*	*	
I. Swine					*			* With other methods		*			IM IV With other methods		IP IV IT IC 100								*							

by exposure to carbon dioxide in an uncrowded chamber. Ether and chloroform are also effective, but pose hazards to attending personnel: both are flammable and explosive, and chloroform is toxic and may be carcinogenic. If animals are killed by ether, special facilities and procedures must be available for storage and disposal of carcasses. Storage in a refrigerator that is not explosive-proof or disposal by incineration might result in a serious explosion. Notices indicating the use or presence of toxic or explosive agents should be conspicuously posted.

LISTING OF METHODS

The choice of agents and techniques for inducing euthanasia is an extremely important issue. The methods listed in Table 1, pages 216-217 have been simplified, abbreviated, and condensed. Many minor differences between species and techniques have been omitted from the table, but may be found in the parent text, *Laboratory Animal Medicine* (Fox, Cohen, and Loew 1984).

REFERENCES

Fox JG, Cohen BJ, and Loew FM (eds) Laboratory Animal Medicine. Orlando, FL: Academic Press, 1984
Guide for the Care and Use of Laboratory Animals. 1978. DHEW Publication No. (NIH) 78-23. Revised. Washington, DC: National Institutes of Health, Public Health Service, U.S. Department of Health, Education and Welfare

30

Euthanasia Agents and Methods

Donald C. Sawyer

Many factors must be considered in selecting the method of animal euthanasia. Most methods require some means of physical control over the animal, but the degree and type of restraint will vary. Determining factors include the species or breed of animal, whether wild or domesticated; the presence or absence of painful injury or disease; the method of euthanasia being considered; and the animal's degree of excitement. Suitable control is vital for satisfactory performance of euthanasia, to minimize the intensity and duration of pain that may be involved, to assure the safety of the person performing the task, and to protect other animals and people. The selection of a method will also depend on the skill of personnel, the number of animals to be euthanatized, and economic factors.

Several criteria are applied to evaluate methods of euthanasia in any given situation. The ability to produce death without causing pain is paramount. For pain to be experienced, the cerebral cortex and subcortical structures of the brain must be functional. In an unconscious animal, the cerebral cortex is not functional and, therefore, the animal does not experience pain. The time required to produce loss of consciousness must be as short as possible; the time required to produce death must also be brief. The method must be effective, reliable, safe, and must minimize any undesirable psychological stress on observers and operative personnel and on the animals involved. Economic factors must be considered and, if drugs are to be used, their availability and abuse potential must be evaluated. In association with research, the method must be compatible with macroscopic and microscopic tissue evaluation.

The methods or agents used for euthanasia terminate life by three basic means: (1) hypoxia, either directly or indirectly; (2) direct depression of neurons vital for life functions; and (3) physical damage to brain tissue.

Methods that deprive tissues of oxygen perform at different sites of action and with different rates of induction of unconsciousness. Muscle movement may be purposeful in response to a painful stimulus, while some motor activity may be only a side effect of the method used for euthanasia. On the other hand, curariform-type relaxants may produce flaccid muscle and no movement. Death eventually occurs because of hypoxia, since the animal cannot breathe, but the animal will remain conscious until cellular function is sufficiently depressed as a result of the lack of oxygen. Although the animal appears relaxed, it can still feel pain, and is stressed and frightened. Agents that do not produce unconsciousness prior to death must not be used alone for euthanasia.

INHALANT AGENTS

Volatile anesthetics such as diethyl ether, halothane, methoxyflurane, or nitrous oxide may be useful for small animals but are not recommended for larger animals because of cost and difficulty of administration. Chloroform can be used but, because of its extreme toxicity, strict safety precautions are required to prevent people from inhaling the gas. Other inhalant anesthetics such as isoflurone and enflurane will produce unconsciousness, but these agents are very expensive.

Nitrogen is an effective means if proper equipment is used, correctly maintained, and proficiently operated. Nitrogen not to be used for animals less than four months of age because young animals are more tolerant to hypoxia. An effective exhaust system is essential to prevent exposure of personnel to high concentrations of nitrogen. The disavantages of this technique are that it is not esthetically acceptable to observers; very young animals are not rapidly euthanatized; rapid nitrogen flow into the chamber may frighten animals and overcrowding may cause undesirable behavior of the animals. The use of nitrogen is prohibited by law in some areas.

Hydrogen cyanide is produced by immersing pellets of sodium cyanide in sulfuric acid. Cytotoxic hypoxia occurs when this gas is inhaled, leading to rapid death. It can be used under field conditions when other methods are impractical. Although rapid in its effect, this agent may cause violent seizures and muscle rigidity prior to death. The gas is irritating to lung tissue, resulting in responses that are objectionable to most observers. In addition, extreme danger from the highly toxic gas threatens the operator. For these reasons, other methods of euthanasia are preferable.

Carbon monoxide combines with hemoglobin to form carboxyhemoglobin, which blocks the uptake of oxygen by red blood cells and leads to fatal hypoxemia. This gas is effective for mass euthanasia and can be drawn from three different sources: (1) a by-product of the chemical interaction between sodium formate and sulfuric acid; (2) properly filtered and cooled exhaust fumes from idling gasoline engines; and (3) commercially available cylinders of compressed carbon monoxide. The advantages of this method are that carbon monoxide produces a rapid and painless death and that unconsciousness occurs without appreciable discomfort. Use for individual or mass euthanasia is acceptable for laboratory rodents, dogs, and cats, provided that strict precautions are followed to prevent discomfort to animals and hazards to personnel (McDonald et al. 1978).

Carbon dioxide can be purchased in cylinders as a compressed gas or in solid form as "dry ice." It is inexpensive, nonflammable, nonexplosive, and presents minimal hazard to the operator when used correctly and with properly designed equipment. In addition the use of carbon dioxide does not result in the accumulation of residues in the tissues of food-producing animals. Pure carbon dioxide is heavier than air, is nearly odorless and in high concentrations, usually has an anesthetic effect that takes place without incidents. Because the gas is heavier than air, adequate levels must be used to prevent climbing animals from avoiding exposure. Also, if dry ice is used, to avoid burns, the ice should not come in direct contact with the animals. This method is effective for use in small laboratory animals, small dogs, puppies, kittens, and cats. Carbon dioxide can also be used in combination with other agents such as carbon monoxide and inhalation anesthestics.

NONINHALANT AGENTS

Noninhalant pharmacologic agents can be administered by a variety of routes, but intravenous administration is the fastest and most reliable means of inducing death. If chemical restraint is required to control a frightened or vicious animal, the use of analgesics, tranquilizers, narcotics, ketamine, xylazine, or other depressants is advised. The combination of atropine, xylazine, and ketamine is effective for capture of free-ranging dogs when administered by a syringe propelled from a capture gun or blowgun. One milliliter of large-animal atropine (2 mg) is combined with 3 ml of xylazine (60 mg) and 1 ml of ketamine (100 mg). This mixture is introduced at a dose of 1 ml/20 lb, usually by the intramuscular route.

Long-acting barbiturates, primarily pentobarbital, are commonly used to produce unconsciousness within seconds. Breathing and heart function cease as a result of the profound depression produced by the drug. The speed of onset is a primary advantage, with minimal discomfort to the animal from the injection. The process of induction is similar to that in anesthesia, except that the amount of drug used will not allow recovery. The best results are produced by intravenous injection, which requires that the animal be restrained by trained personnel. Obviously the procedure is not suitable for very small animals. Current federal drug regulations require strict accounting for the use of barbiturates under the supervision of personnel registered with the U.S. Drug Enforcement Agency. The use of barbituric acid derivatives remains the preferred method of euthanasia of individual dogs, cats, and other small animals.

T-61 (National Laboratories, Somerville, NJ) is a mixture of a general anesthetic, a muscle relaxant, and a local anesthetic. Hypoxia occurs from circulatory collapse and nonreversible paralysis of skeletal muscle, which prevents spontaneous breathing; death follows as a result of severe central nervous system depression. If the drug is introduced too rapidly, the animal will experience pain or discomfort immediately before becoming unconscious. The recommended procedure, therefore, is to give two-thirds of the lethal dose slowly (0.2 ml/sec), then giving the balance more rapidly (1.2 ml/sec). If euthanasia is to be performed in the presence of an owner, a short-acting thiobarbituate may be used to induce anesthesia, followed by T-61 to produce death. Because of the muscle relaxant in T-61, the "last gasp" that occurs with barbiturates does not occur. T-61 is usually more expensive than barbiturates, but it is a suitable substitute when barbiturate derivatives cannot be used. However, it must be administered in recommended doses and at proper injection rates. If the dose is larger than recommended, pulmonary edema and other lung lesions may result, an important consideration when tissues are to be examined following euthanasia.

Chloral hydrate depresses the cerebellum slowly, and magnesium ions injected as magnesium sulfate act at myoneural junctions but exert little, if any, depression on the central nervous system. Used alone, neither of these drugs is recommended, but with pentobarbital added, the combination is particularly useful as a large-animal euthanatizing agent to be given intravenously.

Strychnine, nicotine, and the curariform drugs immobilize the animal and produce death by suffocation. Because the animal is fully conscious for a time prior to death, these drugs should not be used alone. Potassium ions cause immediate cardiac arrest but, again, consciousness persists for a period until hypoxemia is sufficient to produce unconsciousness.

PHYSICAL METHODS

Physical methods such as electrocution, gunshot, captive-bolt pistol, or a blow to the skull are esthetically offensive, but produce instant death when properly handled. Electrocution is humane only when special skills and equipment assure passage of sufficient current through the brain to produce unconsciousness, which is then followed by electrically induced cardiac arrest.

Rapid decompression is a satisfactory method of inducing hypoxia as a method of euthanasia, provided the equipment is properly constructed, adequately maintained, and proficiently operated. Therein lies the problem with this procedure: the equipment is costly to purchase and maintain. Because of these difficulties, other methods are preferable. Moreover, decompression-euthanasia is outlawed in many states.

Additional physical methods such as decapitation and microwave irradiation are used for euthanasia of poultry and small laboratory rodents. However, drowning or exsanguination without first producing unconsciousness is not recommended.

In summary, many factors are involved in the selection of rapid, effective, humane, and esthetically acceptable methods of euthanasia. As technology improves, better methods will undoubtedly be developed, but, it is hoped that the need for mass euthanasia will diminish in the future.

REFERENCES

McDonald LE, Booth HH, Lumb WV; Redding RW, Sawyer DC, Stevenson L, and Wass, WM: Report on the AVMA Panel on Euthanasia. J Amer Veter Medical Association 173:59-72, 1978

Smith CR, Booth NH, Fox NH, Fox MW, et al. Report of the AVMA Panel on Euthanasia. J Amer Veter Medical Association 160:761-772, 1972

31

Animal Disposal: Fact and Fiction

David C. Cooke

Man's infatuation with animals has been a long-term affair going back many thousands of years. Early proof of the human/companion-animal bond is evidenced by the elaborate burials of dogs in Peking, China and the mummified remains of the cats of Luxor in Egypt. Even in America, a recent archaeological excavation at the Koster site in Southern Illinois indicates that dogs had been buried with ritual significance as long ago as 7000 years.

During the past decade, with increasing interest in the human/companion-animal bond, literally hundreds of reasons to justify pet ownership have been discovered and are being studied. In almost any situation, having a pet seems good. Prisons use them, nursing homes use them. The physically handicapped and the mentally retarded benefit from pets. Disturbed children and normal children learn from pet ownership. Pets can be beneficial companions for the elderly, the lonely, the rich, the young, the poor, the educated or uneducated. The unconditional love of a pet is the great equalizer of humans.

As our pets play a role of acknowledged significance in modern lives, we also encounter problems of unique complexity as a result. Man's emotional dependence on pets reinforces the humanization of animals. Their recognized acceptance as family members has been cause for some rapid and radical reassessment on the part of many observers of this social phenomenon. Do animals have souls? Do animals have rights? Do animals increase in value beyond their intial cost or reproductive potential by involvement in a bonded relationship with a human who could not conceive of any monetary value as compensation for the loss of the relationship? These and many other questions are changing public attitudes concerning pet care and pet owner care.

Many aspiring veterinarians might well choose another profession if they were aware of the possible moral, ethical and legal challenges they will face as a result of the increasingly difficult and complex relationship between pets and people. The prospect of performing euthanasia on a loved pet, with all of the attendant emotional possibilities, must be a chore that most veterinarians would rather not encounter. The veterinarian who performs euthanasia on a loved pet does so, increasingly, within a context resembling that of the death of a human, wherein the responsibility is shared by doctor, psychologist, family, mortician, funeral director, cemeterian and clergyman.

In a 1981 interview, James Harris, DVM, was asked why many veterinarians would resist the suggestion that they spend time counseling or attending to the needs of pet owners. Dr. Harris replied, "I've heard the remark 'I became a veterinarian because I don't want to deal with people, I want to work with animals,' more times than I can count. I'm afraid this is the attitude of many veterinarians. Unfortunely there is no sensitivity training in veterinary schools; in fact, the high-pressure, high-volume atmosphere of medical education is quite dehumanizing." (Harris 1981)

In addition to the fact that there is no "sensitivity training" in veterinary schools, however, there is also no training concerning methods for the final disposition of pet bodies. This aspect of pet loss is also left up to the individual practitioner to learn by trial and error.

When discussing euthanasia within the context of the human/companion-animal bond, it is important to acknowledge that mortality in every case is accompanied by the responsibility for arranging the final disposition of the pet's body. Every pet that dies creates a disposal problem for someone, whether the death is natural, accidental or by euthanasia.

What are the pet animal disposal options?

    1. Burying
        a. sanitary landfill along with public refuse and garbage
        b. mass burial (trench burial) on a farm
        c. backyard burial
        d. pet cemetery
    2. Burning
        a. municipal incinerator along with public refuse and garbage
        b. mass incineration in pathological incinerator
        c. individual cremation
    3. Rendering into dog, cat, livestock food and by-products
    4. Miscellaneous
        a. dumping out or burial on public or private lands
        b, sewer (small pets and fish, etc.)

In many people/pet relationships the pet is treated as a human; however, the similarity ends at death. Although there are very specific rules and regulations governing the disposal of human remains which limit the options to cremation, interment or above-ground intombment, there are no regulations governing the disposal of animal bodies.

Over the years, the veterinary profession has assumed the role of responsibility for the disposition of animal bodies. In the past there was little problem, especially in suburban and rural areas, in locating a farmer who would be willing to bury pets in some remote corner of his farm. Many veterinary hospitals buried pets on their own property or used small incinerators to cremate the remains. Since fewer pets existed then, and those that did exist seldom enjoyed the same place in the family that today's pets do, there was not as much concern over the disposition of the body.

Today's methods of animal disposal are undergoing change as a result of stricter environmental regulations. In some areas of the country, municipal incinerators, landfills and town dumps have been repositories for dead pets. As we know, especially in and around urban areas these municipal waste facilities are fast being closed because of their polluting side effects. The New York/New Jersey metropolitan area is a prime example. In addition, most sanitary landfills are fast being replaced by resource recovery plants. I doubt that animal carcasses will have a place among the glass, paper, plastic and metal recoverable-waste categories.

Most of the incinerators used by veterinary hospitals have either burned out or been closed by the EPA because of strict clean-air regulations. Replacement has been nonexistent because of the prohibitive cost of new equipment. Moreover, it is little known that most pathological incinerators, supposedly capable of consuming large volumes of waste, just don't work. Animal carcasses melt before they burn, and equipment manufacturers haven't been able to resolve the problem of containing the fat until it is consumed. This, along with problems of conforming to clean air requirements, not to mention equipment and fuel costs, has had a negative effect on the development of new and functional equipment.

Several years ago the U.S. Government considered classifying veterinary hospital waste as infectious waste, which would have required incineration as a means of disposal (EPA 1980). It was never clear as to whether animal carcasses would have been included in this classification; however, proper incineration would have been impossible to achieve in either case because the equipment to carry out the job doesn't exist.

As concern over waste-disposal methods in this country increases, resulting in closer scrutiny of waste facilities and strict enforcement of rules governing them, our growing pet population is creating a disposal problem of its own. Dr. Alan Beck (1984) states, "More than 20 million unwanted pets are sent to animal shelters to be killed each year." According to pet-cemetery industry figures, the average weight of a pet dog or cat is 40 lb. This means that shelters alone are faced with the disposal of 400,000 tons of euthanatized animal bodies each year, not to mention additional millions of animals that die naturally and accidentally that must also be disposed of. Veterinarians euthanatize an additional 10 million pets, creating another 200,000 tons requiring disposal.

Landfills, dumps and municipal incinerators are steadily being phased out, leaving only one major option for the disposal of America's animals. They are being recycled (cooked) at rendering plants across the nation. The process begins with the animal bodies passing through a hammer-mill which crushes the bones and chops the carcasses up before being mixed with animal waste from butcher shops, meatpacking firms, and slaughterhouses.

The byproducts of the cooking process are bone meal, meat meal and tallow.

Lee Benning, in "The Pet Profiteers," cites a Chicago Tribune Co. 1973 report, confirmed by a pet food company spokesman, that 15% of dry pet food consists of rendering-company by-products.

A pet-food company spokesman said that pet-food labels generally list rendering-industry by-products as "meat by-products" without indicating the type of meat.

The fatty acids are used in hand cream, bath soap, lipstick, shampoo and rinses, mascara, shaving soap, bath oil and baby toiletries.

Feed grain for livestock contains the rendered meal and tallow (Benning 1976).

Although a *Time* article recently indicated that the pet food industry was running out of horse meat, it appears that there are plenty of dogs and cats to take up the slack.

According to 1984 pet-food company pamphlet, describing pet-food packaging nomenclature, regulations by the Association of American Feed Control Officials (AAFCO) govern pet-food labeling in most states. Their definition of meat meal and meat-and-bone meal is, "the dry rendered product from mammal tissues, exclusive of hair, hoof, horn, and hide trimmings, manure and stomach contents, except in such amounts as may occur unavoidably in good factory practice" (Alpo 1984). Can you imagine trying to remove the hair and stomach contents from 600,000 tons of dogs and cats prior to cooking them? It would seem that either the AAFCO definition of meat meal and meat-and-bone meal should be redefined, or it should include a better description of "good factory practice."

Although millions of America's deceased pets are being cooked and processed into pet food, most pet owners don't realize this fact. Does this raise questions of ethics that should be answered by the veterinary profession and the pet food industry?

Consider the introduction of dogs and cats into the human food chain by way of livestock food made from rendered by-products. What happens to all of those toxic products that we use so liberally on our pets? Flea and tick poisons on the pets' coats, heartworm medication, antibiotics, euthanasia materials, and a myriad of other chemicals all go into the rendering process. I wonder if anyone has ever taken the trouble to see if these materials survive the rendering process and become part of the hog and chicken food eaten by animals which we in turn ingest?

Many of the articles and studies concerning pet loss and euthanasia end abruptly with the death of the pet or with an allusion to the idea that the pet was cremated or buried in a pet cemetery. Not only pet owners, but non-veterinary professionals (psychologists, psychiatrists, and social workers) studying pet loss euthanasia and the H/CAB, would have no way of knowing the truth about the disposal of pets in the U.S. Even veterinary associations are apparently not aware of the enormity of the situation.

According to Riise, "Nine out of 10 people, when questioned on the subject, do not know what happens to a deceased pet when it is left with the veterinarian, or they dismiss the question with some variation of 'The vet takes care of it'." (Riise 1981)

In a 1984 *Los Angeles Times* article, Herbert Vida quotes Don Mahan, Executive Director of the Southern California Veterinary Medical Association: "This closer attachment to a pet in modern society makes it more important for an owner to be informed of the options for disposal of the animal. People now are thinking they should at least give it a decent burial. Discussing the disposal of the pet has always been difficult for veterinarians," adds Mahon, who noted that while the association has always urged pet doctors to face the issue head-on, many still sidestep the question. The article continues: "The harsh truth is that pets not buried or cremated are usually sent to disposal plants for rendering and, in the past, an owner who left his dead pet at a veterinarian's office was not aware what happened to its remains" (Vida 1984).

Since there are no laws applying to the disposal of pet animals; and since the veterinary profession has, de facto, assumed responsibility for arranging for final disposition for most pets; and in consideration of increasingly restrictive disposal problems and changing attitudes on the part of pet owners, it seems appropriate that the AVMA and the AAHA, along with individual state Veterinary Medical Societies, now consider adopting guidelines and standards for pet disposal. It also seems appropriate for veterinary schools to provide students information on principles of proper pet disposal along with sensitivity training.

The Professional Animal Disposal Advisory Council (PADAC) has suggested "Disposition Procedures for Pets" to the American Animal Hospital Association for consideration. The recommended procedures are included at the end of this chapter.

Most professionals who have studied pet loss indicate that proper after-death care is a positive and desirable conclusion.

"While pet cemeteries have been ridiculed, they can provide an important function, especially for families who have no backyard to bury their pet in. Ritual burial is part of the individuation and self-healing from the loss of a loved one, as well as a symbol of respect and appreciation" (Fox 1981).

"More or less elaborate burials, even the use of special pet cemeteries, may help owners cope with the loss of an animal companion" (Levinson 1981).

"Among the most important non-medical duties of the veterinarian: to assist in the viewing or disposition of the animal's remains, in accordance with the client's wishes" (Antelyes 1981).

"The owner should be allowed to remain with the pet until he is assured that it is indeed dead, and his wishes about disposal of the body should be scrupulously respected" (Holzworth 1981).

Contrary beliefs notwithstanding, most pet owners, when asked, do care about what happens to their pet's body. At the time of euthanasia they may be intimidated by their own emotions, embarrassed, and have difficulty making rational decisions. Ideally, pet owners should be given disposal-option descriptions in writing, preferably in advance of the euthanasia, to avoid having to make disposal decisions at that time.

I have not mentioned pet cemeteries before this because only a tiny percentage of pets ever make it to a pet cemetery. As of August 1984, pet-cemetery industry figures indicated that there were only 351 operating pet cemeteries in the U.S. Approximately 200,000 pets were handled by pet cemeteries in 1983, a tiny percentage of the many millions of pets in our country. Seven states have no pet cemeteries at all. The chart accompanying this chapter shows numbers of pet cemeteries per state, along with population figures and numbers of veterinarians. As of this writing, it has been impossible to make any correlation between the population, numbers of veterinarians and numbers of pet cemeteries.

The casual observer might think that veterinarians and pet cemeterians would work together to satisfy the needs of grieving pet owners. For some reason this does not happen. I have met and talked to hundreds of pet cemeterians and only a few have indicated a good working relationship with their local veterinarians. This is unfortunate, since most pet cemeterians are sincere, caring people who are experts in the field of pet loss. Use of this resource by veterinarians would transfer much of the emotional burden of euthanasia out of the hospital.

Since becoming Executive Director of the International Association of Pet Cemeteries, Wendell Morse, DVM, has made significant progress in establishing a dialogue between the pet-cemetery industry and the veterinary profession. Creation of a rapport between these two groups can help to ease a burden long assumed by veterinarians alone.

In March 1984, James Quackenbush, in an address to the IAPC, pointed out the difference in value of the relationship between pet owner and pet cemeterian as peers from that of a professional relationship where seeker (pet owner) and giver (veterinarian) are not equal. Mr. Quackenbush observed that the death of a pet occurs in a no-man's land, surrounded by ambivalence. The pet, although not a person, is a family member, and its loss is an occasion for mourning. He indicated the importance of a pet cemeterian as providing more than a business service by understanding and answering the pet owner's needs, by talking, listening and being supportive on both the manifest and latent levels (Quackenbush 1984).

In a 1972 opinion, the AVMA, in its Principles of Veterinary Medical Ethics, says: "The veterinarian who renders a disposal, burial or cremation service should take special care to avoid the impression that veterinarians are caretakers of the quick and the dead. There is potential for unfavorable public relations and questions of ethics when the healer is in a position to profit from the disposition of deceased patients.

In as much as the pet-owning public views burial and cremation in terms of human reference, these services, when rendered for pet animals, should be fully explained so that the differences, if any, will be understood and the client will not be deceived" (AVMA 1984).

The International Association of Pet Cemeteries is currently establishing an Educational Foundation for the purpose of studying pet-animal disposal methods and their legal, moral and ethical implications. One of the foundation's continuing efforts will be to provide information to the public concerning these matters.

It is hoped that representatives of the pet-cemetery industry will someday routinely be consulted by veterinary associations and included in such organizations as the Delta Society and others dealing with pet loss and with the human/companion-animal bond.

The Fall 1984 issue of *People, Animals, Environment: The Bulletin of The Delta Society*, contained a touching article by Dr. Leo Bustad, entitled, "A Liturgy for the Burial of Pets," which describes a ceremony for pet burial written by Richard York for Dr. James Harris. Drs. Bustad and Harris should be commended for their forthright attitudes on the "rightness" of the burial ceremony as consolation for the bereaved pet owner.

Someday, perhaps all bereaved pet owners will be given the opportunity to express their feelings of loss, including the option to freely choose a burial or cremation for their pet without embarrassment.

SUMMARY

Rapidly changing environmental regulations are reducing the number of ways in which pet animal bodies can be disposed of. The emerging reality is that rendering (cooking) may soon be the only disposal method available to veterinarians. These facts mandate that pet owners routinely be given full disclosure options concerning the final disposition of their pets.

Use of the resources offered by pet cemeteries can be of value in alleviating the emotional distress of euthanasia and pet loss within the veterinary practice.

TABLE 1
Pet Cemeteries, Veterinarians, and Human Population by State

	Cemeteries	Veterinarians	Human Population (in Thousands)
Alabama	4	603	3,943
Alaska	0	92	438
Arizona	2	475	2,860
Arkansas	3	343	2,291
California	13	3,401	24,724
Colorado	3	898	3,045
Connecticut	4	382	3,153
Delaware	0	76	602
District of Columbia	0	69	631
Florida	35	1,582	10,416
Georgia	8	833	5,639
Hawaii	1	111	994
Idaho	0	264	965
Illinois	16	1,559	11,448
Indiana	12	947	5,471
Iowa	5	1,125	2,905
Kansas	2	701	2,408
Kentucky	3	562	3,667
Louisiana	3	610	4,362
Maine	0	167	1,133

(continues)

TABLE 1 (continued)
Pet Cemeteries, Veterinarians, and Human Population by State

	Cemeteries	Veterinarians	Human Population (in Thousands)
Maryland	17	838	4,265
Massachusetts	8	601	5,781
Michigan	24	1,327	9,109
Minnesota	3	940	4,133
Mississippi	2	335	2,551
Missouri	10	908	4,951
Montana	1	248	801
Nebraska	3	471	1,586
Nevada	2	167	881
New Hampshire	1	167	951
New Jersey	4	807	7,438
New Mexico	1	233	1,359
New York	20	1,726	17,659
North Carolina	8	789	6,019
North Dakota	1	135	670
Ohio	22	1,427	10,791
Oklahoma	4	735	3,177
Oregon	3	500	2,649
Pennsylvania	40	1,303	11,865
Rhode Island	0	70	958
South Carolina	7	298	3,203
South Dakota	0	202	691
Tennessee	8	674	4,651
Texas	15	2,605	15,280
Utah	2	170	1,558
Vermont	1	134	516
Virginia	14	813	5,491
Washington	3	872	4,245
Wisconsin	9	1,005	4,765
West Virginia	4	160	1,948
Wyoming	0	146	502

TOTAL PET CEMETERIES: 351 (Hoegh Industries, Gladstone, Michigan)
TOTAL VETERINARIANS: 35,606 (1984 AVMA Directory)
TOTAL HUMAN POPULATION: 231,534,000 (Nat'l. Data Book & Guide To Sources; US Dept. Of Commerce, 1984)
TOTAL DOG & CAT POPULATION: 107,000,000 (1984 AVMA Directory)

Professional Animal Disposal Advisory Council
Suggested Standards
Proposed to
The American Animal Hospital Association

DISPOSITION PROCEDURES FOR DECEASED PETS

The recognition of the importance of the human/companion-animal bond as it relates to the veterinary profession, has mandated changes in methods of disposing of pet animal carcasses. Recent legal decisions make it especially important to provide pet owners with a complete description of their options. In view of the fact pet owners view the final disposition of their pets in terms of human reference, it is important the attending veterinarian avoid the responsibility of providing the disposal options whenever possible. Pet disposal services should be turned over to outside contractors whenever possible, in order to avoid implications that veterinarians are purveyors of these services.

Since pet disposal options available to veterinarians vary throughout the country, it is impossible to establish a uniform national disposal procedure; however, the following guidelines will cover most situations when followed as described.

The Guidelines

1. Acceptable methods of pet disposition
   a. Burial (individual or group)
   b. Cremation (individual or group)

In areas where these services are not available, other legal, but less acceptable means of disposition, such as landfills, or rendering may be used.

2. Outline of suggested disposition procedures
   a. A full-disclosure consent form, in triplicate, to be signed by the client,

should be used in all hospitals, relieving the veterinarian of future legal ramifications by describing the pet disposition options offered.

b. In the case where a post-mortem has been performed, closure of the body cavity is strongly recommended.

c. All needles, pacemakers, IV tubes, etc., must be removed.

d. The body should be sealed in a sturdy plastic bag, of sufficient size and strength to contain the entire pet and its body fluids.

e. The body must be properly identified and stored in a freezer.

f. Pets known to have diseases which could be contagious to man and/or other pets, must be identified as such, and should be cremated in accordance with EPA recommendations on the handling of veterinary infectious waste.

REFERENCES

Alpo: If Rover Could Read, Alpo Pet Center, Allentown, PA

Antelyes J: When the pet animal dies, Arch Foundation of Thanatology 9:2, 1981

AVMA Directory, Principles of Veterinary Medical Ethics, Section 3: Guidelines for Professional Conduct, p 413, 1984

Beck A: Family Pet, 131:1 (Spring) p 9, 1984

Benning L: The Pet Profiteers, Quadrangle/The New York Times Book Co., p 189, 1976

Bustad, L: A liturgy for the burial of pets. People, Animals, Environment: Bulletin of the Delta Society 2:2 (Fall 1984)

DVM: EPA recommendations on hospital waste are criticized by AVMA, DVM Magazine, June 1983

EPA: Rules and regulations, Federal Register, 45:98, p 33087, 1980

Fox MW: Pet animals and human well being, in Pet Loss and Human Bereavement, Iowa State Univ Press, 1984

Harris JM: Companion animal practitioner treats pet owners as well as pets, The Latham Letter, 1:2, Winter 1981

Holzworth J: Easing grief over loss of a pet, Archives of The Foundation of Thanatology 9:2, 1981

Levinson BM: Human grief on the loss of an animal companion, Arch Foundation of Thanatology 9:2, 1981

Quackenbush J: Grief Counseling Presentation to the International Association of Pet Cemeteries, Philadelphia, Pa., March 27, 1984

Riise JA: Pet cemeteries—Here is a look past the myths at a viable, valuable industry, Dog Fancy, Nov 1981

Vida HJ: Eternal paws, The Los Angeles Times, Sept 17, 1984

Appendix: Report of the AVMA Panel on Euthanasia

Reprinted with permission from the Journal of the American Veterinary Medical Association, Vol 188, No. 3, 1986, Pages 252-268.

PREFACE

In 1984, at the request of the AVMA Council on Research, the Executive Board of the AVMA appointed a Panel on Euthanasia consisting of six veterinarians and one public representative. The purpose of the panel was to review and update the third Panel Report published in 1978.[1] Since 1978 the panel has become aware of a need for additional information on some aspects of euthanasia. In this report the panel has expanded the information on research uses of animals wherein euthanasia is required, on public disposal of surplus animals, and on slaughter of food animals. The panel is aware that there are euthantizing methods and agents not discussed, but has limited this report to those methods and agents supported by reliable information. The report will be targeted primarily to veterinarians, but will be understandable to a broad segment of the general population. Although the interpretation and use of this panel report cannot be limited, the panel would remind all who refer to it that our overriding commitment is to give professional guidance for relieving the pain and suffering of animals.

INTRODUCTION

Euthanasia is the act of inducing painless death. Criteria to be considered for a painless death are: rapidly occurring unconsciousness and unconsciousness followed by cardiac or respiratory arrest. The distress experienced by people when observing euthanasia or death in any form is an emotional response dependent on the background of the observer. Kinship of people with higher animals, however distant, serves to transfer the unpleasant reaction to human death to death of animals. Such distress occurs even though the observer experiences no physical pain. This distress may be minimized by perfection of the technique of euthanasia. Although not an adequate criterion, observers may mistakenly relate any movement with consciousness and lack of movement with unconsciousness. Techniques in which animals being euthanatized exhibit little or no movement are the most aesethetically acceptable to most people.

Pain must be defined before criteria for a painless death can be established. Pain is that sensation (perception) that results from nerve impulses reaching the cerebral cortex via specific neural pathways called nociceptive pathways. The term nociceptive is derived from noxious stimuli. Noxious stimuli threaten to, or actually do, destroy tissue. They initiate nerve impulses by acting upon a specific set of receptors, called nociceptors. Nociceptors respond to excessive mechanical, thermal, or chemical energies. Endogenous chemical substances such as hydrogen ions, serotonin, histamine, bradykinin, and prostaglandins as well as electrical currents are capable of generating nerve impulses in nociceptors.

Nerve impulse activity generated by nociceptors is conducted to the spinal cord or the brainstem via nociceptor primary afferent fibers. Within the spinal cord or the brainstem the nerve impulses are transmitted to two sets of neural networks. One set is related to nociceptive reflexes and the second set consists of ascending pathways to the reticular formation, thalamus, and cerebral cortex for sensory processing. The transmission of nociceptive neural activity is highly variable. Under certain conditions, both the nociceptive reflexes and the ascending pathways may be suppressed, as, for example, in deep surgical anesthesia. In another set of conditions, nociceptive reflexes may occur, but the activity in the ascending pathways is suppressed; thus the noxious stimuli are not perceived as pain, as, for example, in light surgical anesthesia. It is incorrect to use the term pain for stimuli, receptors, reflexes, or pathways because the term implies perception whereas all of the above may be active without consequential pain perception.[2-6] Pain is divided into two broad categories: (a) sensory-discriminative, which indicates the site of origin and the energy source giving rise to the pain; and (2) motivational-affective in which the severity of the stimulus is perceived and the animal's response is determined. Sensory discriminative processing of nociceptive impulses is most likely to be accomplished by brain mechanisms similar to those utilized for processing of other sensory discriminative input that provides the individual with information about the intensity, duration, location, and quality of the stimulus.

Motivational-affective processing involves the ascending reticular formation for behavioral and cortical arousal. It also involves thalamic input into both the forebrain and the limbic system for perceptions such as suffering, fear, anxiety, and depression. The motivational-affective neural networks also have strong inputs into the hypothalamus and the autonomic nervous system for reflex activities of the cardiovascular, pulmonary, and hypophyseal adrenal systems. Responses activated by these systems feed back into the forebrain and enhance the perceptions derived via motivational-effective inputs. Based upon neurosurgical experience in people, it is possible to separate the sensory-discriminative components from motivational-affective components of pain.[3] On an anatomic basis, it would appear that in animals the sensory-discriminative pathways are smaller, compared with that of people, whereas motivational-affective pathways are more numerous and more diverse in animals.[3,7] Some have speculated that animals need, more than human beings, the motivational-affective input to warn them of impending danger.

For pain to be experienced, the cerebral cortex and subcortical structures must be functional. An unconscious animal cannot experience pain because the cerebral cortex is not functioning. If the cerebral cortex is rendered nonfunctional by any means such as hypoxia, depression by drugs, electric shock, or concussion, pain is not experienced.

Stimuli that might evoke pain in a conscious animal may elicit only reflex responses manifested by movement in an unconscious animal. For this reason, nonpurposeful movements of an animal are not reliable indicators of pain perception. Conversely, an animal can experience pain, even though no body movements occur in response to noxious stimuli, if the animal is given muscle-paralyzing agents such as curare, succinylcholine, gallamine, pancuronium, nicotine, or decamethonium. These muscle paralyzing agents do not induce unconsciousness or depress the cerebral cortex or any neural mechanism involved in pain perception.

As with other procedures applied to animals, euthanasia requires some physical control over the animal. The degree of control and kind of restrain needed will be determined by the animal species, breed, size, state of domestication, presence of painful injury or disease, degree of excitement, and method of euthanasia. Suitable control is vital to minimize pain in animals, to assure safety of the person performing euthanasia, and, frequently, to protect other animals and people.

Selection of the most appropriate method of euthanasia in any given situation is dependent on species of the animal involved, available means of animal control, skill of personnel, numbers of animals, economic factors, and other considerations. This report deals primarily with domestic animals, but the same humane considerations should be applied to all species.

BEHAVIORAL CONSIDERATIONS

The facial expressions and body postures that indicate various emotional states have been described.[8-10] Behavioral and physiologic responses to noxious stimulation include distress vocalization, struggling, attempts to escape, defensive or re-directed aggression, salivation, urination, defecation, evacuation of anal sacs, pupillary dilatation, tachycardia, sweating, and reflex skeletal muscle contractions causing shivering, tremors, or other muscular spasms. Some of these responses can occur in unconscious as well as conscious animals. Fear can cause immobility or freezing in certain species, particularly rabbits and chickens. This immobility response should not be interpreted as unconsciousness when the animal is, in fact, conscious.[10]

In very young animals, autonomic and reflexive reactions are evident, although overt behavioral reactions may differ from those of adults.

The need to minimize fear and apprehension must be considered in determining the method of euthanasia. Distress vocalizations, fearful behavior, and release of certain odors or pheromones by a frightened animal may cause anxiety and apprehension in others. Therefore, whenever possible, animals should not observe euthanasia of others, especially of their own species. This is particularly important when vocalization or release of pheromones may occur during induction of unconsciousness. Gentle restraint, preferably in a familiar environment, careful handling, and talking during euthanasia often have a calming effect on companion animals. However, some of these methods may not be operative with wild animals or animals that are injured or diseased. Where capture or restraint may cause pain, injury, or anxiety to the animal or danger to the operator, the use of tranquilizing or immobilizing drugs may be necessary.

Animals for food or fur should be euthanatized as specified by the United States Department of Agriculture.[11] Painless death can be achieved by stunning the animal before exsanguination. Animals must not be restrained in painful positions before slaughter. Preslaughter handling should be as stress-free to the animals as possible. The use of electric prods or other devices to encourage movement of animals should be eliminated. Proper design of chutes and ramps enables animals to be moved into restraining chutes without undue stress.[12,13]

The ethical and psychologic issues involved with euthanasia of diseased, injured, or unwanted animals is within the purview of this discussion. Moral and ethical imperatives associated with individual or mass animal euthanasia should be consistent with acceptable humane practice. In all circumstances, choice of method should be selected and employed with the highest ethical standards and social conscience. Many issues involving diseased, injured, or unwanted animals and the need for euthanasia have been addressed in conferences cosponsored by AVAM.[14,15]

Distress may occur among personnel directly involved in performing repetitive euthanasia of diseased, injured, or unwanted animals. At the point of terminating the life of an animal, we should be prepared not only to treat the animal but also to consider the people attached to the animal.[16] Constant exposure to or participation in euthanasia procedures can cause a psychologic state characterized by a strong sense of work dissatisfaction or alienation, which may be expressed by absenteeism, belligerence, or careless and callous handling of the animals.[17] This is one of the principal reasons for turnover of employees directly involved with repeated performance of animal euthanasia. This should be recognized as a bona-fide personnel problem related to animal euthanasia, and management measures should be instituted to decrease or eliminate the potential for this condition.

MODES OF ACTION OF EUTHANATIZING AGENTS

Euthanatizing agents terminate life by three basic mechanisms: (1) hypoxemia, direct or indirect; (2) direct depression of neurons vital for life function; and (3) physical damage to brain tissue (Table 1).

Agents that produce death by direct or indirect hypoxia can act at various sites and can cause different times of onset of unconsciousness. With some agents, unconsciousness may occur prior to cessation of motor activity (muscle movement). Thus, even though animals demonstrate muscular contractions, they are not perceiving pain. The uninformed observer may find this difficult to accept.

Conversely, muscle relaxants induce a flaccid muscular paralysis and the animal remains conscious until death eventually occurs as a result of hypoxemia and hypercapnea. While the animal appears relaxed, it is actually in a state of panic and can feel pain. Outwardly this would appear to be an ideal form of euthanasia, but it is not. Agents that do not induce rapid loss of consciousness prior to death include: curare, succinylcholine, gallamine, nicotine, magnesium or potassium salts, pancuronium, decamethonium, and strychnine. *Use of any of these agents alone for euthanasia is absolutely condemned.*

The second group of euthanatizing agents depresses nerve cells of the brain first, blocking apprehension and pain perception, followed by unconsciousness and death.

Some of these agents "release" muscle control during the first stage of anesthesia, resulting in a so-called "excitement or delirium phase," during which

TABLE 1 — Mode of action of euthanatizing agents

	Site of action	Classification	Comments
HYPOXIC AGENTS			
Carbon monoxide	Carbon monoxide combines with hemoglobin of RBC, preventing combination with oxygen	Histotoxic hypoxia	Unconsciousness occurs rapidly; motor activity persists after unconsciousness
Hydrogen cyanide	Depression of oxygen transport at tissue level; no O_2 available in tissue	Histoxic hypoxia	Unconsciousness occurs rapidly; motor activity persists after unconsciousness
Curariform drugs; curare, succinylcholine, gallamine decamethonium	Paralysis of respiratory muscles; oxygen not available to blood	Hypoxic hypoxemia and hypercarbia	Unconsciousness develops slowly, preceded by anxiety and fear; no motor activity
Rapid decompression	Reduced partial pressure of oxygen available to blood	Hypoxic hypoxemia	Unconsciousness occurs rapidly; motor activity persists after unconsciousness
Nitrogen inhalation	Reduced partial pressure of oxygen available to blood	Hypoxic hypoxemia	Unconsciousness occurs rapidly; motor activity persists after unconsciousness
Electrocution when current does not pass through brain	Spastic paralysis of respiratory muscles and ventricular fibrillation; oxygen not available to blood in lungs	Hypoxic hypoxemia	Unconsciousness develops slowly, occurring after violent muscle spasms
DIRECT NEURON DEPRESSING AGENTS			
Anesthetic gases; ether, chloroform, methoxyflurane, halothane, nitrous oxide, and enflurane	Direct depression of cerebral cortex and subcortical structures and vital centers	Hypoxemia due to depression of vital centers	Unconsciousness occurs first; no anxiety or pain; possible involuntary motor activity after unconsciousness; no motor activity after brief period
Carbon dioxide	Direct depression of cerebral cortex, subcortical structures and vital centers; direct depression of heart muscle	Hypoxemia due to depression of vital centers	Unconsciousness occurs first; no anxiety or pain; possible involuntary motor activity after unconsciousness; no motor activity after brief period
Barbituric acid derivatives	Direct depression of cerebral cortex, subcortical structures and vital centers; direct depression of heart muscle	Ultimate cause of death is hypoxemia due to depression of vital centers	Unconsciousness reached rapidly; no anxiety; no excitement period; no motor activity; best to administer by intravenous or intracardiac administration

Agent	Mode of action	Ultimate cause of death	Comments
Chloral hydrate and chloral hydrate combinations	Direct depression of cerebral cortex, subcortical structures and vital centers; direct depression of heart muscle	Ultimate cause of death is hypoxemia due to depression of vital centers	Transient anxiety; unconsciousness occurs rapidly; no motor activity
T-61	Direct depression of cerebral cortex, subcortical structures and vital centers; direct depression of heart muscle	Hypoxemia due to depression of vital centers	Transient anxiety and struggling may occur before unconsciousness when given too rapidly; tissue damage may occur. Must be given intravenously at recommended dosage and rates
PHYSICAL AGENTS			
Gunshot or captive bolt into brain or stunning	Direct concussion of brain tissue	Hypoxemia due to depression of vital centers	Instant unconsciousness; motor activity may occur after unconsciousness
Cervical dislocation	Direct depression of brain	Hypoxemia due to disruption of vital centers	Violent muscle contraction can occur after cervical dislocation
Decapitation	Direct depression of brain	Hypoxemia due to disruption of vital centers	Violent muscle contractions occur subsequent to decapitation
Exsanguination	Direct depression of brain	Hypoxemia	If this method is preceded by and occurs during unconsciousness, there should be no struggling or muscle contraction
Decompression	Direct depression of brain	Hypoxemia	There are numerous disadvantages associated with mechanical problems as well as painful physiologic problems associated with expanding gases
Electrocution through brain	Direct depression of brain	Hypoxemia	Violent muscle contractions occur at same time as unconsciousness
Microwave irradiation	Direct inactivation of brain enzymes by rapid temperature increases of brain	Brain enzyme inactivation	Currently used only in rodents
Rapid freezing	Direct depression of brain	Rapid or near instantaneous cessation of metabolism	Approved only in specialized, well-controlled cases, in small laboratory animals
Air embolism	Direct depression of brain	Hypoxemia due to circulatory collapse	No motor activity occurs when preceded by anesthetics

TABLE 2—Characteristics of agents and methods of euthanasia

Agent	Safety for personnel	Ease of performance	Rapidity	Economic considerations	Tissue changes	Efficacy	Species suitability	Remarks
INHALANTS								
Ether	Flammable and explosive	Easily performed with closed chamber or container	Slow onset of anesthesia	Relatively inexpensive	Slight changes may occur in parenchymatous organs	Highly effective provided that subject is sufficiently exposed	Suitable for cats, young dogs, birds, rodents, and other small species	Acceptable but dangerous
							Administration to larger animals requires specialized equipment and training; onset is slow; vapors are irritating	Not acceptable
Halothane*	Nonflammable and nonexplosive; chronic exposure of animals or personnel to vapor may be harmful	Easily performed with closed container; can be administered to large animals by means of a mask	Rapid onset of anesthesia	Expensive	May occur in parenchymatous organs	Highly effective provided that subject is sufficiently exposed	Suitable for cats and young dogs, birds, rodents, and other small species	Acceptable
Methoxyflurane†	Nonflammable and nonexplosive under normal environmental conditions; chronic exposure of animals or personnel to vapor may be harmful	Slow with closed container; may be difficult to obtain necessary vapor concentration; can be administered to large animals by means of a mask	Slow onset of anesthesia	Expensive	May occur in parenchymatous organs	Highly effective provided that subject is sufficiently exposed	Suitable for cats, young dogs, birds, rodents, and other small species	Acceptable
							Administration to large animals requires specialized equipment and training; slow onset	Not Acceptable
Enflurane‡	Nonflammable and nonexplosive; chronic exposure of animals or personnel to vapors may be harmful	Easily performed with closed container or chamber; can be administered to large animals by means of a mask	Rapid onset of anesthesia	Expensive	May occur in parenchymatous organs, particularly kidneys	Highly effective provided that subject is sufficiently exposed; deep anesthesia may be accompanied by motor activity (twitching)	Suitable for cats, young dogs, birds, and other small species	Acceptable, but not recommended because of motor activity in deep plane of anesthesia
							Useful in large animals in emergency situations	Not acceptable except in emergenices

Agent	Safety	Method	Speed of action	Cost	Lesions	Efficacy	Species	Classification
Isoflurane‡	Nonflammable and nonexplosive; chronic exposure of animals or personnel to vapors may be harmful	Easily performed with closed container or chamber; can be administered to large animals by face mask	High volatility and potency; rapid onset of anesthesia	Very expensive	May occur in parenchymatous organs	Highly effective provided that subject is sufficiently exposed; induction does not appear to be stressful	Suitable for all small animals including birds and rodents	Acceptable
Nitrous oxide	Nonflammable and nonexplosive, but will support combustion; chronic exposure of animals or personnel to gas may be harmful	Easily performed with closed container or chamber	Rapid onset in 100% concentration	Relatively expensive	Hypoxic lesions may occur	Highly effective provided that subject is sufficiently exposed	Useful in large animals in emergency situations; Suitable for cats, small dogs, birds, rodents, and other small species; Not recommended alone for larger animals	Acceptable only in emergency situations; Acceptable; Use in larger animals requires supplementation with other agents
Chloroform	Nonflammable and nonexplosive; chronic exposure of animals or personnel is dangerous because of potential liver or kidney damage and carcinogenicity	Easily performed with closed container; can be administered to large animals by means of a mask	Rapid onset of anesthesia	Inexpensive	Extensive changes may occur in parenchymatous organs	Highly effective provided that subject is sufficiently exposed	Suitable for cats, young dogs, birds, rodents, and other small species; Useful in large animals in emergency situations	Acceptable only in controlled conditions (see text); Acceptable only in emergency situations
N_2	Safe if used with ventilation	Use closed chamber with rapid filling	Rapid	Inexpensive	Changes associated with hypoxemia may occur	Effective except in young and neonates	Suitable for most small species, including mink	An effective agent, but other methods preferable; not acceptable in most animals less than 4 months old
Hydrogen cyanide	Extremely hazardous to personnel	Airtight chamber required unless used under field conditions	Rapid	Inexpensive	Changes consistent with tissue hypoxia may occur	Effective and irreversible	Dens of foxes, badgers, rabbits, and other rodents	Because of extreme danger to operators, other methods are preferred
Carbon monoxide	Extremely hazardous; toxic and difficult to detect	Requires appropriately operated equipment for gas production	Moderate onset time, but insidious, so animal is unaware of onset	Inexpensive when proper equipment is in place	Changes associated with hypoxemia may occur	Effective	Most small species including dogs, cats, rodents, mink, and chinchillas	Acceptable only when properly designed and operated equipment is used
Carbon dioxide	Minimal hazard	Used in closed container	Moderately rapid	Inexpensive	Changes associated with hypoxemia may occur	Effective	Small laboratory animals, birds, cats and small dogs	Acceptable, but time required may be prolonged in immature and neonate animals

(Continued)

TABLE 2—Characteristics of agents and methods of euthanasia (continued)

Agent	Safety for personnel	Ease of performance	Rapidity	Economic considerations	Tissue changes	Efficacy	Species suitability	Remarks
NONINHALANTS								
Barbiturates	Safe except human abuse potential; DEA-controlled substance	Animal must be restrained; personnel must be skilled in IV injection	Rapid onset of anesthesia	Relatively inexpensive	Drug residues	Highly effective when appropriately administered	All species	Acceptable IV (see text)
Secobarbital/dibucaine	Safe	Animal must be restrained; personnel must be skilled in IV injection	Rapid onset of anesthesia	Expensive	Drug residues	Highly effective when appropriately administered	Dogs and cats and some laboratory animals	Acceptable IV
T-61	Safe	Animal must be restrained; personnel must be skilled in IV injection	Rapid onset of anesthesia	Expensive	Drug residues	Highly effective when appropriately administered	Dogs and cats and some laboratory animals	Acceptable IV (see text)
Mixture of chloral hydrate, MgSO$_4$, pentobarbital	Safe except human abuse potential; DEA-controlled substance	Animal must be restrained; personnel must be skilled in IV injection	Rapid onset of anesthesia	Relatively inexpensive	Drug residues	Highly effective when appropriately administered	Large animals, ie, horses and cattle	Acceptable IV
Strychnine/nicotine curariform drugs/MgSO$_4$/KCl	***	****	***	***	***	***	***	Absolutely unacceptable when used alone (see text)
PHYSICAL METHODS								
Captive bolt, gunshot and stunning	Safe, but some concern for mechanical injury; gunshot can be especially dangerous	Requires skilled individuals; however, skills easily developed	Rapid	Inexpensive	Trauma of brain tissues; others unchanged	Highly effective	Usually applied in larger agricultural animals, but can be used for rabbits and guinea pigs	Acceptable (see text for limitations)
Cervical dislocation	Safe	Requires training and skill	Moderately rapid	Inexpensive	Primarily useful if chemical residue-free tissues are needed	Irreversible	Suitable only in chickens, laboratory mice, and rats less than 200 g or rabbits less than 1 kg	Acceptable with prior sedation or light anesthesia (see text)

Method	Safety to personnel	Ease of performance	Rapidity	Cost	Effect on tissue	Effectiveness	Species suitability	Recommendation
Decapitation	Some concern for mechanical injury	Easily performed with minimal training	Moderately rapid; can have consciousness for 13 to 14 seconds	Inexpensive	Primarily useful if chemical residue-free tissues are needed	Irreversible	Suitable for rodents and small rabbits	Acceptable with prior sedation or light anesthesia (see text)
Exsanguination	Safe	Easily performed with minimal training	Moderately rapid	Inexpensive	Minimal	Irreversible	Recommended to ensure death following stunning by captive bolt, or gunshot in large domestic species or rabbits	Acceptable when preceded by other methods that relieve anxiety, consciousness
Decompression	Safe	Requires special equipment that must be operated and maintained by skilled personnel	Relatively slow	Inexpensive	Trauma can occur to tissues when air is trapped in middle ear and gut	Effective if equipment is properly operated and maintained	Primarily for dogs and smaller animals	Not recommended because of numerous disadvantages (see text)
Electrocution	Hazardous to personnel	Not easily performed in all instances	Can be rapid	Inexpensive	Petechial hemorrhages can occur	Highly effective if properly performed	Used primarily in farm animals	Acceptable; however, disadvantages far outweigh advantages in most applications (see text)
Microwave	Safe	Requires training and highly specialized equipment	Very rapid	Equipment is expensive	Primarily used for brain tissue studies	Highly effective	Used in mice, rats, or animals of similar size	Acceptable only in small rodents (see text)
Rapid freezing	Safe	Easily performed	Rapid	Inexpensive	Arrest enzymatic reactions in tissue, usually brain	Effective	Used in small rodents	Acceptable (see text)
Air embolism	Safe	Easily performed	Moderately rapid	Inexpensive	Hypoxemic lesions may occur	Effective if closely monitored	Used primarily in rabbits and other small species	Acceptable only in fully anesthetized animals

*Fluothane, Ayerst Laboratories, New York, NY; Halocarbon Laboratories, Hackensack, NJ; †Metofane, Pitman-Moore, Inc, Washington Crossing, NJ; Penthrane, Abbott Laboratories, North Chicago, Ill. ‡Ethrane and Isoflurane, Anaquest, Division of BOC, Inc., Madison, Wis.

there may be vocalization and some muscle contraction.[18] Although these responses appear to be purposeful, they are not. Death is due to hypoxemia and direct depression of respiratory centers.

With the third group, physical damage to the brain, concussion, or direct electrical flow[19] through the brain produces instant unconsciousness. Exaggerated muscular activity may follow unconsciouess. When electrocution is properly performed, loss of motor function occurs concomitantly with loss of consciousness; with the other methods in this group, muscular contraction may occur. Although this may be unpleasant to the observer, the animal is not suffering.

Electroencephalograms and other physiologic measurements can be employed to measure responses to euthanatizing agents.[1]

CRITERIA FOR JUDGING METHODS OF EUTHANASIA

Several criteria were used in evaluating methods of euthanasia: (1) ability to produce death without causing pain; (2) time required to produce loss of consciousness; (3) time required to produce death; (4) reliability; (5) safety of personnel; (6) potential for minimizing undesirable psychologic stress on the animal; (7) nonreversibility; (8) compatibility with requirement and purpose; (9) emotional effect upon observers or operators; (10) economic feasibility; (11) compatibility with histopathologic evaluation; and (12) drug avilability and abuse potential.

INHALANT AGENTS

Occupational exposure to inhalation anesthetics constitutes a human health hazard. An increased incidence of spontaneous abortion and congenital abnormalities results from exposure to trace amounts of inhalation anesthetic agents.[20] Human exposure levels for volatile liquid anesthetics (ether, halothane, methoxyflurane, ethrane, and isoflurane) should be less than 2 ppm, and less than 25 ppm for nitrous oxide.[21] While there are no controlled studies proving that such levels of anesthetics are "safe," these concentrations were established because they were shown to be attainable under hospital conditions. Effective procedures must be employed to protect personnel from anesthetic vapors.

Inhalant Anesthetics: Ether, Halothane, Methoxyflurane, Enflurane, Isoflurane, Cyclopropane, and Nitrous Oxide

The inhalant anesthetics, primarily ether, halothane, and methoxyflurane, have been used to euthanatize many species.[22] With these agents, the animal is placed in a closed receptacle containing cotton or gauze soaked with the anesthetic.[23-25] Vapors are inhaled until respiration ceases and death ensues (Table 2). Because the liquid state of most inhalant anesthetics is a topical irritant, animals should be exposed to vapors only. Also, air or oxygen must be provided during the induction period.[24]

Other inhalation anesthetics are seldom used for euthanasia, due to low potency (nitrous oxide), high cost (isoflurane, enflurane), or danger (cyclopropane). For example, cyclopropane is highly flammable and explosive, and requires special equipment for administration. Nitrous oxide may be used alone to produce mild analgesia, anesthesia, and death by hypoxemia. Nitrous oxide is nonflammable and nonexplosive, but will support combustion.

Advantages—(1) The inhalant anesthestics are particularly valuable for euthanasia of birds, rodents, cats, and young dogs, ie, animals in which venipuncture may be difficult, and (2) halothane, enflurane, isoflurane, methoxyflurane, and nitrous oxide are nonflammable and nonexplosive under ordinary environmental conditions.

Disadvantages—(1) Struggling and anxiety may occur during induction of anesthesia because anesthetic vapors are irritating and induce excitement; (2) ether is flammable and explosive and should not be used near an open flame or other ignition sources; (3) personnel and other animals can be injured by exposure to these agents; and (4) halothane, methoxyflurane, nitrous oxide, enflurane, and isoflurane are relatively expensive.

Recommendations—Under certain circumstances, ether, halothane, isoflurane, enflurane, methoxyflurane, and nitrous oxide administered by inhalation are acceptable for euthanasia of small animals (ie, birds. rodents, cats, and young dogs). Although acceptable, these agents generally are not used in larger animals because of their cost and difficulty of administration. In emergency situations, halothane, enflurane, or isoflurane may be administered to large animals.

Chloroform

Chloroform is a known potent hepatotoxin and is a suspected carcinogen.[26] Although chloroform is non-explosive, its use in the presence of a flame may result in the production of phosgene gas. Because of its significant hazards to human beings, chloroform can be recommended for euthanasia only under conditions that prevent human exposure.

Nitrogen

Nitrogen (N_2), a colorless, odorless gas, constitutes 78% of normal atmospheric air. It is inert, nonflammable, and nonexplosive.

Euthanasia is induced by placing the animal in a closed container into which pure N_2 is introduced rapidly at atmospheric pressure. Nitrogen displaces oxygen in the container, thus inducing death by hypoxemia. Commercial equipment for N_2 euthanasia consists of a closed chamber, an oxygen monitor to ensure that atmospheric oxygen is 1.5% or less in 45 to 50 seconds, and a timer to assure adequate exposure to the N_2. Because N_2 mixes with room air when the chamber is opened, there is minimal danger to personnel when ventilation is adequate.

In studies by Herin et al,[27] dogs became unconscious within 76 seconds when an N_2 concentration of 98.5% was achieved in 45 to 60 seconds. The electroencephalogram became isoelectric (flat) in a mean of 80 seconds and arterial blood pressure was undetectable in an average of 204 seconds. Although all dogs hyperventilated prior to unconsciousness, the authors concluded that this method induced death without pain. Following loss of consciousness, yelping, gasping, convulsions, and muscular tremors occurred in some dogs. At the end of a 5-minute exposure period, all dogs were dead.[27] These findings were similar to those for rabbits[28] and for a single dog.[1]

Glass et al[29] reported that newborn dogs, rabbits, and guinea pigs can survive an N_2 atmosphere much longer than can adults. Newborn dogs and rabbits survived 31 minutes, and guinea pigs 6 minutes, whereas adult dogs and guinea pigs survived 3 minutes, and adult rabbits 1½ minutes. Nitrogen has been used for euthanasia of mink.[30]

With N_2 flowing at a rate of 39% of chamber volume per minute, rats collapsed in approximately 3 minutes and respiratory arrest occurred in 5 to 6 minutes. Regardless of flow rate, rats exhibited signs of panic and distress before collapsing and dying.[31] Insensitivity to pain under such circumstances is questionable.[32]

Advantages—(1) N_2 gas is readily available, (2) can be rapid and reliable; and (3) hazards to personnel are minimal.

Disadvantages—(1) Very young animals are not euthanatized rapidly; (2) rapid N_2 flow may produce a noise that may frighten animals; (3) the responses by the unconscious animal may be aesthetically objectionable; (4) reestablishing a low concentration of O_2 (ie, 6% or greater) in the chamber before death will allow immediate recovery; (5) in some areas the use of N_2 for euthanasia has been prohibited by law; and (6) when flow rates are low, time to death can be excessively long.

Recommendations—The effect of N_2 can be rapid and is reliable when properly used. However, the manner of death may be aesthetically objectionable. Although N_2 is an effective agent, other methods of euthanasia are preferable. Nitrogen is not an acceptable euthanatizing agent in animals less than four months of age. The use of N_2 requires that the equipment be (1) properly constructed to rapidly attain high concentration, (2) correctly maintained, and (3) proficiently operated. In addition, an effective exhaust or ventilation system must be present to preclude exposure of personnel to high concentrations of N_2.

Hydrogen Cyanide Gas

Hydrogen cyanide gas is one of the most rapidly acting poisons.[33] Cyanide reacts readily with the ferric ion of mitochondrial cytochrome oxidase to form cytochrome oxidase-cyanide complex, inducing cytotoxic hypoxia. The maximum allowable concentration for 8 hours' occupational exposure in industry is 10 ppm. Hydrogen cyanide gas for euthanasia is produced by placing pellets of sodium cyanide in sulfuric acid.

There is no evidence to indicate that the effects of cyanide are painful.[34] Cyanide induces intense respiratory stimulation and may cause excitement resulting in sounds of distress before death. Cyanide possesses a pungent and rather unpleasant smell and, because of its high toxicity, an airtight chamber is required to confine the gas. In the United Kingdom, cyanide is used for euthanasia of rabbits, foxes, and badgers in dens.[35]

Advantages—(1) Hydrogen cyanide gas induces rapid death, and (2) it can be used under field conditions where other agents are impractical.

Disadvantages—(1) The animal manifests violent convulsive seizures and opisthotonos prior to death; (2) the responses are disagreeable to most observers; (3) the gas is very irritating to the respiratory mucosa; and (4) there is extreme danger to personnel.

Recommendations—Although the effect of hydrogen cyandide gas is rapid, reliable, and irreversible, it endangers the operator, and the manner of death is aesthetically objectionable.[14] Other methods of euthanasia are preferable.

Carbon Monoxide

Carbon monoxide (CO) combines with hemoglobin to form carboxyhemoglobin. This blocks the uptake of oxygen by erythrocytes, and leads to fatal hypoxemia.

Clinical signs of CO toxicosis, as originally described, are due to its action upon the circulatory system.[36] These result in generalized vascular dysfunction, characterized by extensive vasodilation and hemorrhage. In people, initial symptoms are headache sometimes combined with nausea, followed by depression progressing to unconsciousness. Because CO stimulates motor centers in the brain, unconsciousness may be accompanied by convulsions and muscular spasms.

Carbon monoxide is a cumulative poison.[37] Distinct signs of CO toxicosis are not induced until the concentration is 0.05% in air, and acute signs do not occur until the concentration is approximately 0.2%. In human beings, exposure to 0.32% and 0.45% of CO for one hour will induce unconsciousness and death.[38]

There are 3 practical methods of generating CO for mass euthanasia.
1) Chemical interaction of sodium formate and sulfuric acid,
2) Exhaust fumes from gasoline internal combustion engines, and
3) Commercially compressed CO gas in cylinders.

Carding[39] used sodium formate and sulfuric acid to generate CO to euthanatize dogs. He found a marked decrease in the average time to collapse and death by increasing CO concentration from 2% to 3% in air.

When CO is produced by combustion, oxides of nitrogen and hydrocarbons, oxygenates of hydrocarbons, and heat must be controlled to prevent discomfort to the animal. This may be done by passing exhaust gases through a water chamber and a metal gauze filter with a cloth screen. The water chamber cools the gas, removes some carbon particles, and entraps the oxides of nitrogen, hydrocarbons, and oxygenates of hydrocarbons. The cloth filter removes carbon particles, allowing relatively clean, nonirritating CO gas to enter the chamber.

An idling engine running on a rich fuel mixture will produce the highest percentage of CO in exhaust gas. Carbon monoxide produced by an internal combustion engine is just as effective as cylinder CO and considerably less expensive.[40] Chamber concentration of CO from piped exhaust gas can quickly reach 8%, resulting in 70% saturation of hemoglobin. Carbon monoxide must be considered extremely hazardous for personnel because it is highly toxic and difficult to detect. An efficient exhaust or ventilatory system is essential to prevent accidental exposure of human beings.

In a study by Ramsey and Eilmann,[41] 8% CO caused guinea pigs to collapse in 40 seconds to 2 minutes, and death occurred within less than six minutes.

Carbon monoxide has been used to euthanatize mink[30] and chinchillas. The animals collapsed in one minute, breathing ceased in 2 minutes, and they were considered dead when the heart stopped beating in approximtely 5 to 7 minutes.

Blood et al[42] reported excellent results with CO for euthanasia of cats and dogs. Several chamber concentrations were tested; a 6% CO concentration gave fastest results. No advantage was observed by further increasing CO concentration.

In a study designed to evaluate the physiologic and behavioral characteristics of dogs exposed to 6% CO in air, Chalifoux and Dallaire[43] could not determine the precise time of unconsciousness. Electroencephalographic recordings revealed a 20- to 25-second period of abnormal cortical function prior to unconsciousness. It is during this period that agitation and vocalization occur. These reactions are not necessarily due to pain, but are probably caused by cortical hypoxemia. The authors concluded the CO meets most accepted criteria for mass euthanasia of adult dogs, but that pretreatment with a tranquilizer (phase I) followed by CO inhalation (phase II) might decrease or eliminate objectionable behavioral and physiologic responses associated with CO inhalation alone.[43] Subsequent studies have shown that premedication with acepromazine significantly decreased behavioral and physiologic responses of dogs euthanatized with CO.[44]

In a comparative study, CO (gasoline engine exhaust) and 70% CO_2 + 30% O_2 were used to euthanatize cats. Euthanasia was divided into 3 phases. Phase I was time from initial contact with gas until clinical signs of effect (eg, yawning, staggering, or trembling). Phase II extended from end of phase I until recumbency and phase III was from the end of phase II until total immobilization.[45] The study revealed that phase I responses were greatest with CO_2 + O_2. Convulsions occurred during phases I and II with both methods. However, when the euthanatizing chamber was pre-filled with CO (ie, "exhaust fumes"), convulsions did not occur in phase III. Time to complete immobilization was greater with CO_2+O_2 (approximately 90 seconds) than with CO alone (approximately 56 seconds).[45] In piglets excitation was less likely to occur when CO was combined with nitrous oxide (N_2O). If excitement did occur, it followed the onset of unconsciousness.[36]

Gasoline engine exhaust piped into an enclosed chamber quickly reaches CO levels in excess of 8%. Saturation of hemoglobin to the 70% level occurs more rapidly when concentrations are greater than 6%, which has been described as optimal. Use of compressed CO allows rapid attainment of an effective chamber concentration. Carbon monoxide produced by a gasoline internal combustion engine and cylinder CO are equally effective,[40] but the gasoline engine costs less to use.

Advantages—(1) Carbon monoxide induces rapid and painless death; (2) hypoxemia induced by CO is insidious so that the animal is completely unaware of it; and (3) unconsciousness occurs without pain or discernible discomfort, when properly administered.

Disadvantages—(1) Safeguards must be taken to prevent exposure of personnel; (2) during chemical generation by sodium formate and sulfuric acid, irritating vapors of sulfuric acid must be removed by passing the CO through a solution of 10% sodium hydroxide; and (3) exhaust gases must be filtered and cooled to prevent discomfort to animals.

Recommendations—Carbon monoxide used for individual or mass euthanasia is acceptable for small animals, including dogs and cats, provided that the following precautions are taken: Personnel using CO must be instructed thoroughly in its use and must understand its hazards and limitations; the CO generator and chamber must be located in a well-ventilated environment, preferably out-of-doors; the chamber must be equipped with internal lighting and viewports that allow personnel direct observation of animals; the gas generation process should be adequate to achieve a CO concentration throughout the chamber of at least 6% within no more than 20 minutes after animals are placed in the chamber; sodium formate- and sulfuric acid-generated CO must have the irritating acid vapors filtered out by passing it through a 10% solution of sodium hydroxide; if CO generation is by combustion of gasoline in an engine, (1) the engine must be operating at idling speed with a rich fuel-air mixture; (2) prior to entry into the chamber, the exhaust gas must be cooled to less than 125 F (51.7 C); (3) the chamber must be equipped with accurate temperature gauges monitored by attendants to assure that internal temperature of the chamber does not exceed 110F (41.3 C), and (4) the exhaust gas must be passed through water and cloth filtration processes to remove irritants and carbon particles before entering the chamber. Exhaust gas piped into a chamber from a cruising vehicle is not acceptable.

Carbon Dioxide

Room air contains 0.04% carbon dioxide (CO_2). Pure CO_2 is heavier than air and nearly odorless. Inhalation of CO_2 in concentrations of 7.5% increases the pain threshold, and higher concentrations of CO_2 have a rapid anesthetic effect.[45-49]

Inhalation of 60% CO_2 results in loss of consciousness within 45 seconds, and respiratory arrest within 5 minutes.[50] Carbon dioxide has been used to euthanatize groups of small laboratory animals including mice, rats, guinea pigs, chickens, and rabbits,[2,51,55] and for humane slaughter of swine for human consumption.[11,56] According to Croft,[57] animals do not detect the CO_2 immediately, and its depressant action takes place almost unnoticed.

Leake and Waters[47] reported the experimental use of CO_2 as an anesthetic agent in the dog. Thirty percent to 40% CO_2 in oxygen induced anesthesia within 1 to 2 minutes, usually without struggling, retching, or vomiting. The combination of 40% CO_2 and approximtely 3% CO has been used experimentally for euthanasia of dogs by Carding.[39] Carbon dioxide has been used in specially designed chambers to euthanatize cats[58-60] and other small laboratory animals.[51,60]

Studies in day-old chickens have shown that CO_2 is an effective euthanatizing agent. Inhalation of CO_2 caused little distress to the birds, suppressing nervous activity and inducing death rather quickly.[52] Because respiration begins during embryonic development, the unhatched chickens' environment may normally have a CO_2 concentration as high as 14%. Thus, CO_2 concentration for euthanasia for baby chickens and other neonates should be especially high. A CO_2 concentration of 60% to 70% with a 5-minute exposure time appears to be optimal.[52]

Carbon dioxide is used for preslaughter anesthesia of pigs. The undesirable side effect of CO_2, as used in commercial slaughter houses, is that the pigs experience a stage of excitement with vocalization for about 40 seconds before they lose consciousness.[56,61] For that reason, CO_2 preslaughter anesthesia may appear less humane than other techniques. The signs of effective CO_2 anesthesia are those associated with deep surgical anesthesia, such as loss of withdrawal and palpebral reflexes.[62]

Advantages—(1) The rapid depressant and anesthetic effects of CO_2 are well established. (2) Carbon dioxide may be purchased in cylinders or in a solid state as "dry ice"; (3) CO_2 is inexpensive, nonflammable, and nonexplosive, and presents minimal hazard to personnel when used with properly designed equipment; (4) CO_2 does not result in accumulation of tissue residues in food producing animals; and (5) CO_2 euthanasia does not distort cellular architecture.[63]

Disadvantages—(1) Because CO_2 is heavier than air, incomplete filling of a chamber may permit a tall or climbing animal to avoid exposure and survive, and (2) in immature animals, the time required for euthanasia may be substantially prolonged.

Recommendations—Carbon dioxide is recommended in small laboratory animals such as birds, cats, and small dogs. Chamber design should allow for precharging with CO_2 and should enable cleaning and removal of dead animals with minimal loss of CO_2. Compressed CO_2 gas in cylinders is preferble to dry ice. Inflow to a euthanatizing chamber can be regulated precisely with compressed CO_2. Optimal flow rate appears to be one that will displace approximately 20% of chamber volume per minute.[31] When using compressed CO_2, O_2 can be added (for example, 30% O_2, 70% CO_2), thus decreasing the discomfort of hypoxia prior to onset of narcosis and anesthesia. If dry ice is used, animal contact must be avoided to prevent freezing or chilling.

NONINHALANT PHARMACOLOGIC AGENTS

Noninhalant agents that can be used for euthanasia are widely diverse in chemical composition.[64,65] Although death can be induced by administering these drugs via many routes (intravenous, intracardiac, intraperitoneal, intrathecal, intramuscular, intrathoracic, subcutaneous, and oral), intravenous administration is preferred because the effect is most rapid and reliable. Intrapulmonic injection should be avoided.

Oral, rectal, and intraperitoneal routes of administration of drugs for euthanasia are inadvisable because of prolonged onset of action, wide range in lethal doses, and potential irritation of tissues. An hour of more may elapse from time of administration to death. Some drugs, such as chloral hydrate and T-61, when given intraperitoneally are irritating and cause abdominal pain. Others may produce tissue changes, depending on dose and route of administration.[25,63]

Because crying and struggling may follow improper intracardiac injection, this route of administration is objectionable. Skill is required to penetrate the heart of an animal with one thrust of a hypodermic needle, especially if the animal is not easily restrained. Intracardiac injection of drugs is not recommended for euthanasia, except in depressed, anesthetized, or comatose animals. Intrathecal use of drugs in unanesthetized animals is not recommended because puncture of the cisterna magna without causing pain and struggling is not possible.

If the animal to be euthanatized is excitable or vicious, use of analgesics, tranquilizers,[44] narcotics, ketamine, xylazine, or other depressants is recommended before administration of the euthanatizing agent.

Barbituric Acid Derivatives

Barbiturates depress the central nervous system in descending order, beginning with the cerebral cortex. Within seconds of intravenous administration, unconsciousness is induced and it progresses to deep anesthesia.[1] Apnea occurs due to depression of the respiratory center, and cardiac arrest quickly follows. Several barbiturates are acceptable, but pentobarbital sodium most commonly is used for euthanasia.

Advantages—(1) A primary advantage of barbiturates is speed of action. This effect depends on the dose, concentration, and rate of injection; (2) the barbiturates induce euthanasia smoothly, with minimal discomfort to the animal, and favorably impress the observer because the animal dies quietly[1]; a cost comparison by Lumb and Moreland[66] indicates that barbiturates are less expensive than most other injectable agents.

Disadvantages—(1) Intravenous injection is necessary for best results, necessitating trained personnel; (2) each animal must be restrained; (3) current federal drug regulations require strict accounting for the barbiturates and, by necessity, these must be used under the supervision of personnel registered with the US Drug Enforcement Agency; and (4) an aesthetically objectionable terminal gasp may occur in the unconscious animal.

Recommendations—The advantages of using barbiturates for euthanasia in small animals far outweigh the disadvantages. The intravenous injection of a barbituric acid derivative is the preferred method for euthanasia of dogs, cats, and other small animals; however, intraperitoneal administration is an acceptable alternative for laboratory rodents. Nervous or vicious animals may require tranquilization[44] or sedation prior to injection of a barbiturate.

Secobarbital-Dibucaine Combination[a]

This mixture contains a short-acting barbiturate to induce anesthesia. The cardiotoxic effects of dibucaine cause cardiac arrest. Limited trials suggest this combination is an acceptable barbiturate euthanatizing agent when given intravenously to dogs and cats.[67-68]

T-61[b]

T-61 is an injectable nonbarbiturate, non-narcotic mixture of three drugs used to induce euthanasia. These drugs provide a combination of general anesthetic,

---

[a]Each milliliter contains 400 mg of secobarbital and 25 mg of dibucaine. Dosage for dogs and cats, IV: 0.22 ml/kg body weight. Repose, Diamond Laboratories, Des Moines, Iowa.

[b]Each milliliter contains 200 mg of N-(2-(m-methoxy-phenyl)-2-ethylbutyl (1)—gamma hydroxybutyramide, 50 mg of 4.4′methylene-bis (cyclohexyl-trimethyl-ammonium iodide), and 5 mg of tetracaine hydrochlorides with 0.6 ml dimethylformamide in distilled water. Produced by American Hoechst Corp., Somerville, NJ.

curariform, and local anesthetic actions. Death results from severe central nervous system depression, hypoxia, and circulatory collapse. T-61 has been used in Germany since 1962 and became available in the United States soon thereafter.[69-72] T-61 has been withdrawn from the United Kingdom market since 1976, but because it is not currently listed as a controlled substance under federal drug regulations, it has gained some popularity in the United States in recent years.

A comparative study of T-61 and pentobarbital (at 57.1 mg/kg of body weight) indicated that either agent induced euthanasia smoothly.[71] Dogs given T-61 received two-thirds of the total dose (0.3 ml/kg of body weight) at a rate of 0.2 ml/second, with the last one-third given at the rate of 1.2 ml/sec. With both pentobarbital and T-61, the electroencephalogram changed from a normal awake pattern to one of low frequency and increased amplitude for approximtely 5 seconds, followed quickly by electrical silence. The pentobarbital-treated dogs required 12 second longer for the occurrence of electrical silence. With both agents, electrocardiographic alterations developed immediately and arterial pressure dropped to zero. Results of this study indicate that painless death is induced by pentobarbital or T-61.[71]

A recent survey[73] and review[74] indicate a need for further controlled studies on the efficacy and humaneness of T-61 as a euthanatizing agent in several species.

Advantages—(1) T-61 may be used intravenously in dogs, cats, horses, laboratory animals, and birds; (2) the terminal gasp[75] that may accompany pentobarbital euthanasia in unconscious animals is not evident with T-61; and (3) it is not regulated or controlled by the US Drug Enforcement Agency.

Disadvantages—(1) T-61 must be administered intravenously because it is painful when administered extravasculary; (2) if T-61 is injected at too rapid a rate, the animal may appear to experience pain or discomfort immediately prior to becoming unconscious; (3) doses larger than recommended may cause pulmonary edema and other tissue lesions; and (4) T-61 is not approved for use in animals intended for human consumption.

Recommendations—If barbiturates cannot be used, T-61 is a substitute, but only when it is administered intravenously by a highly skilled person at recommended dosages and at proper injection rates.[74] Intracardiac or intrathoracic administration is not recommended.

Chloral Hydrate

Because chloral hydrate depresses the cerebrum slowly, restraint during induction may become a problem in some animals. Death is due to hypoxemia caused by progressive depression of the respiratory center. Death may be preceded by gasping, muscle spasms, and vocalization.

Recommendation—Chloral hydrate is not recommended for euthanasia of dogs, cats, and other small animals because the associated signs may be severe and are aesthetically objectionable.

Combination of Chloral Hydrate, Magnesium Sulfate, and Sodium Pentobarbital

This combination has been used for anesthesia of large animals and may be administered in overdosage for euthanasia.[18]

Recommendation—This mixture is an acceptable large animal euthanatizing agent when administered intravenously.

Strychnine

Strychnine or any of its salts, such as strychnine sulfate, increases the excitability of the central nervous system. The animal remains conscious and excessively responsive to stimuli. Strychnine causes violent convulsions and associated painful contraction of skeletal muscles.[76]

Recommendation—Strychnine is absolutely condemned for euthanasia.

Magnesium Sulfate (MgSO₄) or Potassium Chloride (KC1)

Magnesium or potassium ions exert little if any direct depressant effect on the central nervous system. Dosages of $MgSO_4$ previously recommended for euthanasia have been shown to cause complete neuromuscular block and death due to hypoxemia.[77]

Recommendation—Magnesium or potassium salts must not be used alone for euthanasia because of the lack of analgesic or anesthetic effect. Potassium chloride may be adminstered to an anesthetized animal as an efficient and inexpensive way to cause cardiac arrest and death.

Nicotine

Nicotine is an alkaloid obtained from the tobacco plant. Nicotine as a sulfate compound is an odorless, clear, water-soluble liquid. Lethal doses can be absorbed through mucous membranes and intact skin, making it dangerous for personnel.

Nicotine sulfate has been used extensively in the past in capture equipment for immobilizing wild game and feral and domestic dogs. Other drugs have replaced nicotine sulfate because of the high mortality associated with its use.

Nicotine sulfate induces a short period of stimulation, followed by blockade of autonomic ganglia. When injected in sufficient quantity, it induces a muscle relaxant effect, with paralysis of the respiratory muscles and, subsequently, hypoxemic death. Salivation, vomiting, defection, and convulsions commonly occur prior to death.

Recommendation—Because nicotine sulfate is an extremely dangerous drug for personnel, is inhumane for animals, and induces serious side effects prior to death, *it is absolutely condemned for euthanasia.*

Curariform Drugs

Drugs such as curare, succinylcholine, pancuronium, guaifenesin, and other neuromuscular blocking agents induce death by immobilizing the respiratory muscles, causing fatal suffocation. There is no depressant action on the brain.[1] Human patients given these drugs have described periods of full consciousness accompanied by complete muscular immobility and intense anxiety.[18]

Hicks and Bailey[78] administered massive doses of succinylcholine to dogs and observed changes in the electrocardiogram, electroencephalogram, and respiratory responses. They found bradycardia initially and elevated arterial blood pressure. As the myocardium failed, tachycardia was followed by a decrease in arterial pressure. The electroencephalogram indicated no loss of consciousness, as the normal awake wave form progressed to an activated electroencephalogram. The electroencephalographic activity continued long after cessation of respiration (7 minutes) before becoming isoelectric. Urination, salivation, and defecation commonly occurred along with muscular fasciculations. Asphyxial struggling was sometimes accompanied by violent fasciculations and head movements. These authors concluded that dogs given succinylcholine are conscious for prolonged intervals before dying of respiratory and cardiac arrest, and for this reason it should not be given as the sole agent for euthanasia.

Recommendations—Where standard methods of restraint are impractical, impossible, or dangerous, or where manual capture and restraint may cause pain and injury through struggling and anxiety, the use of immobilizing drugs is justified.

Because the immobilized animal is fully conscious and subject to death by suffocation, euthanasia by chemical or physical methods must be accomplished immediately. *Curariform drugs alone are absolutely condemned for euthanasia.*

Other Parenteral Preparations

A number of injectable agents are currently available for immobilizing domestic and feral animals. Drugs such as ketamine HC1 and xylazine are used for immobilization, analgesia, and anesthesia. The effect occurs within minutes following intramuscular injection, making these drugs useful for restraint (ie, phase I of euthanasia). Currently these agents are not included as controlled substances by federal drug regulations. Narcotics also may be used for sedation and analgesia, but detailed records must be kept, and their use properly supervised by a licensed professional registered with the US Drug Enforcement Agency. Although it is possible to cause death with high doses of these drugs, such use would be impractical and may produce convulsions before death.

PHYSICAL METHODS

Physical methods include captive bolt pistol, gunshot, stunning, cervical dislocation, decapitation, exsanguination, decompression, electrocution, microwave irradiation, rapid freezing, and air embolism. It is a requirement that any method of euthanasia be performed by knowledgeable, well-trained individuals. Because trauma often is associated with physical methods for inducing unconsciousness, this requirement is particularly vital. Physical methods are often aesthetically displeasing; however, when properly performed, unconsciousness is rapid, without distress or pain to the animal. In some applications the amount of apprehension of the animals will be less than if chemical means had been used.

Captive Bolt Pistol

This method is used in ruminants, horses, and swine and is being developed for laboratory rabbits. The purpose of both the captive bolt and nonpenetrative percussion methods is to damage the cerebral hemisphere and brainstem so that the animal is unconscious.[79] Penetrating or nonpenetrating captive bolts are powered by gunpowder or compressed air. Nonpenetrating instruments usually are less effective in inducing unconsciousness. Animals must be adequately restrained to ensure proper placement of the captive bolt. The muzzle of the pistol should be placed at a right angle to the skill and directed toward the center of the brain in ruminant species. A multiple projectile has been suggested as a more effective technique, especially on large cattle. In swine, the captive bolt should be directed to the brain from a central point slightly above a line between the eyes.[80]

Evaluation of unconsciousness can be difficult. Some of the methods used are electroencephalography, loss of visually evoked responses, loss of the menace or blink response to a hand brought rapidly toward the eye, and loss of coordinated movements and pupillary dilatation.[62,79,81,82] The signs of effective stunning are immediate collapse and a 15-second period of tetanic spasm, followed by slow hindlimb movements of increasing frequency.

Advantages—A humane method for use in abattoirs and in research facilities when the use of drugs is contraindicated.

Disadvantages—(1) Aesthetically displeasing; (2) nonpenetrating captive bolt pistols cannot be used effectively in mature swine; and (3) death may not occur.

Recommendations—Use of the penetrating captive bolt pistol, when followed by exsanguination or pithing, is an acceptble method of euthanasia for horses, ruminants, and swine when chemical agents cannot be used. Nonpenetrating captive bolt pistols are not recommended.

Gunshot

Under some circumstances, gunshot may be the only practical method of euthanasia. It should be performed by highly skilled and trained personnel utilizing a rifle or pistol appropriate for the situation. The projectile should be accurately placed to enter the brain, causing instant unconsciousness.[83,84]

Advantages—(1) Euthanasia is instantaneous; and (2) under field conditions, gunshot may be the only effective method available.

Disadvantages—(1) It is dangerous to personnel; (2) it is aesthetically unpleasant; and (3) under field conditions it may be difficult to hit the brain.

Recommendation—When other methods cannot be used, competently performed gunshot is an acceptable method of euthanasia. When the animal is appropriately restrained, the captive bolt pistol is preferred to gunshot.

Stunning

Stunning can render an animal unconscious; however, unconsciousness will occur only if a blow to the head is properly executed. If not performed correctly, various degrees of consciousness with concomitant pain will ensue.

Advantages—(1) Stunning is humane when properly performed; and (2) enables collection of blood and other tissues without chemical contamination.

Disadvantages—(1) Stunning is inhumane if improperly performed; (2) it is impossible to ensure constancy of performance by personnel; (3) stunning may be aesthetically displeasing for personnel performing or observing the procedure; and (4) it must be followed by other means to ensure the death of the unconscious animal.

Recommendations—Stunning of laboratory rodents and rabbits by a sharp blow to the head is strongly discourged as a method of euthanasia because of the inherent risk of not rendering animals immediately unconscious. Stunning must be followed by other means to ensure death of the unconscious animal. Any use must be predicated on a case-by-case review by the institutional animal welfare committee or other responsible bodies.

Cervical Dislocation

Cervical dislocation is used to euthanatize poultry, mice, and immature rats and rabbits. For mice and rats, the thumb and index finger are placed on either side of the neck at the base of the skull or, alternatively, a rod is pressed at the base of the skull. With the other hand, the base of the tail or hindlimbs are quickly pulled, causing separtion of the cervical vertebrae from the skull. For immature rabbits, the head is held in one hand and the hindlimbs in the other. The animal is stretched and the neck is hyperextended and dorsally twisted to separate the cervical vertebrae from the skull.[51,80]

Advantages—(1) Cervical dislocation is a technique that may induce immediate unconsciousness; (2) does not chemically contaminate tissues; and (3) it is rapidly accomplished.

Disadvantages—(1) May be aesthetically displeasing to personnel; and (2) its use is limited to poultry, mice, and immature rats and rabbits.

Recommendations—When properly executed, cervical dislocation may be a humane technique to euthanatize poultry, mice, and rats weighing less than 200 g, and rabbits weighing less than 1 kg. In heavier rats and rabbits, the greater muscle mass in the cervical region makes cervical dislocation physically more difficult and, accordingly, it should not be performed. Because unconsciousness may not occur immediately, it is preferable to lightly anesthetize or sedate the animal prior to cervical dislocation.

Institutional animal welfare committees or other responsible bodies must determine that personnel who perform cervical dislocation techniques have been properly trained.

Decapitation With Guillotine

Decapitation is most often used to euthanatize rodents and small rabbits. It provides a means to recover tissues and body fluids that are chemically uncontaminated. It also provides neurobiologists with a means to obtain anatomically undamaged brain tissue for study.[63] In the latter case, the head is immediately placed in liquid nitrogen to halt metabolic processes.

Advantage—Guillotines that are well-designed to accomplish decapitations in a uniformly instantaneous manner are commercially available.

Disadvantages—(1) Decapitation may be aesthetically displeasing to personnel performing or observing the technique; and (2) data suggest that animals may not lose consciousness for an average of 13 to 14 seconds following decapitation.[85]

Recommendation—Until additional information is available to better ascertain whether guillotined animals perceive pain, the technique should be used only after the animal has been sedated or lightly anesthetized, unless the head will be immediately frozen in liquid nitogren subsequent to severing.

Exsanguination

Exsanguination is recommended to ensure death subsequent to stunning or electrocution. Rabbits and other laboratory animals may be exsanguinated to obtain hyperimmune antisera, but because of the anxiety associated with extreme hypovolemia, exsanguination should be done only in sedated, stunned, or anesthetized animals.[86]

Decompression (Hypoxia)

Decompression is a means to induce unconsciousness and death due to cerebral hypoxia. Decompression chambers simulate an ascent to an altitude high above sea level. The higher the altitude, the lower the ambient pressure and the greater the hypoxia. Regardless of altitude, the percentage composition of the atmospheric gases remains the same as at sea level. At sea level, the ambient or barometric pressure is 760 mm of Hg, whereas at 55,000 feet above sea level, the pressure is 68.8 mm of Hg. At sea level, the partial pressure of O^2 is 159 mm of Hg, and at 55,000 feet, it is only 14 mm of Hg. The mean oxygen tension in arterial blood (PaO_2) of dogs is normally about 95 mm of Hg; accordingly, at a simulated attitude of 55,000 feet, the rapid decrease in PaO_2 results in unconsciousness and death.[87]

Data from human studies indicate that decompression at 1,000 feet/minute results in excitement and euphoria, followed by sensory dullness, weakness, dyspnea, and unconsciousness. An optimal rate of decompression in the adult dog has been recommended to be 4,000 feet/minute and for other selected species, approximately 1,100 feet/minute.[88,89] The rate of decompression for equipment most commonly used by animal shelters is 1,000 feet/second for 45 to 60 seconds.[90]

There are adverse physical effects due to rapid decompression, since trapped gases in body cavities (eg, sinuses, eustachian tubes, middle ears, and intestines) follow Boyle's Law and expand proportionally to the level of decompression. The rate of decompression is important, since the slower the rate, the less the discomfort and pain due to expanding gases.

Decompression chambers have been widely used in municipal and humane society shelters as a method for euthanasia of dogs and cats. They are rarely used in laboratory animal facilities.

Advantages—(1) Decompression is safe for personnel; (2) it minimizes operator stress; and (3) it is cost-effective.

Disadvantages—(1) Commonly used chambers are designed to produce decompression at a rate 15 to 60 times faster than that recommended as optimum for animals.[88-90] Although animals are rendered unconscious approximately 10 seconds after exposure to a simulated altitude of 50,000 ft., pain and distress may occur due to expanding gases trapped in body cavities during a portion of the 50- to 60-second period of decompression; (2) immature animals are tolerant to hypoxia, and longer periods of decompression are required before respiration ceases; (3) if decompression rates that are used reflect recommended values, the time for onset of unconsciousness would be 14 minutes (4,000 feet/minute) to 60 minutes (1,100 feet/minute) and decompression then would be a time-inefficient method for shelters and pounds that must euthanatize large numbers of animals; (4) accidental recompression, with recovery of injured animals, can occur due to malfunctioning of equipment or to personnel error; (5) bloating, bleeding, vomiting, convulsions, urination, and defecation, which are aesthetically unpleasant, may occur in the unconscious animal; (6) respiratory or middle ear infections, or both, may cause pain from unequalized pressure; and (7) there may be failure to understand the mechanisms of action of hypoxia and its effects on animals.

Recommendation—Decompression is not a recommended method for euthanasia of animals because of the numerous disadvantages.

Electrocution

Electrocution as a form of euthanasia or stunning has been employed for years in species such as dogs, cattle, sheep, and hogs.[19,64,84,91-95] Experiments in dogs have shown the necessity of directing the electrical current through the brain in order to produce instant stunning with loss of consciousness. In the dog, when electricity passes between fore- and hindlimbs or neck and feet, it causes the heart to fibrillate promptly, but does not produce unconsciousness. The dog does not lose consciousness for at least 12 seconds after cardiac fibrillation, which causes cerebral hypoxemia. These data dictate against use of the methods that direct current through the heart and not directly through the brain. An apparatus that applies electrodes to opposite sides of the head, or in another way directs electrical current immediately through the brain, is necessary to induce immediate unconsciousness. The signs of an effective electrical stun are: extension of the limbs, opisthotonos, downward rotation of the eyeballs, and a tonic spasm changing into a clonic spasm, with eventual muscle flaccidity. This effect should be followed promptly be electrically induced fibrillation of the heart, exsanguination, or other appropriate methods to ensure death.

Advantages—(1) Electrocution is hazardous to personnel; (2) it is not a useful method for mass euthanasia because so much time is required per animal; (3) it is not a useful method for a vicious, intractable animal; (4) because violent extension and stiffening of the limbs, head, and neck occur, electrocution is aesthetically objectionable; and (5) in small animals, electrocution may not result in death because ventricular fibrillation and circulatory collapse do not always persist after cessation of current flow.

Disadvantages—(1) Electrocution is hazardous to personnel; (2) it is not a useful method for mass euthanasia because so much time is required per animal; (3) it is not a useful method for a vicious, intractable animal; (4) because violent extension and stiffening of the limbs, head, and neck occur, electrocution is aesthetically objectionable; and (5) in small animals, electrocution may not result in death because ventricular fibrillation and circulatory collapse do not always persist after cessation of current flow.

Recommendations—Electrocution for euthanasia and preslaughter stunning requires special skills and equipment that will assure passage of sufficient current through the brain to produce unconsciousness followed by electrically induced fibrillation of the heart. Although the method is acceptable if the above requirements are met, the disadvantages far outweigh its advantages in most applications.

Microwave Irradiation

Microwave irradiation is used by neurobiologists as a means to fix brain metabolites without the loss of anatomic integrity of the brain. There are microwave instruments that have been specifically designed or modified for use in the euthanasia of laboratory mice and rats. These instruments, which direct most of their microwave energy to the head of the animal, vary in maximal power output from 2 kw to 20 kw. The kilowattage required to halt brain chemical activity within a specific time depends on the size of rodent within the chamber. A 2,450-MHz instrument (6.5 kw) will elevate the brain temperature of a 30-g mouse to 90 C in 325 msec, whereas a 915-MHz instrument (25 kw) is required to achieve the same temperature within one second in a 300-g rat.[96]

Advantages—(1) Unconsciousness and death occur in less than one second, and (2) this is the most effective method to fix brain tissue chemical activity in small animals.

Disadvantagess—(1) Instruments are expensive; and (2) only animals the size of mice or rats can be euthanatized with currently available instruments.

Recommendations—Microwave irradiation is a humane method to euthanatize small laboratory rodents if instruments that induce immediate unconsciousness are used. Only instruments that provide appropriate kilowattage and directed microwaves can be used. *Microwave ovens designed for domestic and institutional kitchens are absolutely condemned for euthanasia use.*

Rapid Freezing

Neurobiologists require means to accurately measure labile brain tissue metabolites. Rapid freezing of the brain has been used to euthanatize animals and to achieve inactivation of enzymatic activity within the brain. Several techniques are used in rodents: (1) immersion of intact animal into liquid nitrogen; (2) decapitation and immediate immersion of head into liquid nitrogen; (3) freeze-blowing; (4) in situ freezing; and (5) funnel freezing.[97]

Advantages—(1) Rapid freezing provides means to humanely euthanatize rodents if correctly executed and if animals are adequately anesthetized prior to freezing (in situ freezing and funnel freezing).

Disadvantages—(1) Immersion into liquid nitrogen may be used only in animals weighing less than 40 g because heavier animals are not rapidly rendered unconscious; (2) rapid freezing requires very well-trained personnel and appropriate equipment; and (3) rapid freezing may be aesthetically displeasing to personnel.

Recommendations—Animal welfare committees and investigators must ensure that animals are made immediately unconscious either from rapid freezing or prior anesthetic. If a paralyzing drug is given in conjunction with an anesthetic, the amount of anesthetic administered must reflect known dose-effect data for a surgical level of anesthesia. Immersion of unanesthetized animals into liquid nitrogen can be used only in animals weighing less than 40 g. Anesthesia must be employed in animals weighing more than 40 g.

Air Embolism

Intravenous injection of 5 to 50 ml/kg of air induces rapid death in rabbits. However, it may be accompanied by convulsions, opisthotonos, and vocalization.[80] It is an acceptable method only in anesthetized animals.

PRECAUTIONS CONCERNING USE OF EUTHANATIZING AGENTS IN ANIMALS INTENDED FOR HUMAN FOOD

In euthanasia of animals intended for human food, agents cannot be used that lead to tissue residues, unless approved by the US Food and Drug Administration.[98] Carbon dioxide is the only chemical currently used in euthanasia of animals (primarily swine) for human food that does not lead to tissue residue.[11]

PRECAUTIONS CONCERNING LESS COMMON SPECIES

When euthanasia of poikilothermic (cold blooded) animals and aquatic animals is performed, the differences in their metabolism, respiration, and tolerance to cerebral hypoxemia may preclude methods that would be acceptable in terrestrial mammals.

POSTFACE

This panel report summarizes contemporary scientific knowledge on euthanasia in animals and calls attention to the lack of scientific reports assessing pain and discomfort in animals undergoing euthanasia. Many reports on various methods of euthanasia are either anecdotal or testimonial narratives and are therefore not cited in this report. The panel unanimously endorses the need for well-designed experiments to more fully determine the extent to which each procedure meets the criteria used for judging the methods of euthanasia.

The Panel on Euthanasia is fully committed to the concept that whenever it becomes necessary to kill any animal for any reason whatsoever, death should be induced as painlessly as possible. It has been our charge to develop workable guidelines for addressing this need, and it is our sincere desire that these guidelines be conscientiously used by all who exercise stewardship over animals on earth.

References

1. McDonald LE, Booth NH, Lumb WV, et al. Report of the AVMA panel on euthanasia. *J Am Vet Med Assoc* 1978;173:59—72.

2. Breazile JE, Kitchell RL. Euthanasia for laboratory animals. *Fed Proc* 1969;28:1577—1579.

3. Kitchell RL. *Animal pain: perception and alleviation.* Carsten E, et al, eds. Bethesda, Md, Am Physiol Soc, 1983.

4. Kitchell RL, Johnson RD. Assessment of pain in animals. In: Moberg GP, ed. *Animal stress.* Am Physiol Soc, 1983;133—140.

5. Willis WD. *The pain system. The neural basis of nociceptive transmission in the mammalian nervous system.* Basal, Switzerland: S Karger, 1985;346.

6. Zimmerman M. Neurobiological concepts of pain, its assessment and therapy. In: Bromm B, ed. *Pain measurement in man. Neurophysiological correlates of pain.* Amsterdam: Elsevier Publishing Co, 1984;15—35.

7. Dennis SG, Melzack R. Perspectives on phylogenetic evolution of pain expression. In: Kitchell RL, Erickson HH, Cartens E, et al, eds. *Animal pain: perception and alleviation.* Bethesda, Md, Am Physiol Soc, 1983.

8. Beaver B. *Veterinary aspects of feline behavior.* St Louis: CV Mosby Co, 1980.

9. Hafez ESE. *The behavior of domestic animals.* 3rd ed. Baltimore: The Williams & Wilkins Co, 1975.

10. Houpt KA, Wolski TR. *Domestic animal behavior for veterinarians and animal scientists.* Ames, Iowa: Iowa State University Press, 1982;356.

11. Humane slaughter regulations. *Fed Register* 1979;44 (232):68809—68817.

12. Grandin T. Observations of cattle behavior applied to the design of cattle-handling facilities. *Appl Anim Ethol* 1980;6:19—31.

13. Grandin T. Pig behavior studies applied to slaughter-plant design. *Appl Anim Ethol* 1982;9:141—151.

14. *Proceedings of the national conference on dog and cat control.* Denver: Am Vet Med Assoc, 1976.

15. *Proceedings of the national conference on the ecology of the surplus dog and cat problem.* Chicago, Ill: Am Vet Med Assoc, 1974.

16. Bustad LK. An educator's approach to euthanasia. *Lab Anim* 1982;11:37—41.

17. Wolfle TL. Laboratory animal technicians: their role in stress reduction and human-companion animal bonding. *Vet Clin North Am [Small Anim Pract]* 1985;15:441—454.

18. Lumb WV, Jones E. *Veterinary anesthesia.* Philadelphia: Lea & Febiger, 1985.

19. Warrington R. Electrical stunning, a review of literature. *Vet Bull* 1974;44:617—628.

20. *Occupational exposure to waste anesthetic gases and vapors.* Washington, DC: Department of Health, Education, and Welfare (National Institute for Occupational Safety and Health) No. 77-140, 1977.

21. Lecky JH, ed: Waste anesthetic gases in operating room air: a suggested program to reduce personal exposure. *Special report.* Park Ridge, Ill: The American Society of Anesthesiologists, 1983.

22. Booth NH. Inhalant anesthetics. In: Booth NH, McDonald LE, eds. *Veterinary pharmacology and therapeutics.* 5th ed. Ames, Iowa: Iowa State University Press, 1982;175—202.

23. *Chloroform box construction and use.* Denver: American Humane Association, 1969.

24. *Humane killing of unwanted animals.* 2nd ed. Herts, England: Potters Bar, The Universities Federation for Animal Welfare, 1968;19—20.

25. Sawyer DC: Comparative effects of halothane. *Gaines Dog Res Prog* 1976, 2—3.

26. *Registry of toxic effects of chemical substances.* Washington, DC; National Institute of Occupational Health. Department of Health and Human Services Publication No. 83—107,1981—1982.

26a. Chloroform: IARC monographs on the evaluation of the carcinogenic risk of chemicals to humans: Vol 20. 1979.

27. Herin RA, Hall P, Fitch JW: Nitrogen inhalation as a method of euthanasia in dogs. *Am J Vet Res* 1978;39:989—991.

28. Noell WK, Chinn HI. Time course of failure of the visual pathway in rabbits during anoxia. *Fed Proc* 1949;8:119.

29. Glass HG, Snyder FF, Webster E. The rate of decline in resistance to anoxia of rabbits, dogs, and guinea pigs from the onset of viability to adult life. *Am J Physiol* 1944;140:609—615.

30. Vinter FJ. *The humane killing of mink.* London: The Universities Federation for Animal Welfare, 1957.

31. Hernett TD, Haynes AP. Comparison of carbon dioxide/air mixture and nitrogen/air mixture for the euthanasia of rodents. Design of a system for inhalation euthanasia. *Anim Technol* 1984;35:93—99.

32. Stonehouse RW, Loew FM, Quinn JA, et al. The euthanasia of dogs and cats: a statement of the humane practices committee of the Canadian Veterinary Medical Association. *Can Vet J* 1978;19:164—168.

33. Klassen CD. Nonmetalic environmental toxicants: air polutants, solvents, and solvents and pesticides. In: Gilman AC, Goodman LS, Gilman A, eds. *The pharmacological basis of therapeutics.* 6th ed. New York: MacMillan Publishing Co, Inc, 1980;1638—1659.

34. Sanford J. Euthanasia of domesticated animals by injection of drugs. In: *Humane destruction of unwanted animals.* Herts, England: Potters Bar, The Universities Federation for Animal Welfare, 1976;18—21.

35. Scott WN. The use of poisons in animal destruction. In: *Humane destruction of unwanted animals.* Herts, England: Potters Bar, The Universities Federation for Animal Welfare, 1976;33—42.

36. Lambooy E, Spanjaard W. Euthanasia of young pigs with carbon monoxide. *Vet Rec* 1980;107:59—61.

37. Haldane J. The action of carbonic oxide in man. *J Physiol* 1985;18:430—462.

38. Bloom JD. Some considerations in establishing diverse breathing gas purity standards for carbon monoxide. *Aerosp. Med* 1972;43:633—636.

39. Carding AH: Mass euthanasia of dogs with carbon monoxide and/or carbon dioxide: preliminary trials. *J Small Anim Pract* 1968;9:245—259.

40. Moreland AF. Carbon monoxide euthanasia of dogs: chamber concentrations and comparative effects of automobile engine exhaust and carbon monoxide from a cylinder. *J Am Vet Med Assoc* 1974;165:853—855.

41. Ramsey TL, Eilmann HJ. Carbon monoxide acute and chronic poisoning and experimental studies. *J Lab Clin Med* 1932;17:415—427.

42. Blood DC, Johnston DE, Blackwood JD. Carbon monoxide euthanasia. A report to the Committee of the Victorian Division of the Royal Society for Prevention of Cruelty to Animals. (Information provided for the 1972 Report of the AVMA Panel on Euthanasia.)

43. Chalifoux A, Dallaire A. Physiologic and behavioral evaluation of CO euthanasia of adult dogs. *Am J Vet Res* 1983; 44:2412—2417.

44. Dallaire A, Chalifoux A. Premedication of dogs with acepromazine or pentazocine before euthanasia with carbon monoxide. *Can J Comp Med* 1985;49:171—178.

45. Simonsen HB, Thordal-Christensend AA, Ockens N. Carbon monoxide and carbon dioxide euthanasia of cats: duration and animal behavior. *Br Vet J* 1981;137:274—278.

46. Klemm WR. Carbon dioxide anesthesia in cats. *Am J Vet Res* 1964;25:1202—1205.

47. Leake CD, Waters RM. The anesthetic properties of carbon dioxide. In: *Current researches in anesthesiology and analgesia.* 1929;8:17—19.

48. Mattsson JL, Stinson JM, Clark CS. Electroencephalographic power-spectral changes coincident with onset of carbon dioxide narcosis in rhesus monkey. *Am J Vet Res* 1972;33:2043—2049.

49. Woodbury DM, Rollins LT, Gardner MD, et al. Effects of carbon dioxide on brain excitability and electrolytes. *Am J Physiol* 1958;192:79—90.

50. Glen JB, Scott WN. Carbon dioxide euthanasia of cats. *Br Vet J* 1973;129:471—479.

51. Hughes HC. Euthanasia of laboratory animals. In: *Handbook of laboratory animal science.* Vol III. Melby, Altman, eds. Cleveland: CRC Press, 1976;553—559.

52. Jaksch W. Euthanasia of day-old male chicks in the poultry industry Int. *J Stud Anim Prob* 1981;2:203—213.

53. Kline BE, Peckham V, Hesit HE. Some aids in handling large numbers of mice. *Lab Anim Care* 1963;13:84—90.

54. Kotula AW, Drewniak EE, Davis LE. Experimentation with in-line carbon dioxide immobilization of chickens prior to slaughter. *Poult Sci* 1961;40:213—216.

55. Stone WS, Amiraian K, Duell C, et al. Carbon dioxide anesthetization of guinea pigs to increase yields of blood and serum. *Proc Care Panel* 1961;11:299—303.

56. Hoenderken R. Electrical and carbon dioxide stunning of pigs for slaughter. In: *Stunning of animals for slaughter.* Eikelenboom G. ed. Boston: Martinus Nijhoff Publishers, 1982;59—63.

57. Croft PG. Anaesthesia and euthanasia. In: *UFAW handbook on the care and management of laboratory animals.* 3rd ed. Baltimore: The Williams & Wilkins Co, 1967;160—172.

58. Euthanasia (carbon dioxide). In: *Report and accounts.* Herts, England: Potters Bar. The Universities Federation for Animal Welfare 1976—1977;13—14.

59. Hall HW. The anaesthesia and euthanasia of neonatal and juvenile dogs and cats. *Vet Rec* 1972;90:303—306.

60. McArthur JA: Carbon dioxide euthanasia of small animals (including cats). In: *Humane destruction of unwanted animals.* Herts, England: Potters Bar. The Universities Federation for Animal Welfare, 1976;9—17.

61. Laursen AM. Choosing between CO_2 and electrical stunning of pigs. A preliminary examination of stress and ethics. In: *Stunning of animals for slaughter.* Eikelenboom G, ed. Boston: Martinus Nijhoff Publishers, 1983;64—72.

62. Blackmore DK, Newhook JC. The assessment of insensibility in sheep, calves, and pigs during slaughter. In: *Stunning of animals for slaughter.* Eikelenboom G, ed. Boston: Martinus Nijhoff Publishers, 1983.

63. Feldman DB, Gupta BN. Histopathologic changes in laboratory animals resulting from various methods of euthanasia. *Lab Anim Sci* 1976;26:218—221.

64. Hatch RC. Euthanatizing agents. In: Booth NH, McDonald LE, eds. *Veterinary pharmacology and therapeutics.* 5th ed. Ames, Iowa: Iowa State University Press, 1982;1059—1064.

65. Lumb WV. Euthanasia by noninhalant pharmacologic agents. *J Am Vet Med Assoc* 1974;165:851—852.

66. Lumb WV, Moreland AF. Chemical methods of euthanasia. *Lab Anim* 1982; 11:29—35.

67. Herschler RC, Lawrence JR, Schiltz RA. Secobarbitaldibucaine combination as a euthanasia agent for dogs and cats. *Vet Med/Sm Anim Clin* 1981;1009—1012.

68. Wallach MB, Peterson KE, Richards RK. Electrophysiologic studies of a combination of secobarbital and dibucaine for euthanasia of dogs. *Am J Vet Res* 1981;42:850—853.

69. Eikmeier H. Experience with a new preparation for painless destruction of small animals. (T-61). *Die Blauen Hefte Tieraerztl* 1962;5:22—23.

70. Kuepper G: T-61 used in large animals. *Die Blauen Hefte Tieraerztl* 1964;8:32—33.

71. Lumb WV, Doshi K, Scott RJ. A comparative study of T-61 and pentobarbital for euthanasia of dogs. *J Am Vet Med Assoc* 1978;172:149—152.

72. Quin AH. Observations on a new euthanasia agent for small animals. *Vet Med* 1963;58:494—495.

73. Rowan AN. T-61 use in the euthanasia of domestic animals: a survey. *Adv Anim Welfare Sci,* in press.

74. Barocio LD. Review of literature on use of T-61 as an euthanasic agent. *Inst J Stud Anim Prob* 1983;4:336—342.

75. Fowler NJ, Foster SJ. The last gasp. *Vet Rec* 1970;86:145.

76. Franz DN. Central nervous system stimulants. In: Goodman LS, Gilman A, eds. *The pharmacological basis of therapeutics.* 5th ed. New York: Macmillan Publishing Co, Inc, 1975;359—366.

77. Bowen JM, Blackman DM, Heavner JE. Effect of magnesium ions on neuromuscular transmission in the horse, steer, and dog. *J Am Vet Med Assoc* 1970;157:164—173.

78. Hicks T, Bailey EM Jr. Succinylcholine chloride as a euthanatizing agent in dogs. *Am J Vet Res* 1978;39:1195—1197.

79. Blackmore DK. Energy requirements for the penetration of heads of domestic stock and the development of a multiple projectile. *Vet Rec* 1985;116:36—40.

80. Clifford DH. Preanesthesia, anesthesia, analgesia, and euthanasia. In: *Laboratory animal medicine.* Fox, Cohen, Loew, eds. New York: Academic Press, 1984;528—563.

81. Blackmore DK. Differences in behavior between sheep and cattle during slaughter. *Res Vet Sci* 1984;37:223—226.

82. Blackmore DK. Non-penetrative percussion stunning of sheep and calves. *Vet Rec* 1979;105:372—375.

83. Anis GW. Euthanasia of domesticated animals by shooting. In: *Humane destruction of unwanted animals.* Herts, England: Potters Bar. The Universities Federation for Animal Welfare, 1975.

84. Carding T. Euthanasia of dogs and cats. *Anim Reg Stud* 1977;1:5—21.

85. Mikeska JA, Klemm WR. EEG evaluation of humaneness of asphyxia and decapitation euthonasia of the laboratory rat. *Lab Anim Sci* 1975;25:175—179.

86. Gregory NG, Wotton SB. Time to loss of brain responsiveness following exsanguination in calves. *Res Vet Sci* 1984;37:141—143.

87. Booth NH. Effect of rapid decompression and associated hypoxic phenomenia in euthanasia of animals: a review. *J Am Vet Med Assoc* 1978;173:308.

88. Barber BR. Use of a standard autoclave for decompression euthanasia. *J Inst Anim Technol* 1972;23:106—110.

89. Smith DC. Methods of euthanasia and disposal of laboratory animals. In: *Methods of animal experimentation,* Vol 1. New York: Academic Press, 1965;167—195.

90. High altitude (low pressure) euthanasia. Denver, Colo, *Operational Guide for Euthanasia,* 1969.

91. Croft PG, Hume CW. Electric stunning of sheep. *Vet Rec* 1956;68:318—321.

92. Loftsgard G, Braathen S, Helgobostd A. Electrical stunning of mink. *Vet Rec* 1972;91:132—134.

93. Roberts TDM. Correspondence: electrocution cabinets. *Vet Rec* 1974;95:241—242.

94. Roberts TDM. Cortical activity in electrocuted dogs. *Ve Rec* 1954;66:561—567.

95. WHO Joint FAO/WHO Expert Committee on Meat Hygiene. Second Report. *WHO Tech Rep Ser 241* 1962.

96. Medina MA, Diam AP, Stavinoha WB. Inactivation of brain tissue by microwave irradiation in cerebral metabolism and neural function. Chapter 8. Passoneau RA, et al eds. Baltimore: The Williams & Wilkins Co, 1980.

97. Passoneau RA, Hawkins RA, Lust WD, et al, eds. *Cerebral metabolism and normal function.* Chapters 2—8. Baltimore: The Williams & Wilkins Co, 1980.

98. Booth NH. Drug and chemical residues in the edible tissues of animals. In: Booth NH, McDonald LE, eds, *Veterinary pharmacology and therapeutics.* 5th ed. Ames, Iowa: Iowa State University Press, 1982;1065—1113.

Subject Index